Amateur

WoodCarving

A Guide

This Edition Published in aid of:
SSAFA
The Armed Forces charity

Published in 2021 with the permission of others as indicated.
Printed & Bound in Great Britain 2021
Published by Whittington, Fursdon, Exeter, EX6 6LJ, UK. E-mail: books@fursdonfarm.uk
ISBN Donated by: GMC Publications Ltd
Castle Place, 166 High Street, Lewes, East Sussex BN7 1XU, UK
ISBN 978-1-91519-106-9

Typeset:
Rokkitt: Vernon Adams
SIL Open Font License: https://github.com/googlefonts/RokkittFont
Roboto:
Apache License: https://fonts.google.com/specimen/Roboto
Balava
GNU Licence: http://www.softerviews.org/fonts.html
Rubrics 1 2 3 4 CD Numbers
Public Domain/GPL: http://www.fontgrube.de/en/contact.htm
Rubrics 1 2 3 4 Square Frame W95 Negative
CC BY 3.0: http://www.onlinewebfonts.com

In support of:

ssafa | the Armed Forces charity

Front Cover: Author's Coursework, Geisler-Moroder Carving School Austrian *see page 63*

Contents

Introduction

This book is aimed at "the amateur" as in the traditional meaning of "***....a person who takes part in a sport or other activity for enjoyment, not as a job...***" rather than in the modern more fashionable derogatory meaning of the word. A subtitle of "***A Gentleman's Guide...***" could have been added a century ago, prior to the modern pejorative meaning of the word "amateur". In the Victorian period of the late 19th and early 20th century, it was becoming apparent to some that the industrialisation of society was leading to a decline in the traditional craft training and skills. As we again saw in the late 20th century, all the traditional woodworkers, from carpenters and joiners, through to wheel-wrights, cabinet makers and carvers, who had previously followed a traditional craft training to gain skills and to increase their income, were increasingly unable to pass these skills on due to the ever increasing commercial pressures of earning a living in an industrial society, where price had become king. While trades such as carpenters and joiners were under pressure, their skills were in a "must have" for construction work. However, the woodworkers most at risk were those specialists, such as woodcarvers, where their output was not "essential" to trade. Not only that, but much of the production of basic decorative carving, such as panels and decorative mouldings (that we can still admire in the few well preserved grand houses finished in the late 19th & 20th century) was being industrialised. This simple, repetitive work had been previously the woodcarver's "bread and butter", as the semi-skilled preparatory work done by apprentices (under the supervision of the master carver) provided much of the profit for their masters.

Along with the loss of work to mechanisation went the decline in the master's profit, that was needed to fund the training of apprentices and their employment as journeymen. So started the inevitable vicious circle leading to the decline in traditional skills.

One of the better known reactions to this decline was the birth of the "***Arts & Crafts***" movement in England, pioneered by Barnsley and others, (later reflected in the "***Mission Style***" of North America), but less well know was a proliferation of printed work where the amateur, or "gentleman" woodworker, that is, a person who had time and education on their side, tried to record and emulate the art of the professional, in an area of his own personal interest. Many of these books for the "amateur woodworker", so often on small private print runs, were aimed at both gentlemen and ladies of the professional classes, who increasing had the spare time and money to follow a "hobby". The authors often had the background, time and contacts, to devote to the production of well researched and illustrated books, now sadly most lost to history. The current fashion for digital books, has resurrected some of the more noteworthy tomes, such as "***A Manual of Wood Carving, by Charles G. Leland - 1891*** (Revised by J J Holtzapffel 1909)[1]. Fortunately, an amateur's interest in woodcarving has not been lost with them.

For as long as people have been woodworking, they have been adding decorative enhancements to their work. Surviving examples of early woodcarving vary from simple embellishments to tools and utensils, (probably an amateur carver, possibly by the tool-maker or even the owner or user), to the highly skilled ornamental carving and wood-sculpture that has survived due to its "monumental" purpose, such as that from Celtic and Viking graves and early ecclesiastical relics and structures — almost certainly the work of dedicated itinerant professional carvers, working as part of a team. This would have been

[1] *Project Gutenberg http://www.gutenberg.org/files/42949/42949-h/42949-h.htm*

funded and supported by an appreciative patron with deep pockets.

The monumental works, such as the ornamental carving and wood-sculpture by acknowledged masters such as Grinlin Gibbons in England and Tilman Riemenschnieider in Germany (and more recently the renowned restoration of Windsor Castle after the fire in the late 20th century) were well known internationally and continued to be recognised, so the trade prospered. However, the amateur and "folk" work has long been in decline, especially outside the few nations (predominantly in European timber producing areas), where owning and using knives is a tradition retained today. In such knife owning societies, decorative carving permeated the whole woodworking environment and is now often been protected in their craft training schools. For example, the early recognition in late 19th century Finland of the decline in competence with hand tools, led to the introduction of measures designed round the need to preserve such skills, through formal craft education and training. By the early part of the 20th century this had developed into the Swedish ***slöyd*** training tradition[2]. In nations, with a preserved tradition there remains a public disposition to pay a fair commercial rate for traditional products. This has in turn supports a market environment where decorative carving can continue to flourish. Unfortunately, this tradition does not pertain to the United Kingdom or North America where "market forces", in both education and retail, have nearly driven decorative carving to extinction.

Publication of this book has been made possible by the assistance of Jonathan Bailey & Emma Foster at The Guild of Master Craftsman (GMC) Publications[3] who arranged for the donation of the ISBN.

Proceeds from the book all go to SSAFA[4], the Armed Forces charity.

[2] 1892 The Teachers Hand-book of Slojd By Otto Salomon: https://archive.org/details/teachershandbook00salo
[3] The Guild of Master Craftsman (GMC) https://www.guildmcgroup.com
[4] SSAFA, the Armed Forces charity https://www.ssafa.org.uk

Chapter One - Basic Carving Tools

Carving tools are a Mecca for tool junkies, so what tools do you really need?

Carving tool terminology is, at best confusing, but also arcane with older English terms mixed in with common usage. Traditionally tools are numbered based on "***The London List***"[1], where the numbers convey a three dimensional description. The original "home" for the manufacture of the English carving tools was probably in London (Depford), where it was allied to shipbuilding & maintenance at The London Docks, and home to the likes of Grinlin Gibbons and his workshops. The history of the "***London List***" probably also evolved from here, starting with the Addis brothers' feud in the mid-19th century, where the older Addis (SJ) remained making tools in London, while the younger Addis (JB) went to the "new" steel centre at Sheffield to manufacture tools for Ward & Payne, who subsequently sold them throughout the world. The confusing nature of tool descriptions was recognised by Ward & Payne, so in the late 19th century (through to the mid 20th century), they listed the (Sheffield made) JB Addis Tools in their catalogue under the description "***London Pattern***", a description that was probably an attribution to elder Addis (SJ) and that has outlived the various Addis brands.

Tools in UK are described in three dimensions:

1. first as viewed from the sharp end;
2. next as viewed from the side;
5. then finally viewed from above.

Viewed from the sharp end, tools come in a graduated range of profiles, each in a range of widths. The numbers start with N°1 (a straight or "firmer"), N°2 (a flat skew), with curved gouges numbered N°3 to N°10. One mystery to new carvers is that European sweep number are apparently one sweep greater than the equivalent ***London List*** numbers. This is simply explained by the Continental lists calling a London N°2 (straight skew or corner firmer) as a Continental N°1-S, so renumbering curved gouges from N°2 to N°9, one short of the equivalent London List profile N°3 to N°10.

The widest range of profiles still in UK production is probably by Henry Taylor. The use of secondary numbering is well illustrated in their catalogue[2] (although they do have the unique use of the prefix 1 (as in 1 1-13) in the tool number stamped on their blades, to denote their short length "amateur" tools.

Generally, having numbered the tool as seen from the sharp end, the list then goes onto add a prefix digit to describe:

Side view:

a. 'Long-Bent' or curved - where the whole tool is curved or bent

b. 'Short-Bent' or spoon-bent - where just the end is bent.

c. Within the 'Short-Bent' another digit is used for 'Front' or 'Back' bent where the short end is bent up or down.

Top view:

b. 'Fishtail' or 'Pod'- flared either just at the end or along their length - useful in tight corners as they provide a better view of where you are carving.

c. 'Skew' or 'Corner' - where the chisel end is at an angle to the blade.

Then there's '***Parting tools & Veiners***': including 'V' Parting-Tools (at 45°, 60°. 90°) and "Veiners"/ "Grooving or Fluting Tools" -

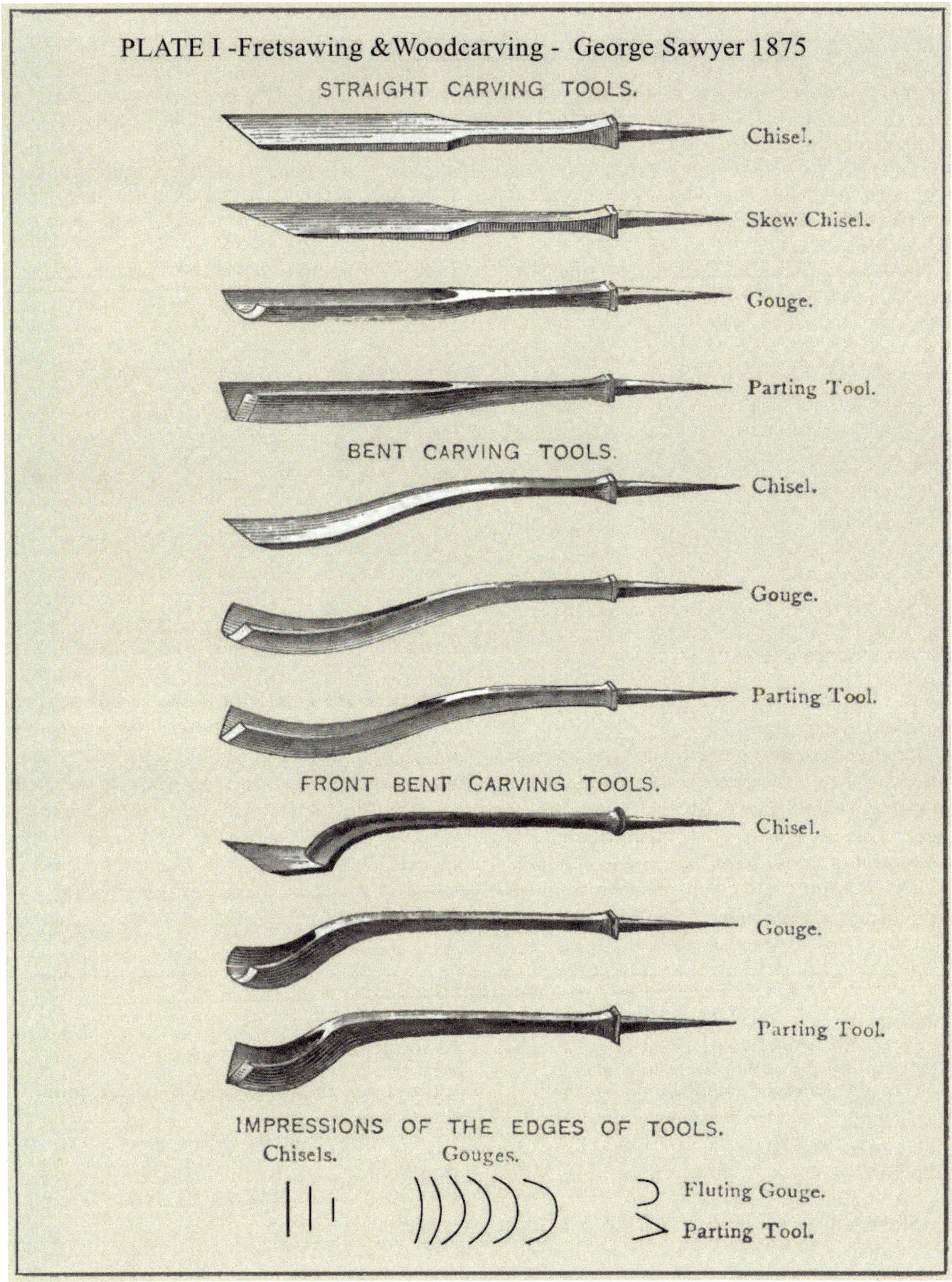

PLATE I -Fretsawing & Woodcarving - George Sawyer 1875

TOOL TIP

Simplistically, the tool's curve is an arc of a circle - however it is also said that it is an arc of a spline, (although I suspect that it's actually less to do with mathematics and originally more to do with hand forging physics, as the wings of a blade will cool faster than the centre, so distorting the arc from the shape that was forged). Whatever the science, it makes the scribing an arc simple with successive tools:

A. To link between the gouge profiles, (for example to carve a classic Acanthus scroll), you start at the centre with a No 7 then rotate it and push it away from you with your thumb in a slicing cut;

B. To continue opening out the curve, just change to the edge of a N°5 again with a thumb powered slicing cut;

C. End the curve in the same way with a N°3. In this way, by using the corner of the tool you can steer it out from its own curve following the line of the pattern.

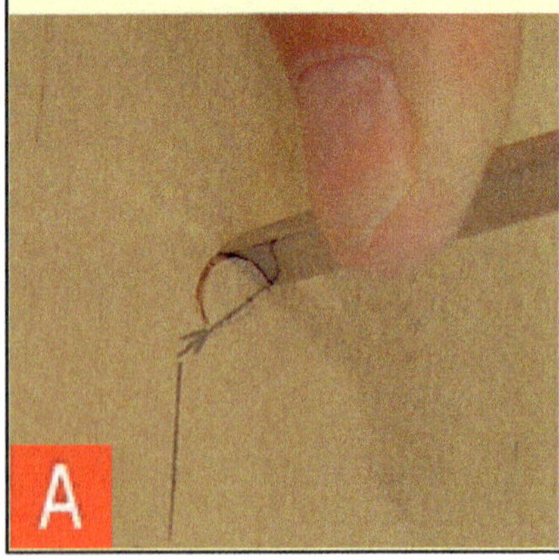

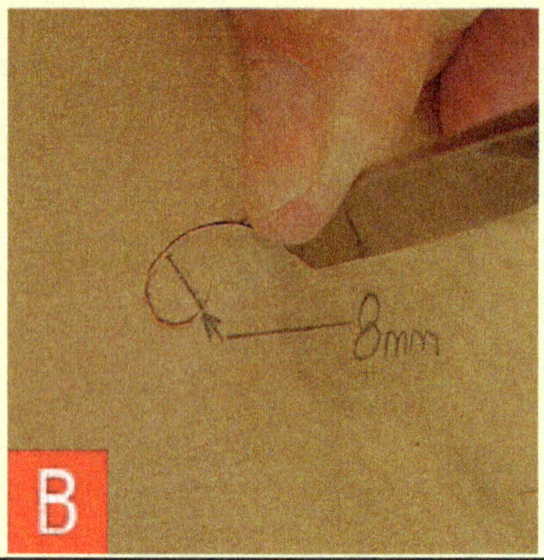

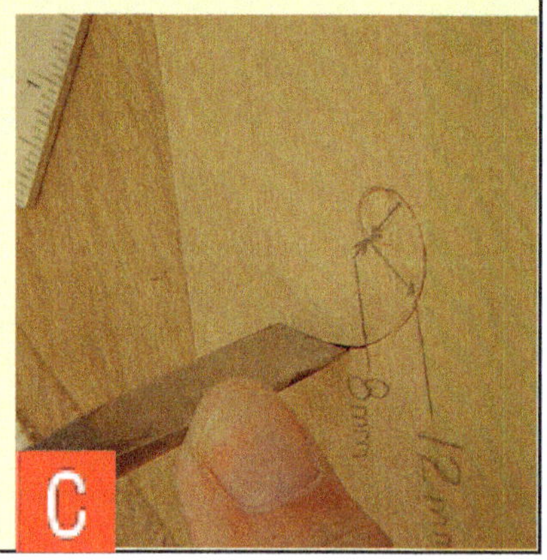

where the U-shaped sweep is a semi circle with elongated shoulders - a N°11.

Conventionally, the N°1 & N°2 or so called "*firmers*" are sharpened with a double bevel, while the description "chisel" will still be used where a straight tool is sharpened with a single top-bevel like a carpenter's chisel.

As to which tools you "***need***" - well answering the question "***what woodcarving tools should I need...***" is in the same category as "***...what car should I buy...***" - everyone has an opinion, but both the answers really start with another question "***...so what do you want to do with....***" My suggestions for a basic set of tools, are influenced by my carving training (which was mainly in Europe - for decorative & furniture carving), plus an interest in restoration work, all backed by a reasona-

London/Sheffield List

Straight
- Straight (firmer) #01
- Skew/corner #02 (continental #1S)
- Gouges #03-#11 (continental #02-#10)

Long Bent
- Gouges #12-20

Short Bent
- Straight chisel - #21
- Skew - right - #22 left - #23
- Gouges #24-#32

Back Bent
- Gouges #33-#38

Veiner
- Straight #11, curved #20, & spoon #32

Parting or V-Tools
- 60°V - #39; 30°V - #41; 90°V - #45

Long Bent
- 60°V - #40, 30°V - #42, 90°V - #46

Short Bent
- 60°V - #43, 30°V - #44

bly equipped amateur workshop. For example, if I need a straight bladed I have a carpenter's toolkit on which to fall back.

1 I also have some carpenter's or "***chippy's***"[1] gouges - ("shouldered" chippy's tools on left, un-shouldered carvers on right). Traditionally, it was more common to find a chippy's gouge referred to as an ***Incannel Firmer Gouge*** and forged as a standard length (long) chisel with the bevel on the inside of the blade. This was in common with the chippy's straight blade chisels where the flat side is presented to the work-piece. I believe that the use of "shoulders" on the tool were simply structural in that many chippy's jobs could easily lead to "tool abuse"

2 Woodcarving tools come in a bewildering array of shapes and size and are a Mecca for tool junkies, so compiling a list of "best buys" is really dependant on what your background is and what you want to carve. The handle shapes and available blade lengths can vary, as different parts of Europe (and the Far East), have different traditions from England, where short tools were once referred to as "amateur" or "ladies pattern". You even have the enterprising Flexcut™ brand who have re-invented the concept of the multi-blade carving set, pioneered by the X-Acto™ carving tool sets in the 1930's, where X-Acto diversified their expertise in surgical knife manufacture into the expanding hobby market.

3 For example, while in England a carving tool's handle is now predominantly short and round (on the right), elsewhere in Europe, handles tend to be octagonal and longer (on the left) or English (round) on the right - it does it matter - not a lot, (although an octagonal handle is less likely to roll off the bench!). Another regional difference is in the method of attaching the

[1] *"Chippy" is UK-English slang that covers all the time-served woodworking trades involved in various forms of construction and maintenance, including carpenter, joiners and shipwrights.*

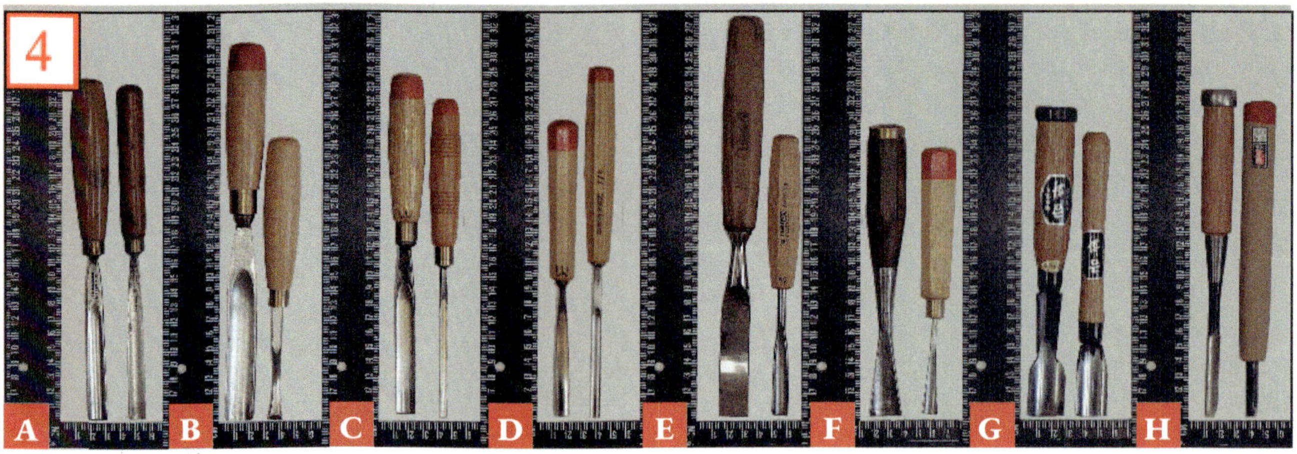

handle - in UK & Europe now almost universally a tang inserted into the handle while socket handles are more common in Asia - see Chapter 11 on page 83.

4 The illustration above shows some of the regional variations (left to right):

England: A; the old Addis tools all had a short round handle - still the prevalent UK form, B; Sorby; uniformly round C; Henry Taylor; default is round (although they give alternatives including octagonal handles); **Elsewhere in Europe:** handles tend to be octagonal, in Middle Europe D; Austria (Stubai) & Germany (*Kirschen.de* or Two Cherries[3]) make shorter tools (left side) and Swiss (*Pfeil.ch*[4]) with longer handles (right side) and two blade lengths 85mm & 110mm Then E; Check Republic (*Narex.cz*)[5] - who make both amateur & professional tools) **in the Far East:** F; China; G South Korea; and H Japan; Does it matter - not a lot, although an octagonal handle is less likely to roll off the bench!). Another regional difference is in the method of attaching the handle - in UK & Europe now almost universally a tang is inserted into the handle with a ferrule for strength, while socket handles are more common in Asia, although their smaller "detail" chisels usually have just a tang, often in a longer-thin handle.

5 In the Far East, the better carving tools are still often laminated steel (where the cutting edge of a thin layer of high carbon steel is forge-welded with heat and a hammer to a softer steel shaft):

A with a socket for the handle on the striking tools,

B reserving the tang fitting for the lighter "hand" tools.

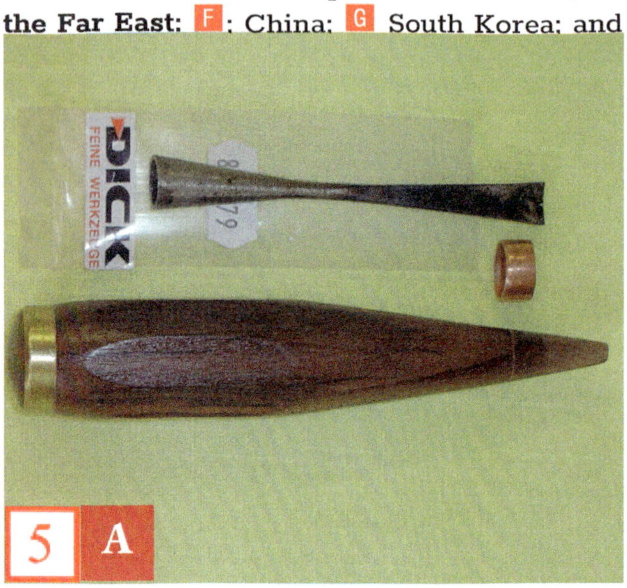

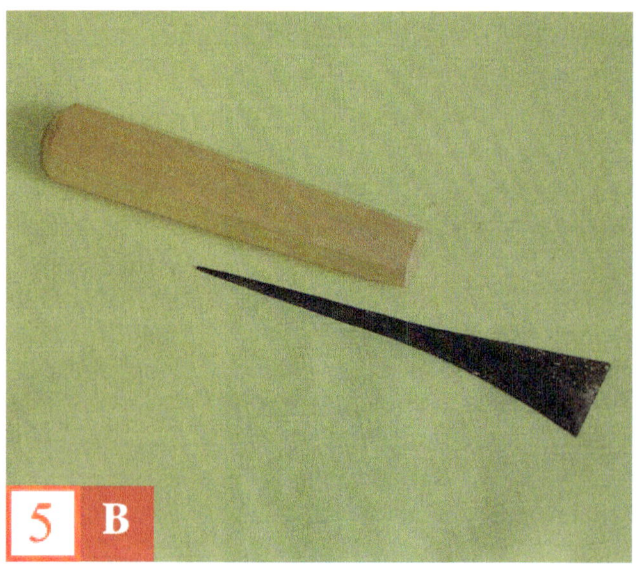

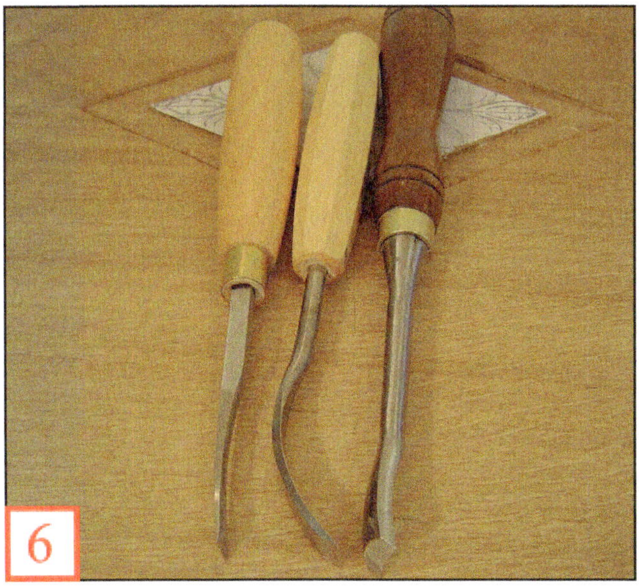

6 Care is needed to differentiate between value and cheap, The one on the right (less than £5) is the latter and is just too clumsy to even adapt. "Real" tools (on the left) start are two to three times that price and are much finer in section with better quality steel.

7 Athough often priced attractively, "sets" often have tools you won't use so can be a false economy - the only "set" I've found irresistible (and luckily worthwhile) is the German Dictum Chinese set, from DICTUM™ in Germany - see page 91 - where a set of 18 is in 2021 now at €60 (c£50 or c£3 each) - no replacement for a basic kit, but ideal as an inexpensive supplementary set[6].

8 My personal preference and recommended selection is for use in traditional decorative carving, such as the 17th century acanthus style, so I'm using shorter, lighter weight tools (on right) than would be required for say sculpting (on left).

9 The Carver's toolbox is predominantly curved section "gouges", where the choice is further complicated by the special terminology used within the range of carvers tools. As to which tools you really need for a starter kit, a small collection of half a dozen should suffice. For decorative

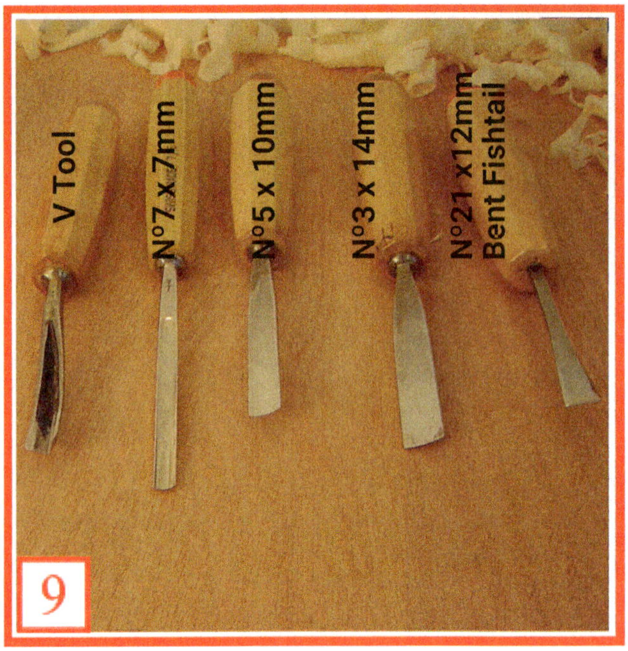

carving, I find a set of just five essentials, plus three supplementary tools will get you a long way. As you progress it is important to have a "set" of common sweep, such as a N°5 in varying widths, plus a couple of selected complementary sizes, for example N°3>N°5>N°7.

10 While my original three supplementary tools were chosen from the Sheffield makers to fill the gaps, they have been superceded by a N°3, 6 & 8 from the Chinese

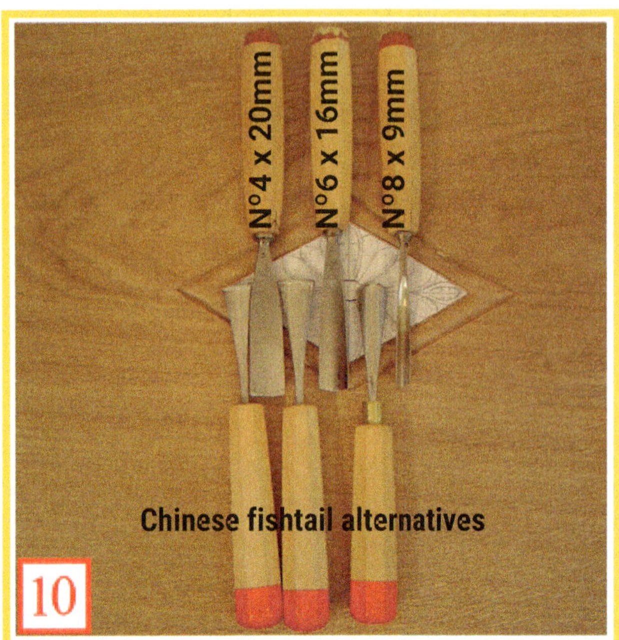

set, which also bring fishtails into the options.

11 Again, with a Continental "bent" I am also a great believer in having a carving knife in my toolbox, whether it be a chip-carving blade or a Slöyd knife, as they can reach into corners that other can't.

12 Another useful tool that is occasionally indispensable is a small draw knife which is easier to use than the less expensive double handled Slöyd splitting-knife I started off with. Having mentioned "tool box" - the only imperative is that blades are not stored loose, as not only will blade selection be a health hazard but they will tend to chip their beautifully honed and polished blades.

13 You will also need some form of mallet. I started with a regular chippy's mallet ('cos that's what I had), graduated to a carver's mallet, (where the round head more easily makes contact with the tool) but now primarily use a small brass mallet, as this is ideal for setting-in and tapping gently for my ornamental carving.

14 Finally there is the "*Tailed Apprentices*" (which could be said to start with the electric kettle and the vacuum cleaner) but those aids more specifically aimed at woodcarving are the power chisel and the various form of powered abrasion (from the numerous Ar-

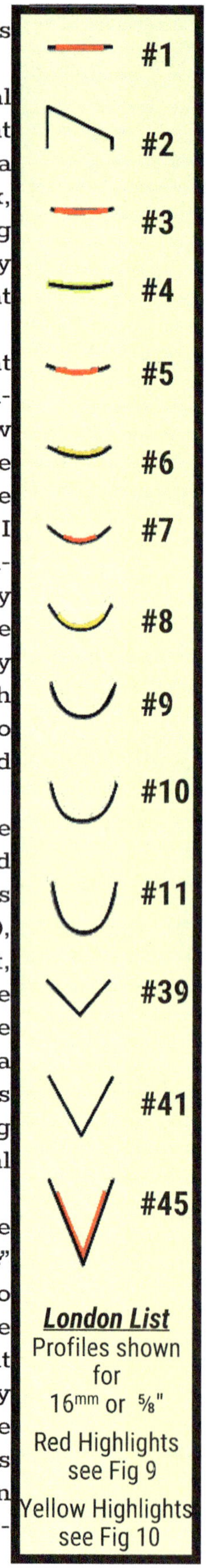

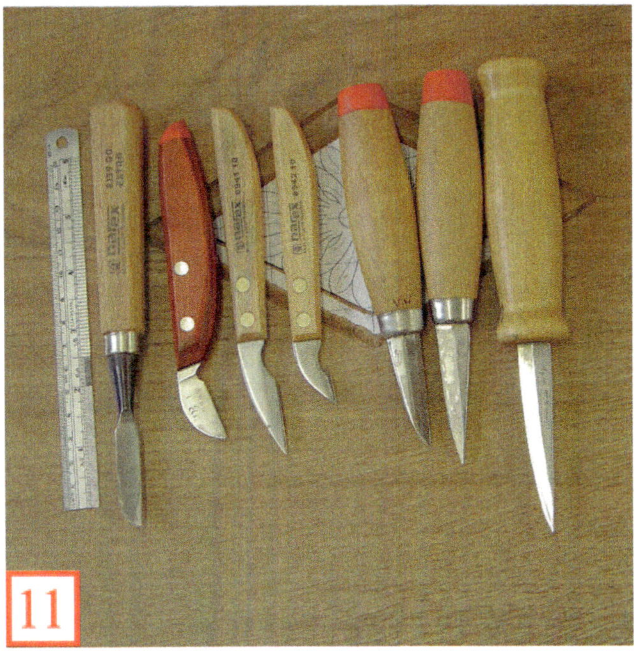

11

12

bortech® machines to the Powerfile™ and imitators). Power tools are significant labour saving devises for the wood-sculptor but when it comes to relief carving, it is really only the power chisel that is sufficiently controllable to help in roughing out. In my experience the more compact the device, the better. I have used the old US manufactured *Ryobi DC500*, which was a relatively light "in-line" machine and found it effective for roughing-out in harder woods like oak.

15 My power chisel only really worked well when equipped with replacement blades from Flexcut™ (who also have an adapter available for using them by hand). While the *Ryobi DC500* is no longer made, the use of a compact power carver (rather than the modern "multi-tools") can be of assistance in roughing out. As always, the cost-benefit has to consider the *full* price, as most reviews I have seen also emphasise the need for re-

13

14

placement blades to add to the basic see the true cost.

16 In addition to "Carving" tools, there are some workshop tools that are necessary. The first is a saw for roughing-out blanks, the second a drill. At the basic level, a hand driven fret-saw and drill will suffice, but in this modern day, you're more likely to already have a power jig-saw and electric drill at home than an old fret-saw and hand drill or brace & bit.

17 The power router can also assist. In addition there are a number of drawing and measuring instruments that should already be common in a workshop, again with their "***battery powered***" replacement - a computer, laptop or "tablet".

18 I have never regretted an early purchase of a small "table-top" band-saw for roughing out my wood carving. From my experience, I would recommend buying one and then making sure to invest in a good quality blade for it, as it is a tool that greatly improves both accuracy and speed of preparation.

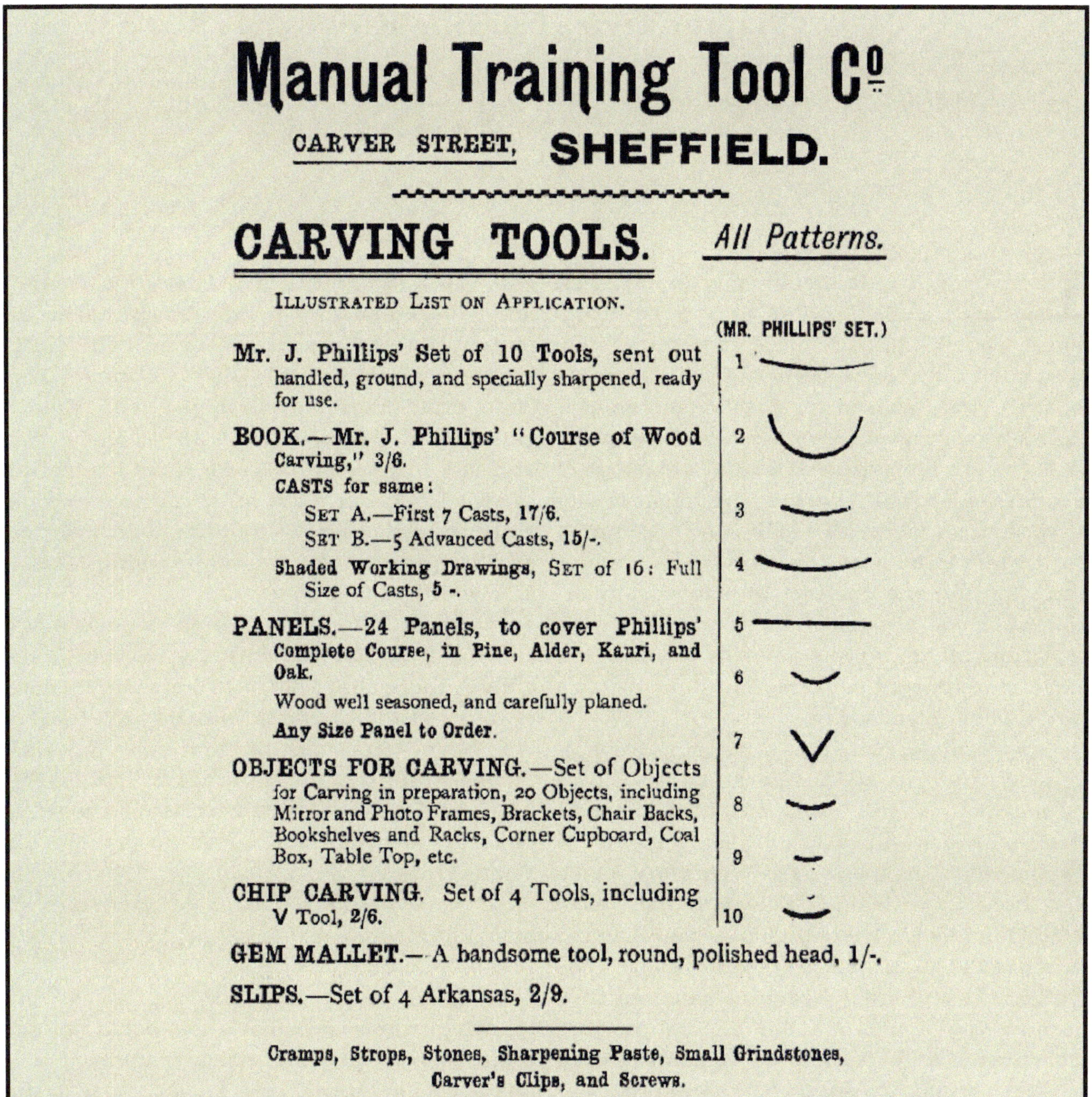

Manual Training Tool Co

CARVER STREET, **SHEFFIELD.**

CARVING TOOLS. *All Patterns.*

ILLUSTRATED LIST ON APPLICATION.

Mr. J. Phillips' Set of 10 Tools, sent out handled, ground, and specially sharpened, ready for use.

BOOK.—Mr. J. Phillips' "Course of Wood Carving," 3/6.

CASTS for same:

SET A.—First 7 Casts, 17/6.

SET B.—5 Advanced Casts, 15/-.

Shaded Working Drawings, SET of 16: Full Size of Casts, 5 -.

PANELS.—24 Panels, to cover Phillips' Complete Course, in Pine, Alder, Kauri, and Oak.

Wood well seasoned, and carefully planed.

Any Size Panel to Order.

OBJECTS FOR CARVING.—Set of Objects for Carving in preparation, 20 Objects, including Mirror and Photo Frames, Brackets, Chair Backs, Bookshelves and Racks, Corner Cupboard, Coal Box, Table Top, etc.

CHIP CARVING. Set of 4 Tools, including V Tool, 2/6.

GEM MALLET.—A handsome tool, round, polished head, 1/-.

SLIPS.—Set of 4 Arkansas, 2/9.

Cramps, Strops, Stones, Sharpening Paste, Small Grindstones, Carver's Clips, and Screws.

NOTE FROM OLD TOOL LIST (above) The Manual Training & Sloyd Tool Company was also using this address as was the London Mantle Warehouse. On 19th January 1893 the following report appeared in the Sheffield Daily Telegraph: *"The Sheffield Sloyd School at no 16 Fargate is the first of its kind in Great Britain. It's primarily designed to prepare teachers for Sloyd classes in schools. Classes are open to the general public and instruction covers the use of all carpentry tools and their sharpening, plus the principles of their construction, the characteristics and technical uses of timber, the making of working drawings and the making of Sloyd models"*

Read more at: *http://www.thestar.co.uk/retro/retro-sheffield-tour-of-lost-fargate-pubs-1-7388096*

[1] *Addis: A Famous Name in Carving Tools By Geoffrey Tweedale*

[2] *https://www.henrytaylortools.co.uk/downloads/htt_brochure.pdf*

[3] *Two Cherries: https://www.kirschen.de/en/Carving_Carving-Chisels-short-pattern_p10.html*

[4] *Pfeill: https://pfeiltools.ch/katalog/#page-14*

[5] *Narex: https://www.narextools.cz/en/carving-tools*

[6] *2008 WC #101 - Mar-Apr 2008 Chinese CarvingTools Pt 1 & WC #102 May-Jun 2008 - Chinese CarvingTools Pt II*

Chapter Two - Carving Knives

The knife for wood-carving probably pre-dates the chisel by a long way. As a carving tool, it is still relevant today.

In my youth (admittedly now in the "last century"), the carrying of a fixed blade knife "sheath-knife" was common, especially for country dwellers and scouts. As a consequence, what passed for "health and safety" (know then only as "***common sense***") required that a youth be instructed in the safe usage of a knife and possibly also in the mysteries of their sharpening. As a result, it was common for a knife to be used for many tasks, including whittling and carving. In many continental countries, especially those with a strong tradition of forestry, skill with a knife has been more deeply embedded in their culture, so remains intact today.

For example, Norwegians have traditionally made and carried knives and to this day, a "***Tollekniv***" is still often included in their national dress, much as the Scots include a "***sgian-dubh***" in theirs. The traditional blade for these Scandinavian knives is still made from laminated steel, giving a long lasting sharp edge on a tough, flexible blade. The Tollekniv and it's Scandinavian cousins, formed the model for the general-purpose Scandinavian Craft Knife or "***slöjdkniv***" used in the formal teaching of hand-craft. or "***Educational Slöjd***", first introduced in Finland in the mid-19th century, later expanded in Sweden and the rest of Scandinavia following the establishment of a teachers' training college in 1875 at Nääs Castle (***Nääs Slott & Slöjdseminarium***). A Swedish-American, Gustaf Larsson, trained there before emigrating and going on to establish the Slöyd teachers' training programme at the North Bennet Street School, Boston in 1891[1], where slöjd education in the USA is still thriving today, and the descendants of "***Educational slöjd***" are still compulsory across Scandinavia, although Norway has integrated arts and crafts into one school subject called "***forming***". This hand craft tradition, combined with such a widespread competence with a blade, has strongly influenced the widespread retention of wood carving skills in countries such as Norway, including the traditional Scandinavian "flat-pane" style of figure-carving tackled solely with a slöjdkniv.

There is a link between a popular knife carving tradition and forestry, in that areas where there has been a long indigenous practice of the growing and use of softwood, also have a tradition of figure-carving with knives, from the Alpine areas of middle-Europe to the Appalachian areas of the USA (where the craft is referred to by the old English term of "***whittling***"). "***Educational slöjd***" took off as a means of general craft education in many nations at the turn of the 19th/20th century.

It never really took hold in UK as the teaching profession, even then, could not see their way to putting a sharp knife in the hands of juveniles, preferring to use the chisel as the basic woodworking tool. The advent of "Educational Slöjd" introduced the world to Scandinavian knives, which had been up to then somewhat hidden from sight although many knife companies in the industrial west had been using Scandinavian blades in their products, but re-branding them, such as shown in the extract from a 1900 New York catalogue opposite. The correlation between softwood and knife blades is a practical reflection of the difficulty in mak-

THE TEACHER'S

HAND-BOOK OF SLÖJD

AS PRACTISED AND TAUGHT AT NÄÄS

CONTAINING EXPLANATIONS AND DETAILS OF EACH EXERCISE.

By OTTO SALOMON,

Director of the Nääs Seminarium.

ASSISTED BY CARL NORDENDAHL AND ALFRED JOHANSSON.

III. The Knife.

ble ife.

The *knife* is the *slöjder's* indispensable and most important tool, and it is the *first* to be placed in the hands of a beginner. It is therefore important to select for slöjd suitable knives of the best quality. The blade of the slöjd knife should be made of good steel, about 4 inches long, and not more than $\frac{3}{4}$ inch broad. The edge should be straight, and the two faces which form it should extend over the entire breadth of the blade. The back of the knife should not be more than $\frac{3}{16}$ inch thick. The blade ought not to taper to a dagger-like point, but should terminate as is shown in Fig. 46. The best angle for the edge is 15°. The other end of the blade terminates in a *tang* which slots into the handle.

Fig. 46. Slöjd-knife—Nääs pattern. $\frac{1}{3}$.

A commoner, though by no means so suitable form of knife is shown in Fig. 47. Directions for using the knife are given in Chap. V.

Fig. 47. Slöjd knife. $\frac{1}{3}$.

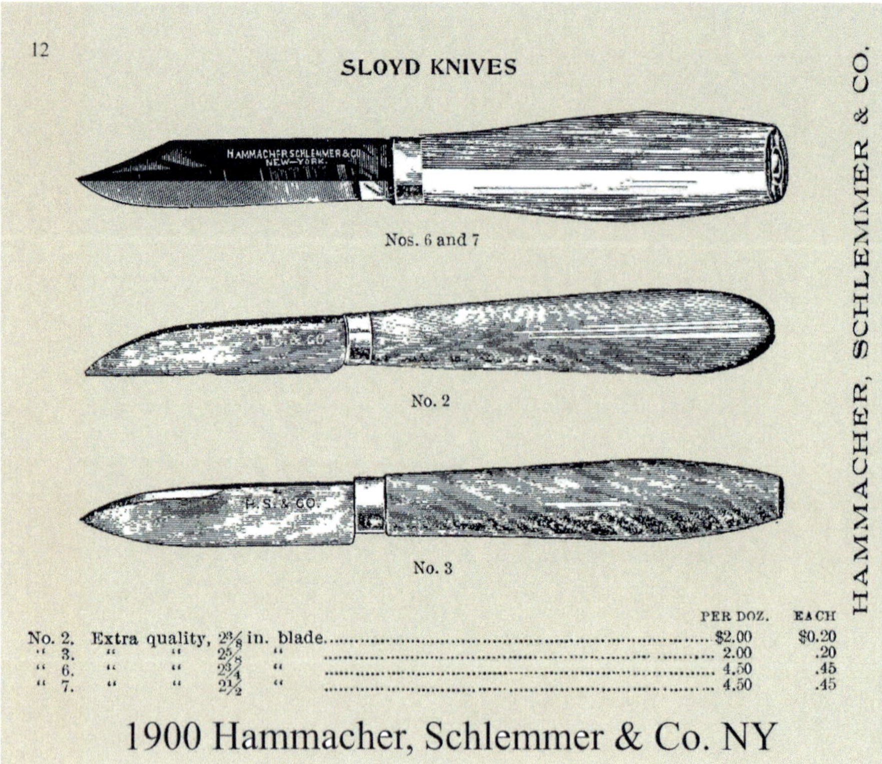

1900 Hammacher, Schlemmer & Co. NY

ing a clean cut in softwood and greenwood with a chisel, as the wedge shape of the chisel edge will tend to crush the grain, while a knife can be used more effectively to make a clean cut by slicing across the gain. Until recently the Scandinavian[2] carving or slöjd knives were predominantly made from laminated steel. There are still a couple of Norwegian traditional knife manufacturers plus the Swedes making "classic" or "*Tollekniv*. However, the only mass-producer of the traditional slöjd or carving knifes is Morakniv®, the current home of the former *Frosts Knivfabrik*, and they now come in both "traditional" - birch handled laminated steel, and a "basic" knife — plastic handled (thinner) carbon steel blade. Finns also have the "*puukko*", which is presumably the model for the original slöjdkniv. The other useful "traditional" Scandinavian carving knife is the double-handled *späntkniv* (transliterates as "splitting-knife" which is in fact a push-knife — the reverse of better known draw-knife).

1 As with other carving tools there is no need to buy a "set" as you may not use them all. However, the "set" of Scandinavian wood-carving knives consists of:

A a long blade knife - where the sharp blade curves up to meet the spine - the original slöjdkniv (#105/106 - 80mm) where the #105 has the birch "safety handles"

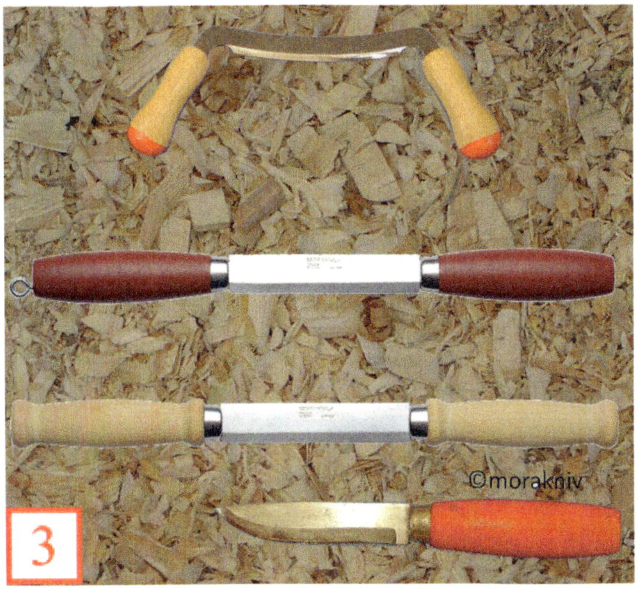

B and the #106 the traditional Scandinavian barrel handle in birch or alternatively/additionally a shorter version of the knife (#120 - 60mm);

2 To supplement these, there is a short chip carving blade #122 - (60mm) with a straight edge and a spine that curves down to the tip, giving a more robust point - somewhat different in shape from the more curved chip-carving blade common in middle-Europe and UK shown underneath.

3 The push-knife (***späntkniv)*** (#220 with either birch "safety" handles or "classic red" barrel handles, has a similar 114mm blade to say the small flexcut drawknife above it. If you want a full set, the traditional general purpose ***Tollekniv*** has a pointed 100mm utility blade.

I will include an illustrations of the practical use of the different knifes for a "flat plane" carving of a Troll on the top of a fence post. Unfortunately, the common fence post is now a fast grown Baltic pine that has been

LAMINATED STEEL BLADES

Both the Vikings and Saxons made and used laminated steel for knives. Although widely used in Scandinavia to the present day, the practice apparently declined in England after the Norman conquest and died out almost completely post industrialisation (apart from a few special plane irons). Hand-made laminated blades are still made by folding a strip of high carbon steel into the middle of the blade and forge-welding the layers together with heat and a hammer. Commercial laminated steel for knife blades is a triple layer, with a high-carbon RC 61-62 steel laminated between two layers of flexible medium-carbon steel, all pressure-welded together by heat and rollers. The composite blade then has the benefits of a hard steel (sharp) edge with a flexible (tough) body. While a hand-made folded-laminate may give greater strength to a general-purpose Tollekniv, the industrial laminate actually provides a better steel for a Slöydkniv, as it extends the hard (sharp) edge right to the very point. The hallmark hard edge can be seen clearly on a laminated blade with the naked eye as it is a slightly lighter colour. This change in metallurgy also gives rise to the attractive patterns in Damascene steels

pressure treated — a poor carving timber at best, further degraded by the tanalising process that has replaced creosote (apparently because if you eat creosote you get cancer!). This turns the outer layers to rot-resistant mush (although modern tanalising is apparently more environmentally friendly, some care should still be exercised in its handling and disposal).

4 Due to the difficulties in roughing-out with a chisel, I started with a saw to notch the main features and to knock off the corners. With a basic shape established and the pattern re-sketched, the double handed ***späntkniv*** is then ideal for the next stage of roughing-out, as the twin handles can be used to give the blade some leverage on larger chunks, yet fine shavings can still be taken with care.

5 Unlike a traditional draw-knife, which is shaped to facilitate "drawing" or pulling, the ***späntkniv*** can be re-orient-

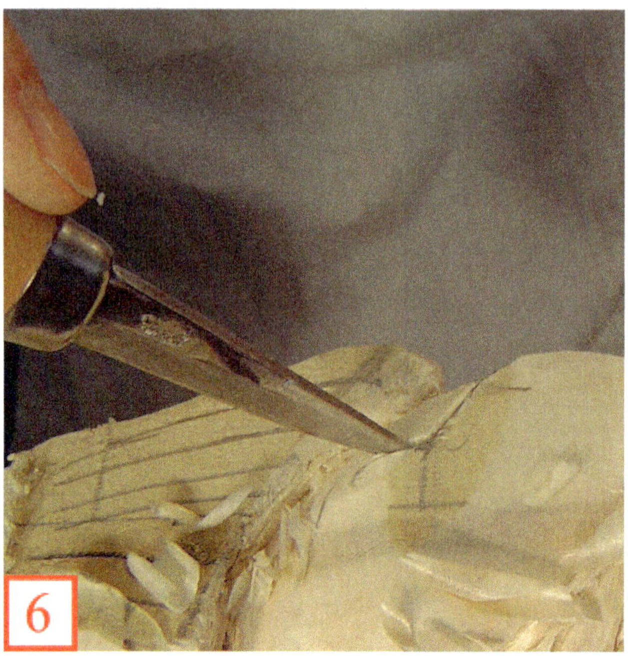

8

9

ed from pull to push, so reversing the angle of attack when used as a double handed "push-knife" — a great asset in carving.

6 With its long, tough knife blade, the long slöjd knife can replace a straight chisel for stop-cuts, using downward pressure while sliding the blade along the stop-line .

7 The waste can then be eased out by an opposing slicing cut - but be careful not to leaver the blade as it's very easy to snap the long pointed hard-steel tip.

8 The 'V'-tool can be replaced by the use of the short blade chip-knife, where a pair of angled parallel incisions can be used to intersect along the line of the required groove.

9 This straight blade is also useful for removing waste by using a paring cut, by rocking the blade into the stop-cut in much the same way that a chef's knife is rocked when dicing vegetables. As in peeling potatoes, it is a good idea to keep the opposing thumb well away from the blade. (although the cut from a sharp knife does heal quickly, avoidance is better than cure).

SCANDINAVIAN GRIND:

No - it's not "inappropriate material", just another *"secret ingredient" of the slöjd knife. The standard knife bevel is ground at a 30º for the main bevel with a 40º secondary bevel, giving a strong structural cutting edge, much in line with a plane blade. As the laminated blade is tougher, you can use the Scandinavian Grind at 25º with no secondary bevel, as the greater strength of the hard steel core is well supported by the flexible mild steel outer blade (by contrast a Nº1 Carving Chisel has a 30º bevel, with or without a secondary bevel). By convention, bench plane has an effective cutting angle of 45º and the Bevel-up plane - for end grain - has an effective cutting angle of 25º ,so you can see the Scandinavian Grind is a better compromise for adapting to grain direction.*

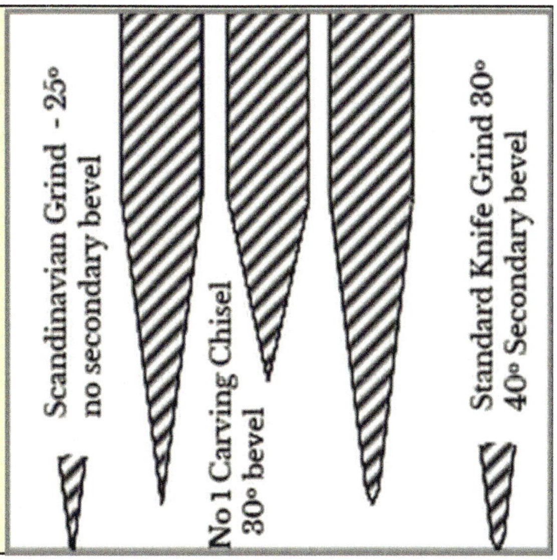

[1]. Hoffman, Benjamin & Rodha, Eva; (1892). The Slöyd System of Wood Working in American

[2] In this chapter I have referred to "Scandinavia" as in the English common usage, when using knife terminology in the context of Norway and Sweden. Educational Slöyd, is a system of handcraft-based education started by Uno Cygnaeus in Finland in 1865 so I have included the Finns' puukko blade (also references to the Sami) neither of whom are ethnically Scandinavian. Perhaps the more accurate reference would be "Nordic" (or "Norden" in Scandinavian and Germanic languages) but a less common term in English usage.

FLAT PLANE CARVING:

Harley Refsal is a Norwegian-American woodcarver and international authority on flat-plane carving. He provides this definition:

"Norwegian figure carving is a flat-plane style that emerged in the mid-18th century; Norwegian carving itself dates to well before the Viking Era (800-1050). Using a single carving or whittling knife, Scandinavian woodworkers created small, six-to-nine- inch figures that likely began as children's toys. The figures, which typically depicted farm animals and country folk, also appealed to adults. Transportable and affordable, the carvings provided a small income source, especially during the winter months. The tradition grew in popularity throughout the 19th century and into the 20th century but began to decline after World War II. In the past twenty years, the tradition has undergone a revival in Scandinavia and among Scandinavian Americans. Today, this style of carving involves roughing out a figure with an axe or band saw, then using a Swedish slöjdkniv to carve figures"[1]

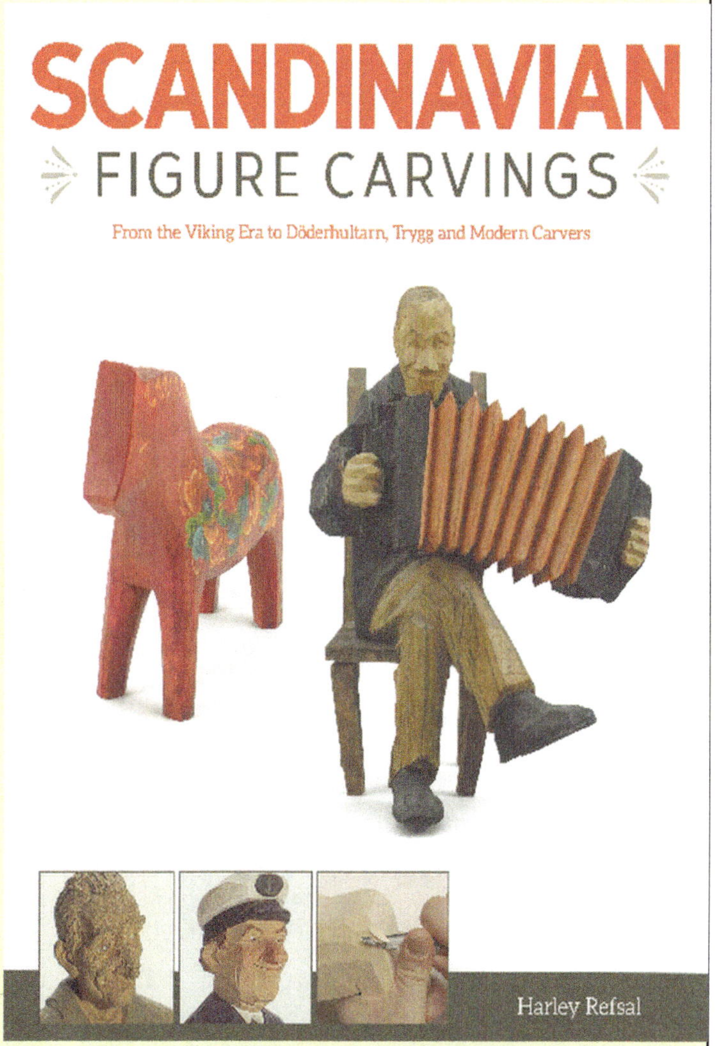

[1] *Scandinavian Figure Carving: Fox Chapel ; 2015 ISBN: 978-1565238756*

Chapter Three - Sharpening

Unless you were born in the last century, there's a good chance you did not have the opportunity to learn tool sharpening at school. Modern technology can go some way to help.

The theory of sharp tools is one of those dichotomies of physics where you need a thin edge for sharpness but a thick edge for strength. This is complicated by the chemistry of steel, where various elements are added to iron to form steels with different characteristics. Historically this has been further complicated, first by iron and then later by steel becoming the material of weapons, so developments in edge "technology" were the closely guarded trade secrets of the specialist (sword)-smiths. The secrets were so carefully guarded that they occasionally became lost in time, such as the original secrets of "Damascus Steel[1]" - a complex ancient sword steel where a raw product from Indian was forge welded in the Middle-East into a complex laminated steel for sword blades. In a similar manner the Viking "Laminated Steel", still common in the Saxon period in England died out with the Norman conquest but is still much evident in the Scandinavian peninsula.

A blend of the techniques remains much in evidence in the highest quality hand-forged tools in Japan, where the banning of swords in the late 19th century left a lot of skilled sword-smiths to turn their skills and technology to tool-making. All these ancient crafts were aimed at solving the same problem faced by the wood-carver - how to get a steel that will give a strong, long lasting, sharp edge. The manufacture of the steel is but one part of the equation, with the shape of the edge being its counterpart. The simple geometry of a tool edge is based on the narrow angle of an obtuse triangle, where the smaller the angle the sharper (but weaker) the edge. While the strength and durability of the edge will be influenced by the characteristics of the steel, the simple correlation is that the smaller the angle, the sharper the edge. Interactively, this has led to the standard knife bevel ground at a 30° for the main bevel with a 40° secondary bevel, giving a strong structural cutting edge, much in line with a plane blade. As a laminated knife blade is tougher, you can grind at 25° with no secondary bevel, as the greater strength of the hard steel core is well supported by the flexible mild steel outer blade. A Carving Chisel has 20° bevel for softwood or hand paring increasing to a 25° or even 30° bevel in hardwood or for roughing with a mallet (this can be with or without a secondary bevel). By convention, a bench plane has an effective cutting angle of 45° and the Bevel-up plane - for end grain - has an effective cutting angle of 25°.

To add to the complex equation of edge profiles, a flat grind stone produces a "flat ground" edge while a rotating grind-stone will produce rapid results with a "hollow ground edge". Either way, a hollow ground blade usually ends up with a flat edge secondary bevel when honed. The evangelicals of the sharpening world can go to some lengths to pit one against the other, but practically, what you need is a sharp tool, that will keep its edge and minimise your non-carving time in the process. Tool steel has more to contribute to this than the esoterica of sharpening, with edge tools available in various grade of steel from the "High Carbon" O1 steel of the traditional Sheffield tools through the more durable (but possibly

GRINDSTONES

SIZES USUALLY STOCKED

Diameter.	14 to 16	16 to 18	18 to 20	20 to 22	24 to 26 inches.
Weights..	25 " 35	38 " 50	51 " 70	75 " 90	100 " 110 lbs.
Face......	1½ " 2	1¾ " 2¼	2¼ " 3	2½ " 3	2½ " 3¼ inch.

Weight of Grindstones

RULE—Square the diameter (in inches); multiply by thickness (in inches); then by .00363; the product will be the weight of the stone in lbs.

Grindstones, under 200 lbs. .... $1.15 per 100 lbs.
" 200 to 1000 " .... 1.90 " " "
" over 1000 lbs. price on application.

MOUNTED GRINDSTONES

SAMSON

Nos.	1	2	3
Stone weighs...	100 to 110	70 to 80	40 to 50 lbs.
Each..........	$4.00	3.75	3.50

CCOKE

KITCHEN GRINDSTONES

MOUNTED

Iron Frame and Wood Stand.

8 inch Diameter................per dozen $10.80
9 " " .... " 12.00

COOKE EMERY GRINDERS

6 × ¾ inch Emery Wheel........per dozen $16.50

KITCHEN GRINDSTONE

96

1398 RICE LEWIS & SON, Toronto - *Mounted Grindstones* - Pg 96

Hand Sharpening

less sharp) A1 steel found in some modern chisels. The addition of alloys also affects hardness and edge holing, where small quantities of alloys such as chromium, tungsten manganese or molybdenum are introduced. This is more popular on continental Europe where tool makers such a Narex have developed Chrome Manganese (Cr-Mn) as a low-alloy high-carbon steels for modern chisels. Laminated steels are still popular in traditional Scandinavian knife making (see Chapter 2) and in the hand made chisels from China and Japan (see Chapter 11 - page 85).

When a lad at school, I remember being let loose with the rest of the class on "sharpening". Armed with a double sided "***Carborundum***" stone we set-to and collectively ruined the edges on the assembled chisels. A week later, when we returned to the subject, now with the suitably blunted set of "***hand sharpened***" chisels from the previous session, we were then introduced to the ***Eclipse Honing Guide*** and the resulting magic of sharp tools.

1 The Eclipse Honing Guide[1] and its clones, are both easy to use and inexpensive (about £5) (Lie-Nielsen have a nice video on how to fettle the clones). Sadly, there is no similar bargain for the woodcarver.

2 The best actual woodcarver's jig is probably the Tormek SVS32 "Short Tool Jig" which knocks spots off its clones that are less than half the price but very much less sophisticated. Unfortunately, you may have to add the price of some sort of compatible mechanical sharpening device to be able to use the jig.

3 The simple way to use the Tormek Short Tool Jig without any machine is to fabricate a sledge from off-cuts (see page 34) which can house a length of 12mm bar. This provides a suitable reference surface to keep the tool edge at a constant angle to the abrasive while the jig allows it to be rotated along the width of the blade,

Bench Grinders

Mechanical sharpening machines have been around for a long time. All the regular power sources have been applied to them in turn, from hand cranks through foot treadles, to water wheels, steam engines, even a small mechanical drive whetstones aimed at the itinerant craftsman or amateur. The modern power source is a small electric motor, popular in the mechanical workshop for the best part of a century. Unfortunately, these machines were developed primarily for the "black" trades of metalworking and are not well suited to the sharpening of hand tools by the untrained. For a woodcarver, the basic problems with a stock bench grinder are that the standard wheels are too coarse and they rotate too fast, with a resulting tendency for "operator error" to ruin an edge by overheating, hence "***blueing***" (which indicates a loss of the steel's temper). Modern bench grinders are much quieter as they tend to be powered by "Induction" motors rather than the older "Universal" (or brush) motors that are noisy.

4 The shortcoming of the basic bench grinder of the cheap coarse abrasive wheels can be mitigated somewhat by the fitting of replacement grinding wheels that are wider and of "softer" grit. Wide wheel grinders are available "off the shelf" aimed more at turners, but cost about twice as much as a basic one (although for a fair comparison, you would need to add in the £10 premium for a 1" (25mm) wide white wheel to the basic grinders' price).

5 To fill the gap in the market, enterprising companies have developed and introduced lower speed sharpening machines specifically designed for wood-working tools, such as the Swedish Tormek whetstone "system" £300-£500 (now with its various imitators now down below the £100 mark).

6 The British Robert Sorby belt linisher "system" cost slightly over £250. This and the Tormek have found favour with wood-workers in UK.

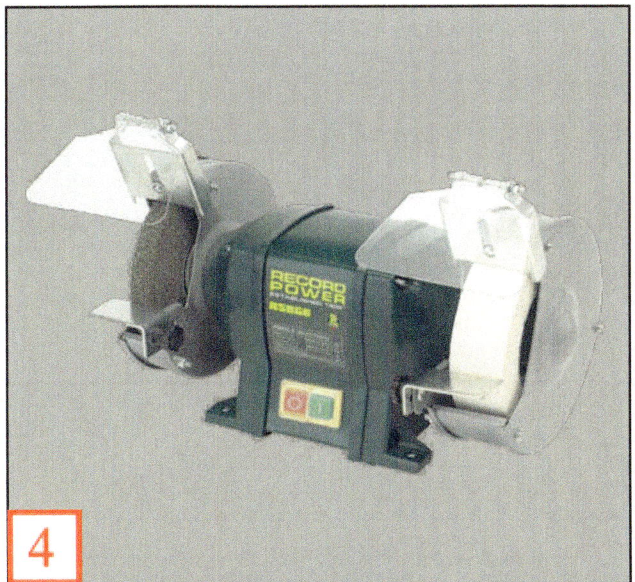

4

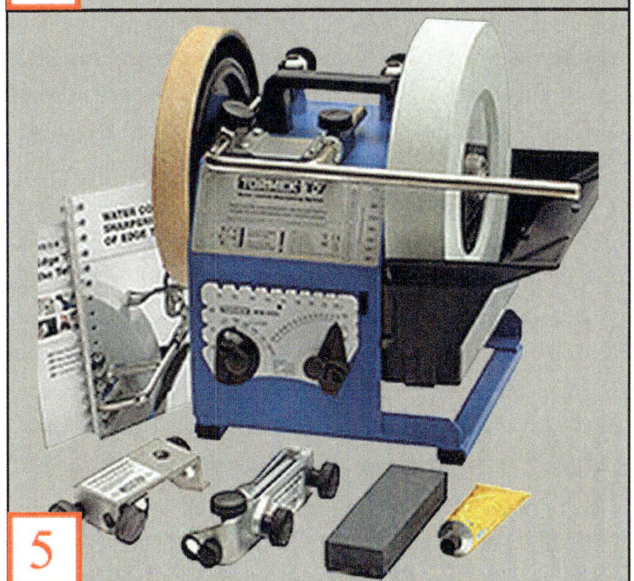

5

6

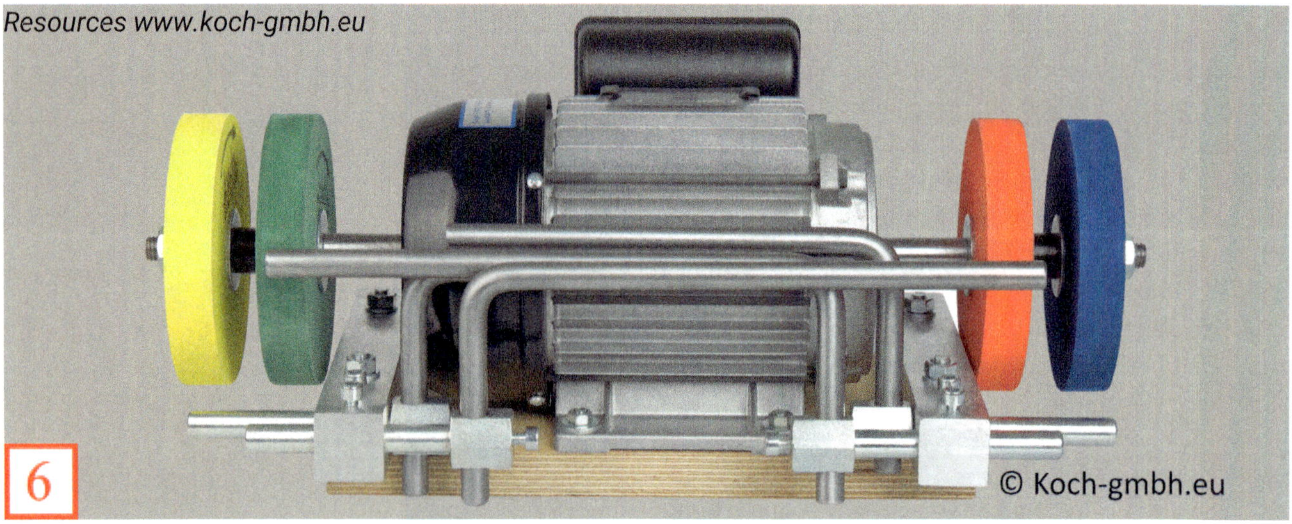

7 In addition to the UK developments, the patented German Koch system, costing upwards of £300 is the only system specifically developed for wood-carvers and is one that impressed me when I attended a wood-carving course in Austria - page 65.

The high-end "systems" such as the Koch, have much in common — slower speed abrasive, "idiot proof" adjustments and high quality sales pitch — unfortunately another thing that all these high end "systems" also share is a premium price. All these premium systems are excellent general purpose machines, especially when "bundled" with the jigs you need or otherwise "*on offer*"; just remember to factor in the extra cost of any additional jigs you will need that are not "*included*" in the price. If you are starting from scratch, the basic price of a good Tormek clone is hard to beat.

However, as a woodcarver, if you have already invested in an electric bench grinder what are the options?

I will deal with the options in order based on which one you already have:

1. The "standard" twin wheel 6"grinder
2. The twin ended Wetstone grinder
3. The twin ended Belt-Sander adapted bench grinder.

KURT KOCH SYSTEM
PATENT EP 0446871 A1 - abstract

The Kurt Koch patent relates to the combination of a "thermo-reactive" buffing compound with a laminated (felt) wheel (Fig -3) that has been manufactured so that felt (A) is inter-layered with grinding grit (B) so that it is embedded in its structure. When the wheels rotate (away from the operator) buffing compound is applied, so that the friction caused from contact with a tool melts the carrier (releasing lubricant and grinding grit) which, combined with the wheel's embedded grit, sharpens the tool without risk of over-heating. The Koch green compound is 2,400 grit, the blue 3,500 grit with a correspondent difference between their colour-coded wheels that have a similar differentiation between "fine" (wheel 1) and "coarse"(wheel 2) in Fig 1 & 2.

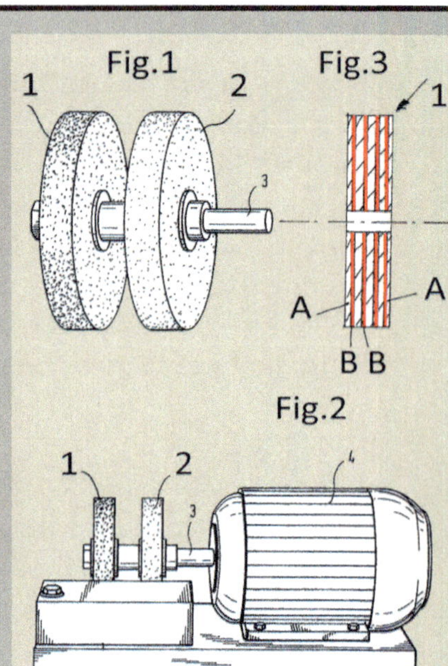

Option 1: Rotate the "Basic" Grinder

8 The "standard equipment" for a budget 6" bench grinder seems to be a 36 grit wheel paired with a 60 or 80 grit wheel — both rather too coarse for carving tools. In addition, these wheels are set-up to rotate towards the operator, for aggressive steel removal. It is relatively simple to change the direction of rotation on a standard bench grinder, (so that it's turning away from the operator thus making it more suitable for carving tools), in that just rotating the guards and running the grinder with the the switch on the back achieves this (albeit in a slightly impractical way)

9 If you don't mind invalidating the warranty & CE/OSHA certification (and potentially shelling out for a Portable Electrical Equipment Test (PAT) - see page 36) - it's relatively simple to rotate grinder on its base, by removing the base-plate cover, then the four screws holding the motor body, rotate it, then replace the screws and base. (I would strongly advise that you clearly mark the new direction of rotation on the motor housing and wheel guards during this procedure, to avoid any potential problems in the future). You can then replace the stock wheels with finer and/or wider wheels and add a decent tool rest. For example the Tormek SVS32 "***Short Tool Jig***" can be used with a suitable length of 12mm (~½") bar ins a fabricated mounting bracket..

10 Moving up the price range, the Tormek "***XB-100 Base***" and a support arm can be mounted on a wooden spacer, or you can actually purchase as a complete Tormek "***BGM100 Bench Grinder Assembly***" if you have deep pockets and don't want the hassle of "adapting" its mounting for your own use.

Option 2: Upgrade the Whetstone Grinder

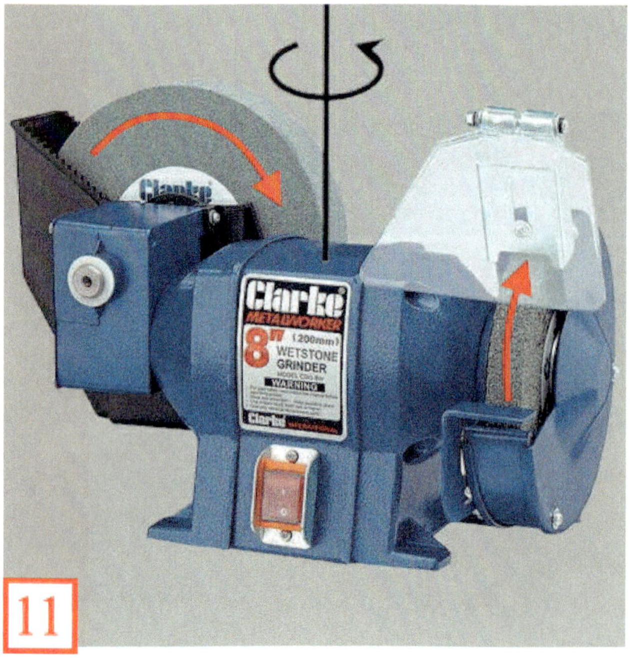

11

12

11 With the introduction of the "clones" of the Tormek, the twin-ended wetstone grinder is now less common. They do still exist in this category and are inexpensive, but all have the problem that a relatively coarse 8" wetstone (80 grit compared with 220 grit on a Tormek) paired with a 60 or 80 grit 6" wheel, which is also moving in the "wrong" direction, plus the tool rests are a joke. However, if you already have one of these budget machines, it really needs re-equipped with a better a quality wetstone, which will cost £25 - £65. Unless it's the old "improved" variation with a decent tool rest, you can still easily add a Tormek style tool-rest, which will greatly improve the accuracy.

12 To do this you start by removing the gearbox cover and replacing it with a larger metal plate with the Tormek XB-100 Base mounted on it. If you then want to make use of the shaft at the other end, unfortunately its rotation cannot be altered, as this form of machine cannot be rotated on its base. However, rotating the stone cover flange 180° and approaching the machine from the rear has a similar practical effect.

13 You can then fit a soft felt wheel for finishing carving tools and even mount a leather honing wheel out-board for stropping (Record WG250/N Profiled Leather Honing Wheel).

14 Finished assembly: Right>Left;
Tormek Tool rest above fine grain stone; Stubai felt wheel on original shaft; Record leather wheel on extension shaft.

13

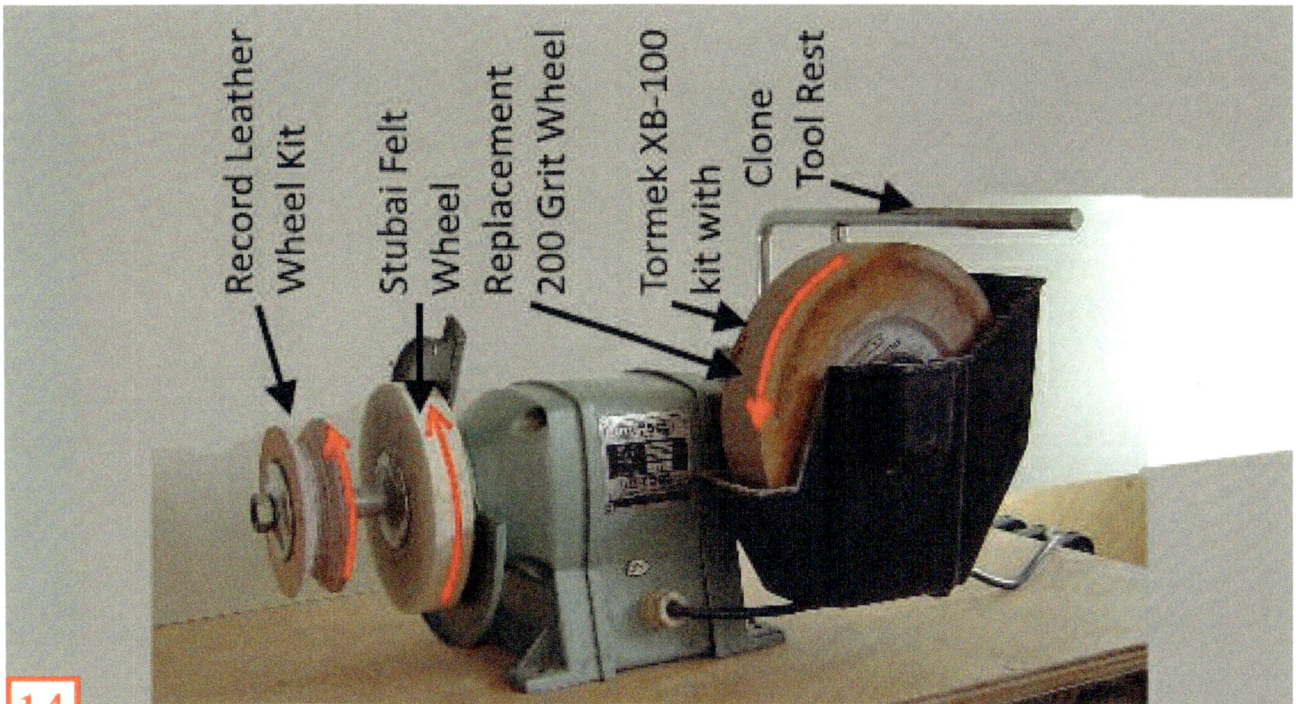

14

Note: the guards have been removed for the photo

SHAFT EXTENSIONS

Shaft extensions are available from Creusen (at a price) for both RH and LH M12x1x75 threads that are now commonly used on budget bench grinders in UK. I found that the budget offerings were heavy and not well enough machined or balanced to double up on a shaft, although the Record WG250/N *Profiled Leather Honing Wheel* does come with a well made RH shaft extension. This proved ideal for the replacement wheels on the wetstone grinder, but the linisher needs the wheels put onto the LH thread, of which the budget offerings, even when cut down to size, caused too much vibration. As a result, I resorted to purchasing some 20mm *Threaded Inserts* (made for the motor trade - hence well balanced) along with suitable threaded rod. Leaving half the 25mm thread depth free for the spindle, a length of threaded rod was silver-soldered in place, although epoxy would probably do just as well.

PAT Test - Portable Appliance Testing

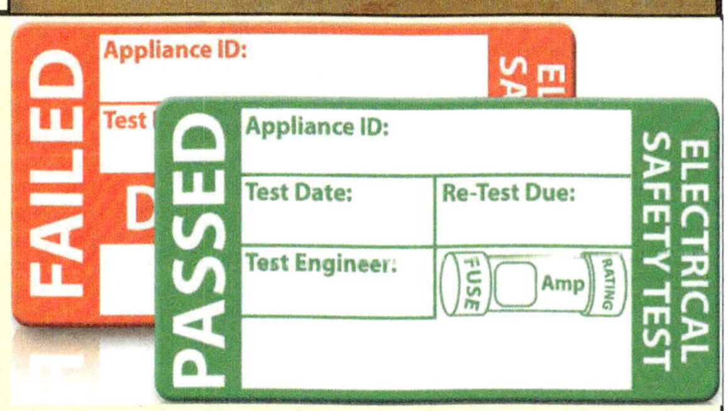

The "PAT" test is the name of a process in the UK by which electrical appliances are routinely checked for safety. The formal term for the process is "in-service inspection & testing of electrical equipment". Testing involves a visual inspection of the equipment and any flexible cables for good condition, and also where required, verification of grounding (earthing) continuity, and a test of the soundness of insulation between the current carrying parts, and any exposed metal that may be touched.

Option 3: Convert the Linisher

15

16

15 With the twin ended Belt-Sander/grinder, the first task is to reverse the direction of rotation so it's set up with the shafts turning away from you (see Option 1). Then remove the wheel guard and grind-stone and the sanding belt assembly, to replace them on the opposite ends (the wheel you should discard or put on e-bay as it will be replaced by a felt wheel). While the belt guard is dismounted, re-drill it so that it goes back onto the motor in the vertical, rather than the original 30° angle.

16 What is now needed is a Tormek compatible tool-rest which, for just the SVS32 "Short Tool Jig" can be based on a 12mm bar or for wider use, the Tormek XB-100 Base mounted on a spacer. You will also need at least one (and possibly more) of the Tormek (or compatible) jigs to use with this tool rest).

17

18

17 The "Tormek SVS-32 Short Tool Jig" is essential for carving tools and a compatible "Square Edge Jig" is also useful for general sharpening.

18 Now to the Koch-like end of the machine. A non-abrasive "Hard Felt" wheel is placed onto the shaft vacated by the coarse grind wheel, followed by a LH Spindle Adapter onto which an undersized 5" Soft Felt wheel is secured by a second LH Spindle Adapter, with a Record WG250-N Profiled Leather Honing Wheel to finish the lot. Before replacing the end wheel cover, a 15mm hole needs to be drilled in the end to enable the end of the shaft extension to protrude.

19 The two wheel covers are used to secure an extended wheel guard over the left hand side. A shaft end-support (arrow) is fabricated from an off-cut of 15mm brass tube or copper pipe to take the excess strain off the bearing and to damp any out-of-balance vibration. (The larger wheel guard was sourced from e-bay and held between the two wheel covers by lengths of threaded rod).

20 A simple ply tool rest was added with the top edge cut at 30° tangentially to the large felt wheel. It's also worth looking at the various belts that go with the Sorby system to get an idea of different types and uses (although their belts are too long for a "shed" linisher (at 50 x 686 you can use the specification of their abrasive to search for other suitable sharpening belts).

Option 3: Converted Linisher.

Sharpening Stones

21

22

The old catalogues list a long array of natural oil stones with geographic names such as India, Arkansas, Washita (Rosy Red) Hindustan, Belgian Blue, along with natural Sandstones & Emery. Most were also available as "slips" (small pieces of shaped stone) - see below.

21 These were supplemented at the end of the 19th Century with vitrified grinding wheel of Emery powder (aluminium oxide) fired in clay fallowed by the manmade "stones" of carborundum (synthetic Silicon Carbide). Some of these survive today, including the inexpensive synthetic Carborundums. Now these are supplemented by the use of synthetic "diamond" bonded to steel plates, and hard ceramic "stones" which come out as significantly more expensive.

22 The investment in a quality diamond sharpening plate is highly recommended as they remain flat and "sharp" much longer than the more traditional stones. With double sided plates available at less than the price of two separate plates, these often form the "best buy". For carving tools, the solid surface plates are superior to the perforated plates, the latter snag the corners of gouges. A useful inexpensive alternative is to glue a sheet of "wet & dry" paper to a hard, flat surface.

23 These "flat plate" abrasives have limited use for the inner bevel, so a collection of shaped "slips" are required for honing the inner bevel. These can be supplemented (or replaced) by rotary abrasives for hand held machines, like the Dremel.

23

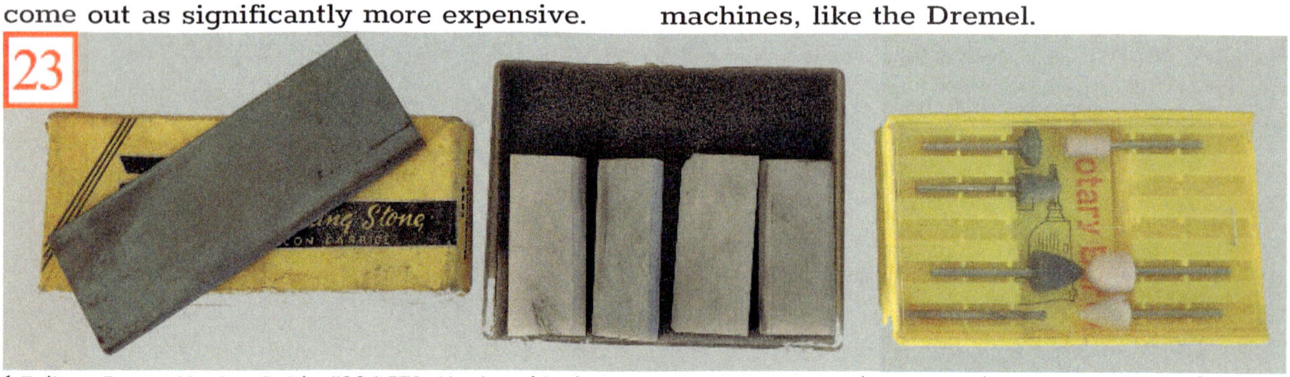

[1] *Eclipse Patent Honing Guide:#924,579. Honing chisels &c. JAMES NEILL & CO. (SHEFFIELD) Ltd. Feb. 21, 1962 [April 18, 1961], No. 13880/61*

OIL STONES

ARKANSAS

Unmounted			Price
6 x $1\frac{3}{4}$ x $\frac{3}{4}$ inch	Regular	Each,	$2.50
6 x $1\frac{3}{4}$ x $\frac{3}{4}$ "	Soft	"	1.00
8 x 2 x $1\frac{1}{8}$ "	Regular	"	4.90
8 x 2 x $1\frac{1}{8}$ "	Soft	"	2.00

In Cherry Cases			Price
6 x $1\frac{7}{8}$ inch	Regular	Each,	$1.70
6 x $1\frac{7}{8}$ "	Soft	"	1.00
8 x 2 "	Regular	"	2.25
8 x 2 "	Soft	"	1.35

WASHITA

ROSY RED

Unmounted		Price
6 x $1\frac{3}{4}$ x $\frac{3}{4}$ inch	Each,	$0.35
8 x 2 x $1\frac{1}{8}$ "	"	.65

In Cherry Cases		Price
6 x $1\frac{7}{8}$ inch	Each,	$0.65
8 x 2 "	"	.80

Our Rosy Red Washita Stones are warranted to have a fine even grit and to be free from hard or soft spots.

LILY WHITE

Best, extra fine grit, 8 x 2 x $1\frac{1}{8}$ inch, Each, $0.75 | Regular, 8 x 2 x 1 inch.......... Each, $0.50

INDIA

India Stones are even and clear grained throughout, have remarkable cutting qualities and are adaptable to all required shapes. A composition stone perfect in make up and in all good working points.

Medium			Price
No. 0.	8 x 2 x 1 inch	Each,	$1.00
" $1\frac{1}{2}$.	7 x 2 x 1 "	"	.75
" 2.	6 x $1\frac{5}{8}$ x $\frac{3}{4}$ "	"	.50
" 3.	4 x 1 x $\frac{1}{2}$ "	"	30
" 24.	$4\frac{1}{2}$ x $1\frac{1}{2}$ x $\frac{5}{8}$ "	"	.40
" 29.	6 x 2 x 1 "	"	.60

Fine			Price
No. 0.	8 x 2 x 1 inch	Each,	$1.50
" 24.	$4\frac{1}{2}$ x $\frac{1}{2}$ x $\frac{5}{8}$ "	"	.60
" 29.	6 x 2 x 1 "	"	.90

MISCELLANEOUS STONES

Queer Creek Stones,	8 x 2 x $1\frac{1}{8}$ inches	Each,	$0.40
Hindostan "	8 x 2 x $1\frac{1}{8}$ "	"	.15
Sand "	8 x 2 x $1\frac{1}{2}$ "	"	.10
Emery "	8 x 2 x 1 " (Nos. 60, 80, 100, 120 and 150)	"	.30

HAMMACHER, SCHLEMMER & CO.

1900 Hammacher, Schlemmer & Co

"Importers and Dealers in Fine Tools for All Trades, 209 BOWERY, NEW YORK"

Tool Profiles.

A The tool profile starts from the geometry forged into the blade by the blacksmith (or the factory). The cutting edge is then ground by the carver to suit the intended use. I have discussed the "standard" bevels earlier in relation to knives - see Page 18 -. Using the Eclipse Guide as a *"standard"*, this indicates for bench-chisels: either a 25° bevel or a 30° bevel, with most factory grinds delivering the former. Looking at a bench-chisel only gives a "guide" as even there the thinner "paring chisel" will be ground to 30°. A carving tool for "sculpting" will reflect the environment of a bench-chisel, but for ornamental carving it's going to be more like the paring-chisel, with the majority of carving tools coming from the factory with the outer ground straight with a 20° bevel. Most tools will need "finished" by the carver and a tool that is used (inverted) for decorative carving, may need this outer-bevel decreased towards a minimum of about 15° and finished with a short inner bevel. The thickness of the tool then becomes significant in the dichotomy between strength & sharpness. For this reason, for my decorative carvings, I preferred the thinner tools from say Henry Taylor or Europe over the thicker tools from Ashley Isles or Record-Irwin. This seems to have been taken up by Chris Pye with Ashley Isles as they now offer a range of thinner *"Chris Pye Finishing Gouges"*[1]. There is a new N°2½ in this range which has a slightly reduced curvature, in a similar way to the N°3 Chinese Detail Tool I use (see pg 9). Chris Pye's text[2] well describes the function of the inside bevel and the "relaxed" profile.

B In UK, carving tools come with the outside ground straight with wings in-line with the front edge. In Europe, where architectural carving traditions use the tool inverted more for paring, the wings tend to be ground back by the carver, with inner surface and micro-bevel polished. I noticed this trend emphasised in the Korean tools I use (see Pg 87), where the edge has a pronounced fingernail profile with a highly polished inside, which I have found most effective when the tool is used inverted for paring & finishing.

C Carving tools are often modified by the craftsman to meet a "niche" requirement that they have, a trend that is supported by the manufacturers in the array of named "special products" they provide. I have described in Chapter 11 a "paring" chisel that I find useful, where it started as a ½" (12mm) fish-tail where I have bevelled the edges

[1] *https://www.ashleyilestoolstore.co.uk/carving-tools/chris-pye-finishing-gouges/chris-pye-finishing-gouge*

[2] *https://toolsforworkingwood.com/extra/chrispye-gouges.pdfhttps://toolsforworkingwood.com/extra/chrispye-gouges.pdf*

Business End of Carving Tool

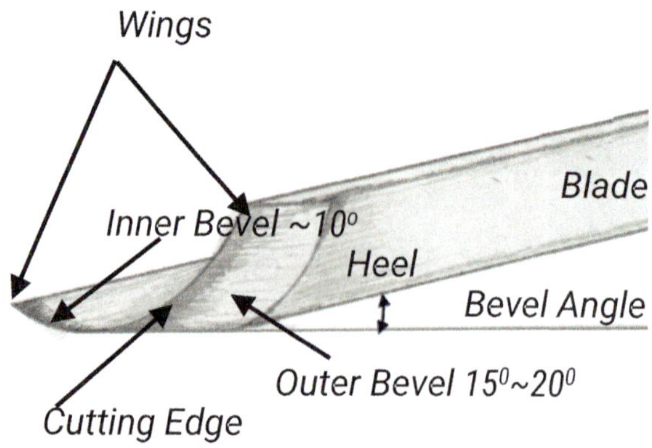

A

B UK Straight Grind v Korean Fingernail

C Modified tool - with Edge Bevel added

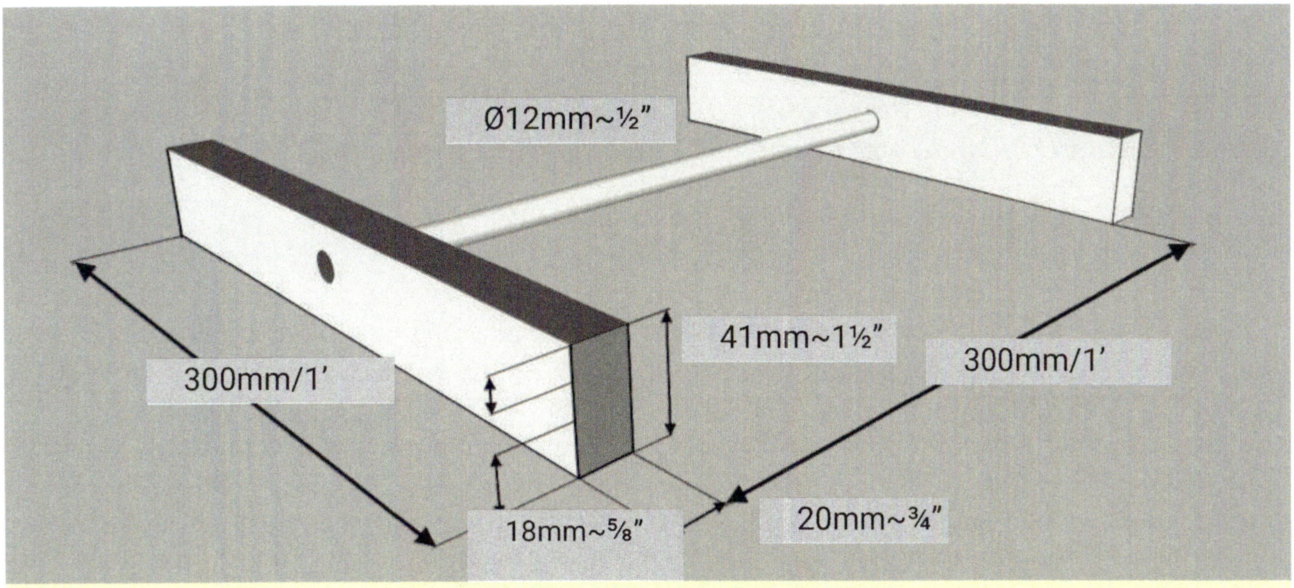

MAKING A SHARPENING SLEDGE

A The The easiest way to use the sharpening jigs without any machine is to fabricate a sledge from off-cuts to house a length of 12mm (~½") bar (don't try tube from a "Shed" as it lacks the accuracy of steel bar). To maximise the efficiency of the design, I made my sledge so that when used one way it gave a 30° bevel and the other way a 25° bevel. Either way, you will also need a granite tile (any of the good tile merchants) with sheets of abrasive stuck to it in the best *"scary-sharp"*[1] tradition. The dimensions in the diagram above are given as a guide only, the only critical measurements are those required for the sharpening geometry. For example, the 30° bevel is achieved when the height of the bar is at ½ x blade length.

B The machine jig can then be used to accurately slide a carving tool along the abrasive, taking care to rotate it as you go (this is where the updated Tormek SVS32 *"Short Tool Jig"* design really comes into its own as it will stay on the bar, while sliding & rotating. It is much more difficult to keep a "clone" in contact with the bar.

C The Eclipse style jig can also be used to sharpen straight tools

[1] *Scary Sharp: https://en.wikipedia.org/wiki/Scary_sharp*

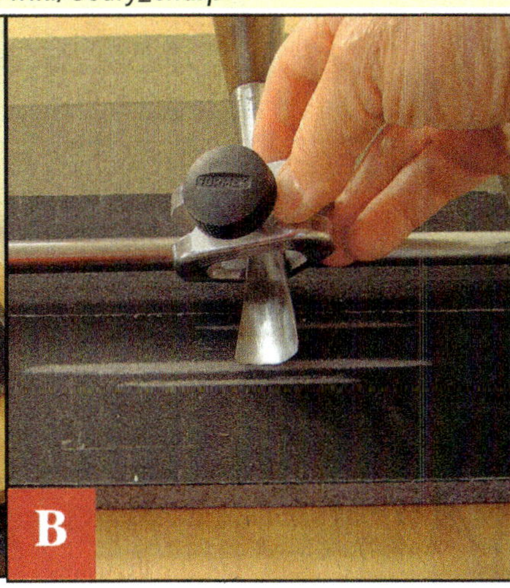

Chapter Four – Work Holding

Carving uses very sharp tools,
so it is very important that your work is firmly anchored.

If you look at the illustration from 1765[1] in an old French Encyclopaedia opposite, starting at "*fig 66*" onwards, there is little new in the field of "work holding". Back then they had the twin-screw vice of the Workmate® (*fig 68&69*), the metal hold-fast (*fig 70*) (available then from your local blacksmith), along with an array of suitable holes in bench tops and legs - but I doubt many of us now have the need (or the space) to cut a hole in the floor to work on long of timber beams as in fig 69. I've not used, nor will mention further the shaving horse (*fig 65-67).* I have seen the shaving horse used by carvers and the variations opposite could provide templates for someone to exploit?

There are many different ways of holding work for carving, but the foundation of most of them is some sort of work-bench. You may have to add to a bench some extra clamps for securing the work to gain the best use of the bench. If you want to understand the full potential that a workbench offers, I would recommend the excellent book by Chris Swartz[2] that walks you through all the many variations on bench design and construction, but most usefully makes you think about what you want to achieve with your workbench.

1 The main components of a bench for decorative carving (which is principally the carving of surfaces) are a flat surface and the means of clamping your work to it. With the use of an end-vice and the addition of bench dogs, inserted in holes in the surface, you have a bench that provides great flexibility for work holding. I was luck to have inherited my father's English joiners'

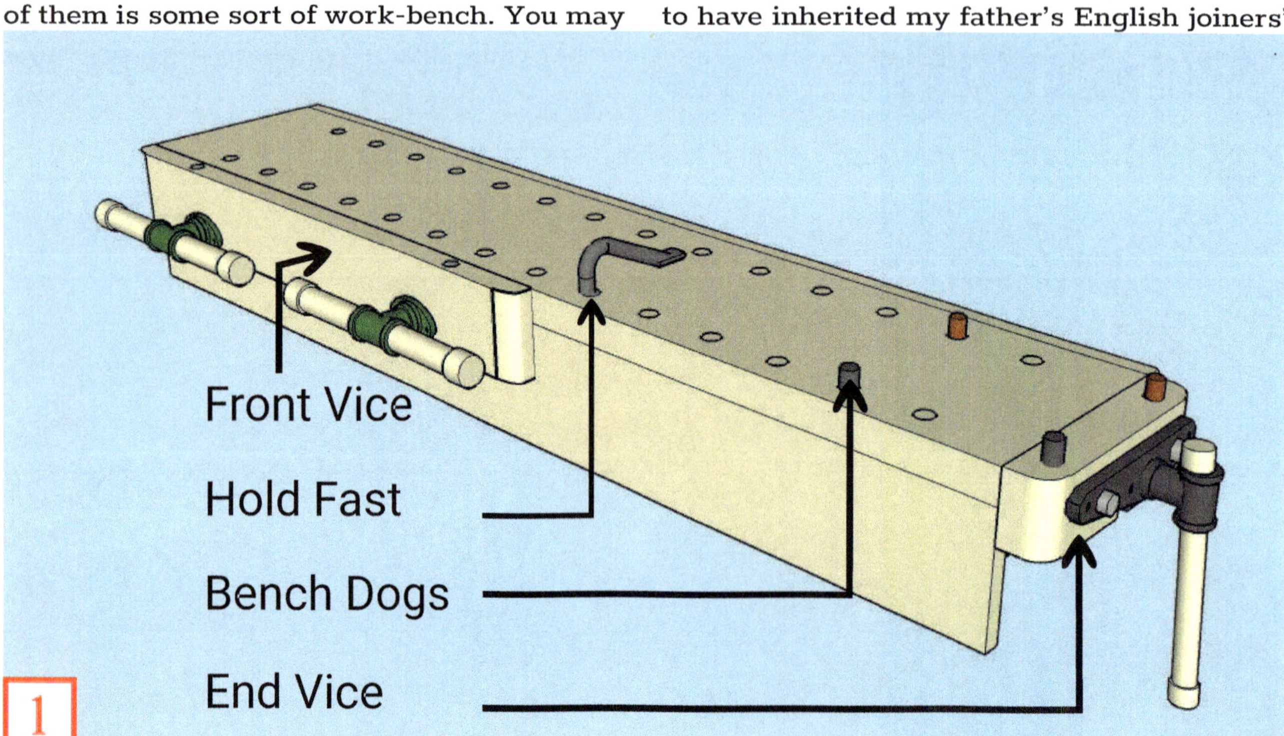

1

Diderot Encyclopédie - 1765 - Ébèniste et Marquéterie. Vol IV Pl IX

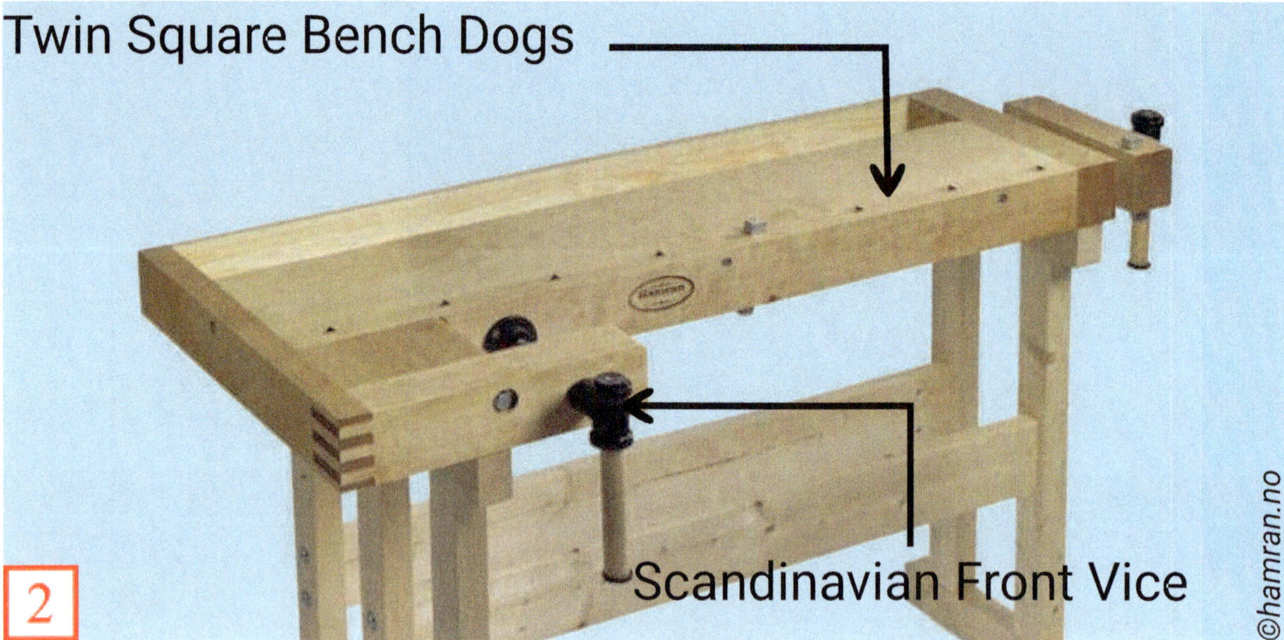

bench that provided the necessary solid surface, but lacked an end-vice. If like me you are adapting an existing bench, then the end-vice has to be retro-fitted, so the use of round bench-dogs (de facto standard at ¾" or 19mmØ) is the simplest solution, but square dogs, common in older benches, work just as well. A benefit of a joiners' bench is the front apron provides scope for holes for additional front dogs and hooks.

2 The old traditional Scandinavian workbench also had an end-vice plus a front vice without guide bars, thus giving you an open space to secure work at 90°,which, with the linked use of a leg clamp at the other end, gives great flexibility. I have a "school" bench (***Skolehøvelbenk***) from Hamran[3] in Norway that has the ideal configuration. Hamran seems to be the only remaining manufacturer of these benches with the "traditional" front vice, as the more commonly available Scandinavian work benches seem to have moved to the cost effective use of ironwork with integral guide bars. A good point is that the Scandi-bench top is usually thin enough to enable the use of clamps.

3 If you are going to modify an existing bench, then an end-vice is the first preference for carving, as this will enable you to reach three sides of your carving with ease. There are many sources and types[4] of end vices;

A the single vice-screw, (note: most are setup for fitting through an apron)

B the vice-screw with guide rods, (available also with quick-release).

4 The easiest compromise, but possibly more expensive, is simply to fit a Record N°52 with a wooden face that is

4

large enough to take bench-dogs holes (or any of the less expensive "cloned" 230mm/9" iron vices) .

5 If you are modifying a bench, also think about securing work to the front as this can also be useful for enabling the edge of a carving to be attacked. This could either be a twin-screw vice (with wider applications than just carving) or by adding a front bench hook to supplement the conventional front vice, providing a "third hand" to clamp the "other end" of the work. This may only work easily if you have an English style joiners' bench with a front apron to drill for dogs, although clamps can be used in leg holes on most Scandi-benches.

6 Coupled with an end-vice there is the need for bench dogs (¾" or 19mmØ) and possibly a hold-fast or bench-hook. Again there are several commercial offerings, all with they're own unique selling point. However, I find that short lengths of hardwood dowel can work just as well as do the majority of 20mm "Workmate[5]" plastic dogs. The old iron bench-hook has its uses, although the modern hold-fasts with a screw action are a superior investment for carving[6] and they have wider applications than just holding carvings; coupled to leg holes they can form a "third hand" to a front vice.

5

6

7

8

9

7 There are also times when you would want to be able to rotate a carving, more commonly with wood sculpture, but also helpful when carving pattresses. This is where a special carvers' vice like the face plate-vices (previous page) come into their own. These are available from multiple sources, either for bench mounting or as clamp mounting, such as Record Tools[7] or their clones.

8 A less expensive adaptation that will enable a 90° flip and variable rotation is the use of a basic 6" iron vice mounted on a length of scrap timber. This can be secured in you bench vice and sloped at any required angle. Old 6" vices can be bought at flea markets for small change, or a clone can be bought new for upwards of £15, so it is an economic and adaptable "tool" for occasional use.

9 Another variation on that theme is simply a (wooden) clamp in a vice - here the old Jorgensen Hand Screw Clamps make the best combination, as their jaws are able to be set non-parallel plus they won't damage your tools on accidental contact.

10 When carving with a knife the use of a vice is not needed and can even be

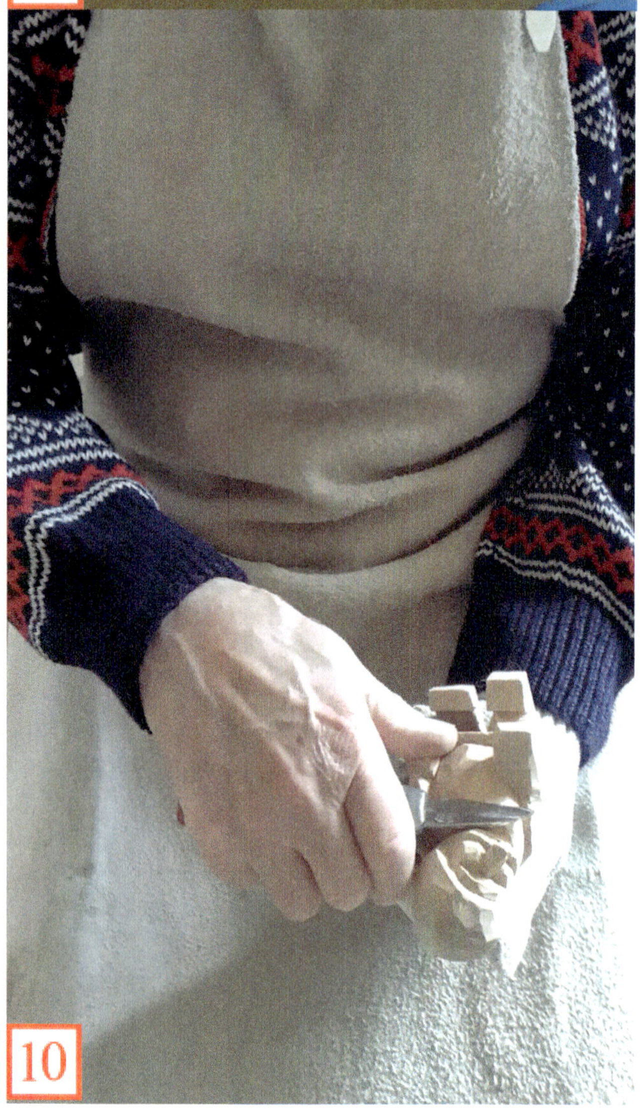

10

Portable Carving Vice

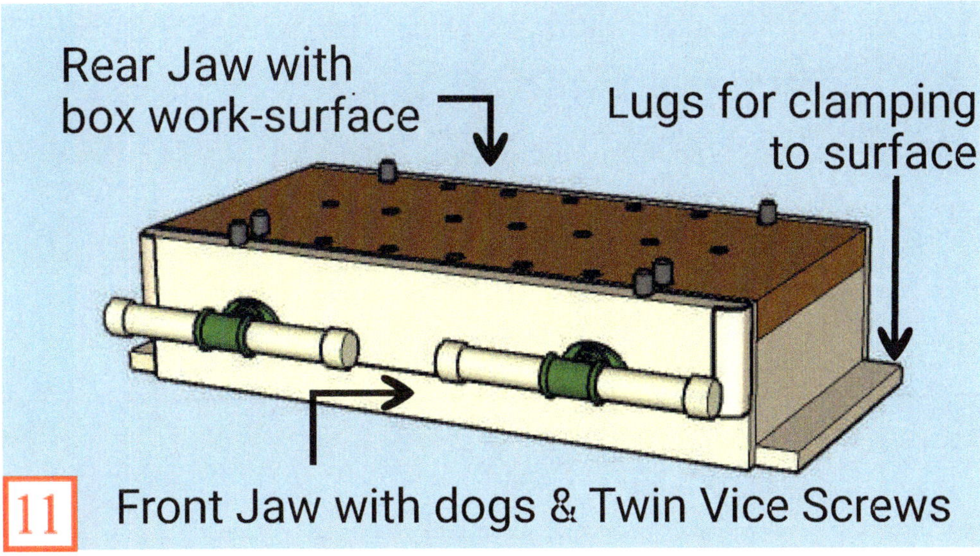

impractical. If hand carving, I would recommend using a kevlar glove (that should conform to EN388:2016[8] (or ANSI/ISEA 105-2016[9], the equivalent in the USA) on the hand that "holds". An added precaution for hand carving, especially when sitting down to carve, is a suitable leather apron, to protect the lower regions from the worst of any accidental blade-damage.

I have written this book to bring carving to the woodworker. As a result, this chapter has been written on the premise that you already have a work bench available, so I have described how best to hold carving to an existing bench. There are scenarios, that are not uncommon for a woodworker, that can result in the lack of a "proper" workshop being available. Lack of space in the home is the most common, which was a frequent problem that I had with the peripatetic lifestyle of serving in the armed forces. The solution to this problem is either a "knock-down" work-bench (which is where my Norwegian *Hamran* bench came from, as the solid top is easily removed from the "knock-down" base) or a portable carving vice that can be secured to any available surface.

11 The latter is where making a "Moxon"[10] vice can be a solution. While there are many sources of plans and hardware "kits" available for this, it is in essence a couple of vice screws holding jaws together in a manner that has apparently been around since the 16th century. To use this setup effectively for woodcarving,the main face needs to be thick enough to take ¾" dogs and the back face needs to be extended with a deep box which has been drilled to accept the ***dog-mates*** as a working surface.

12 Another portable carvers' vice is what I would call the "***Scandi-light***" vice, which is a bench-top vice that was available commercially as a "***Carvers' Bench***" from Messrs Hammacher & Co in New York as early as 1900, but can be reproduced easily with a vice screw on the end of a box structure, with the top surface thick enough to be drilled for dogs and with the bottom section extended enough for lugs to clamp it

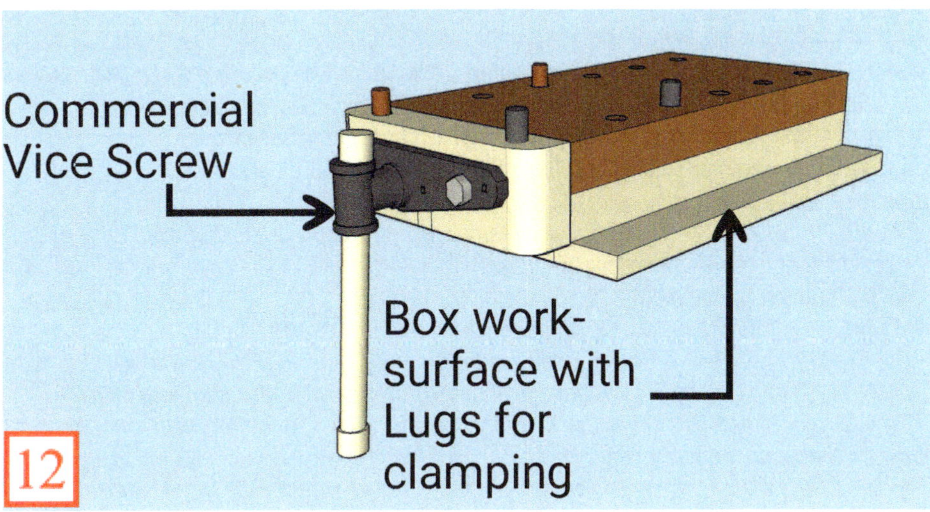

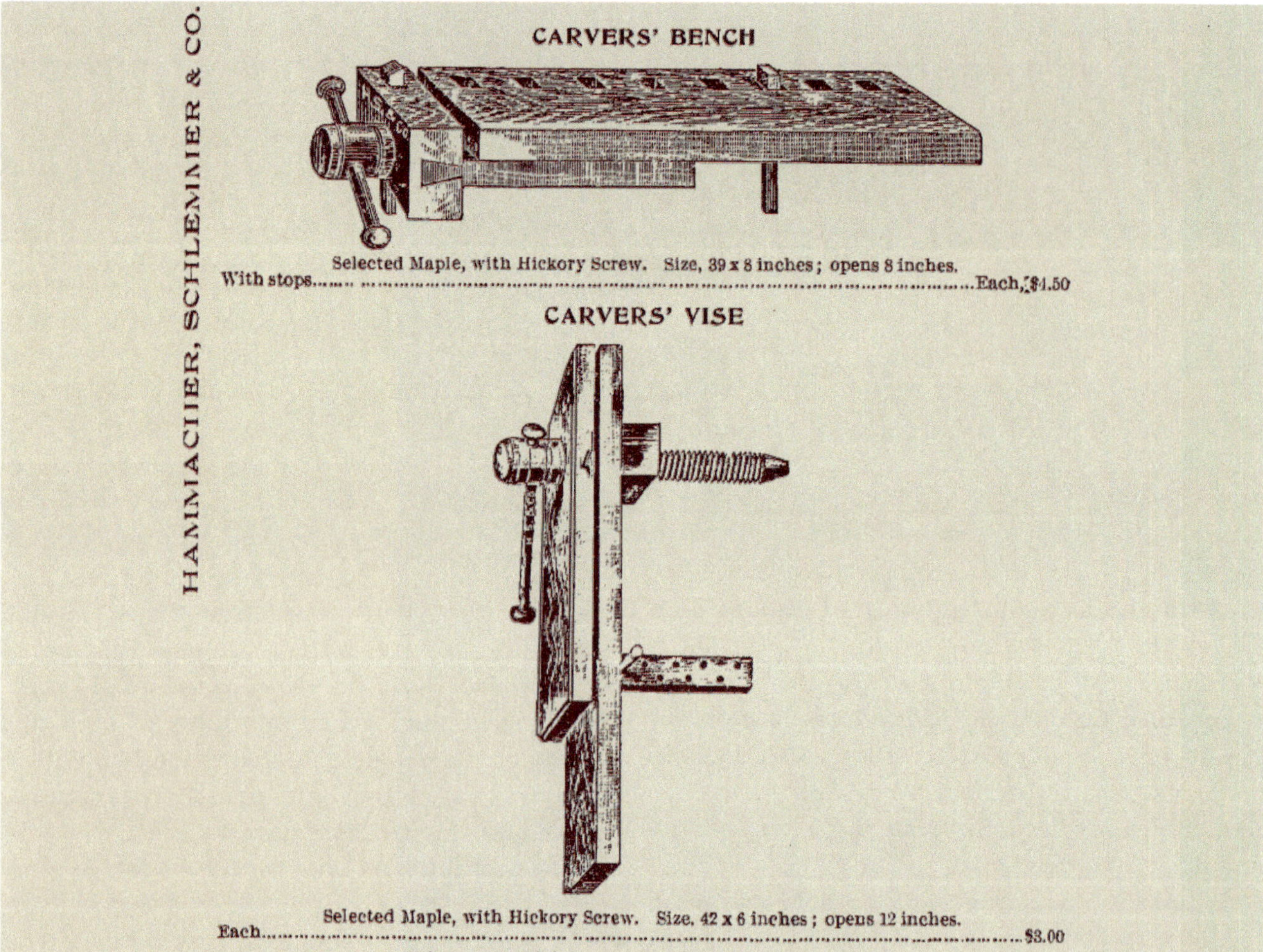

The portable carvers' vice is not new.
This plate from a Catalogue published in New York in 1900 offered two variations.

to a table top. Current commercial versions are made by Sjöberg[11] of Sweden as their "***Smart Vise***" series. A table top vice can be secured to a suitable surface, or in the jaws of a Workmate® style folding bench and can hold a carving securely.

[1] *Plate IX: Tools - Adjustable tools: vice or bench vice; a different [type of] bench vice; another [type of] press. https://quod.lib.umich.edu/d/did/*

[2] *Workbenches, Revised Edition: From Design & Theory to Construction & Use;May 2016:ISBN-13: 978-1440343124*

[3] *Hamran Snekkerverksted ASNorway; http://www. hamran. no/høvelbenker/*

[4] *Assorted Vice Screws https://www. fine-tools. com/spindel. html*

[5] *"Workmate" used as generic term for folding benches of the type: https://en. wikipedia. org/wiki/Black_%26_Decker_Workmate*

[6] *Sjöberg HOLDFAST ST03: https://www. sjobergs. se/en/products/hobby/239. php?id=1036&cat=30&lang=en&artnr=33637*

[7] *RECORD Carver's Vice RPCV130: http://www. recordpower. co. uk/product/carvers-vice#. WrpqAT-5uUk*

[8] *HSE EN388: http://www. hse. gov. uk/foi/internalops/oms/2009/03/om200903app5. pdf*

[9] *ANSI/ISEA 105-2016 https://webstore. ansi. org/standards/isea/ansiisea1052016*

[10] *Chris Schwartz explains the name he coined: https://www. popularwoodworking. com/woodworking-blogs/chris-schwarz-blog/questions-moxon-vise*

[11] *Sjöberg Smart Vice: https://www. sjobergs. se/en/products/hobby/238. php?id=1100&cat=29&lang=en&artnr=33274*

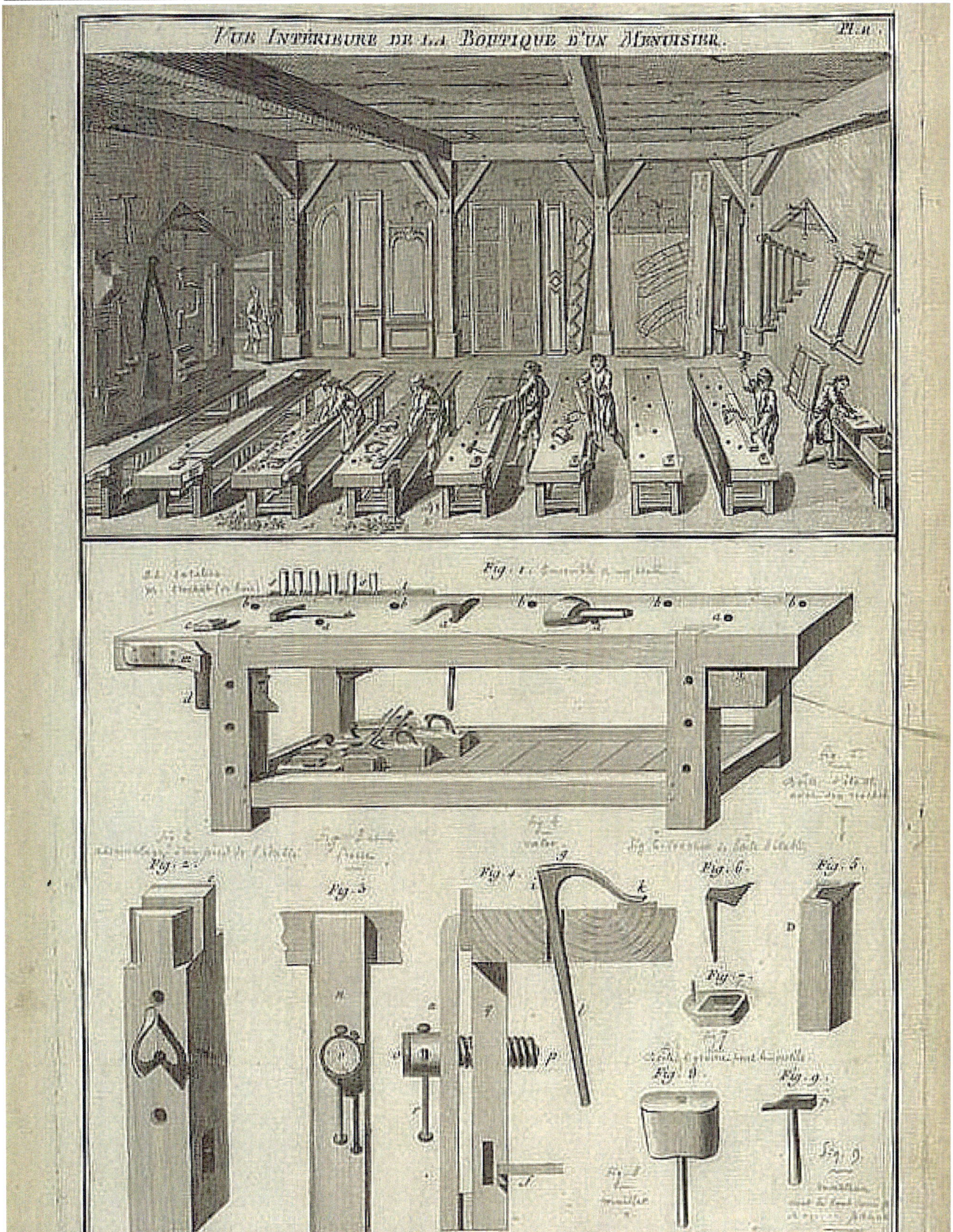

18thC Work holding: Pl 11: L'art du menuisier: 1769
[Paris: Académie Royale des Sciences]

Chapter Five – Finishing

Having invested time and energy in a carving, it needs finished to set it up for display.

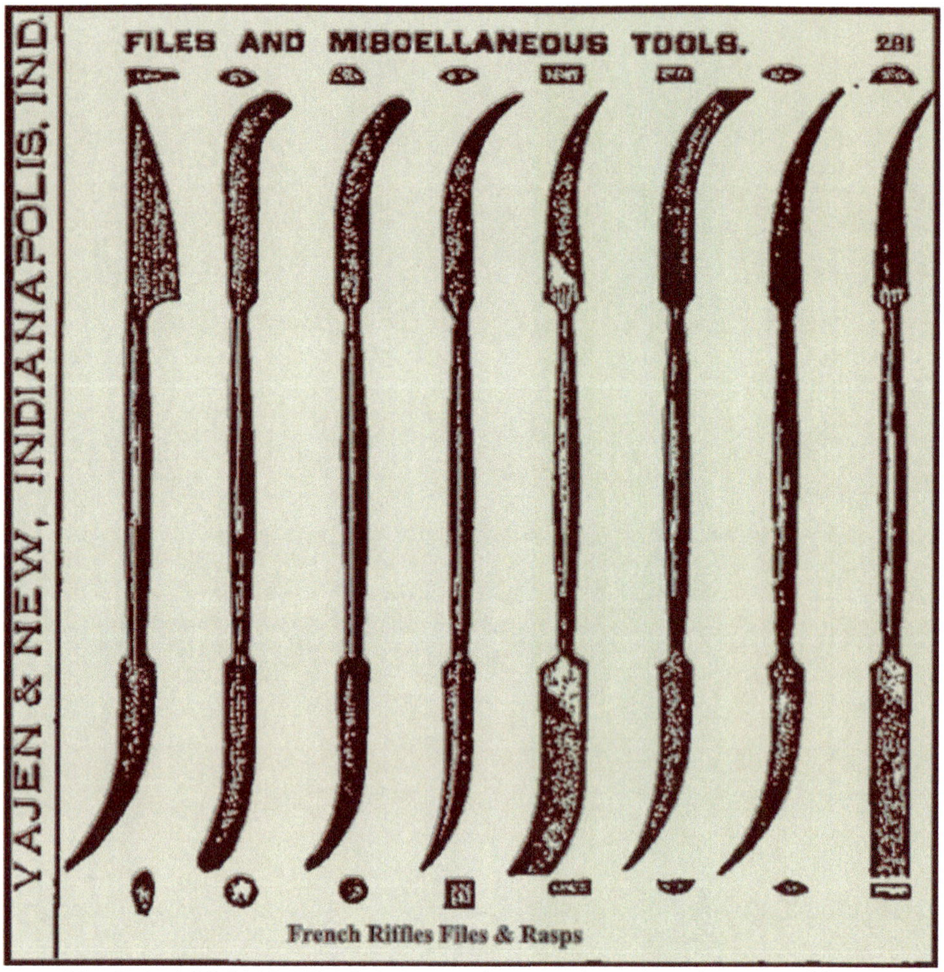

Fig 5-1: 1884 VAJEN & NEW Indianapolis - Catalogue Rifflers pg

Any use of abrasive on a carving is to be discouraged, as it is going to leave abrasive residue in the wood. This in turn will harm the edge of your tools, leading to a cycle of re-sharpening & honing. Small imperfections can be removed with a fine needle file, riffler file,or an abrasive "plate" such as the (discontinued) ***Sandvik Sandplate*** or its nearest replacement the Japanese NT[1] ***NT Dresser S-10P***. Rifflers are extensively used in sculpture and traditionally, the best results are obtained from expensive hand-cut files, although fine diamond plate needle files and the abrasive plates come close.

When the carving is complete (and only after you will definitely not return to it with edge tools), it can be burnished by the use of an extra-fine flap wheel mounted on a hand drill. This is especially beneficial if the carving is to be finished with a painted or with a gilded surface.

Painting of carvings has a long tradition throughout Europe and in Norway, Lars Kinsarvik (1846-1925),is credited with developing the Dragon Style of painted carving. This "***Dragestil***" re-creating ornamental themes taken from the Viking Age. His ideas were the Norwegian reflection of the "Arts & Crafts" movement in England and the "Mission Style" furniture in the US where a return to traditional furniture construction was emphasised but in Kinsarvik's case, then tempered by the ornate vernacular traditions and cultural identity of Norway. His ornate carved and painted furniture was in at the birth of "Art Nouveau", forming part of the Norwegian exhibition at the 1900 Paris

Fig 5-2: Sanvik "Sandplate"

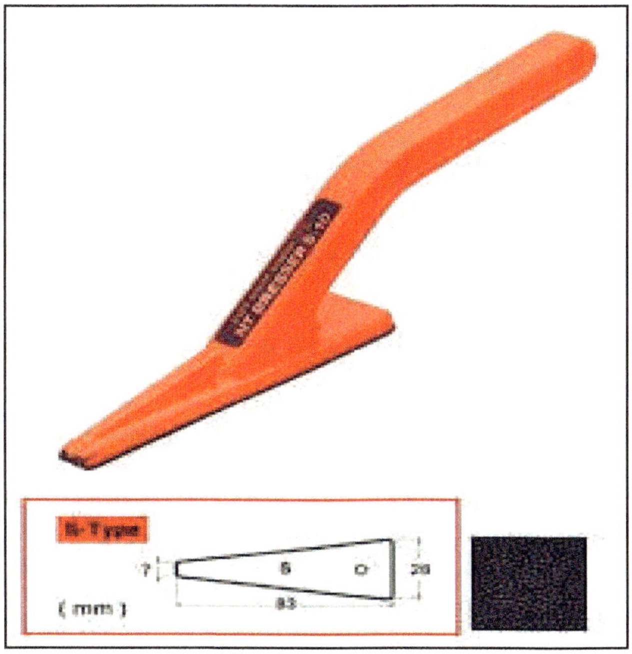

Fig 5-3: NT Dresser S-10P

World Fair (1900 Paris) . This tradition is still alive in Norway still has a keen following with spectacularly furniture and effects painted in the "***Rosemaling***" style, such as

Fig 5-4: "Rosemaling" style painted finish,

the colour plate at the end of this chapter. It is a style still taught in Norwegian craft schools, a finish that attracts premium prices in their domestic market. In addition, it remains common to paint the caricature carvings of the "Flat Plane" tradition, which will include the various mythical Trolls and traditional Christmas characters carved in Scandinavia. Should you wish to leave your carving without paint, it can still be coloured with stain or French Polish, the latter being a common finish for restoration work, as it seals the wood while leaving a transparent finish that will develops a patina as it ages. Where the carving is a component of a restoration project, the main piece will determine the possible use of stain and the final finish that you use. (Do remember to test any stain on a trial carving, as the random grain exposed by a carving can cause unexpected difficulties in colour matching).

I do often finish carvings with a liberal application of oil, either the ubiquitous Danish oil, (Walnut Oil is better substitute for boxes, or, where food contact may occur), followed by a top coat of good quality wax polish.

Fig 5-5: "Natural" style painted finish,

For external work, creosote works well, but the other modern preservatives can also provide a range of colours from clear to shade of brown. I would not normally recommend varnish on a carving, but its selective use on an external carving (or French polish internally) can seal a portion of the work, allowing contrast with its surround.

For example, the features of this Wood Spirit were sealed between the base and topcoats of a dark preservative, making the face stand out on the final work. The "art " of colour matching is subjective and comes from a build-up of the colours of wood stain plus the hue of the over-laid French Polish. This can be "tweaked" by the colour of the wax polish used to finish it all. If a dark oak finish is needed, the darkest Garnet polish is used (Button Polish gives a brighter red/brown finish, better suited to mahogany, while Garnet Polish is richer and darker, more suited to old oak with Blonde Polish available to be used as a transparent seal coat).

You need to apply several coats over a number of days, as a new coat will re-dissolve underling coats that are fully hard. Keep going until an acceptable colour match is achieved and fully hardened-off before touching it up with coloured wax polish.

Fig 5-6: "Creosote" finish

[1] NT Dresser S-10P http://www.ntcutter.co.jp/cat14A.htm

Fig 5-6: "Norwegian Traditional painted" finish[1]

[1] https://digitaltmuseum.no/011023246857/tine

Chapter Six - Simple Ornamentation

Before you can start, you need a "cunning plan". This can be a very simple geometric design prepared with a few tools.

The use of geometric designs for ornamentation has its roots in antiquity, but only reached its full potential once the theory of geometry was better understood. Simple designs can be achieved using iterative techniques, but a basic knowledge of the arcane science of geometry greatly helps in the design for larger or more complex objects. The designer's tools include a ruler and a basic school drawing compass, although the more advanced draftsman's scale rules plus a bow compass and dividers do make life easier. Otherwise items such as standard carpentry cutting gauges can be useful for edge ornamentation and, for those educated in the computer age without the benefit of tuition in technical drawing and geometry, computer design software all have the necessary geometry tools built in to them to make draw simple shapes and then make multiple linear copies easily- that's how the illustrations for this article were prepared using the inexpensive TurboCAD or the freeware Sketchup. The common geometric shapes are squares and circles which can be simply subdivided, (squares into triangles and circles into arcs and sectors). Adding offsets into the mix and a bewildering array of complex patters can be achieved with basic step-and-repeat techniques.

Λ For example, starting with dividing a couple of parallel line into equal segments (squares) and adding diagonals (that give a sharp tip) you have the basis of the many varieties of the "hound's tooth"[1] . These patterns can either be simply incised with a sharp tip or have the third dimension of relief added by "Chip-Carving", to create various "egg-box" shapes. In its simplest form Chip-carving is based on a triangular cut, which gives four different borders.

1 In the first section they are composed of the same triangular cut but different-

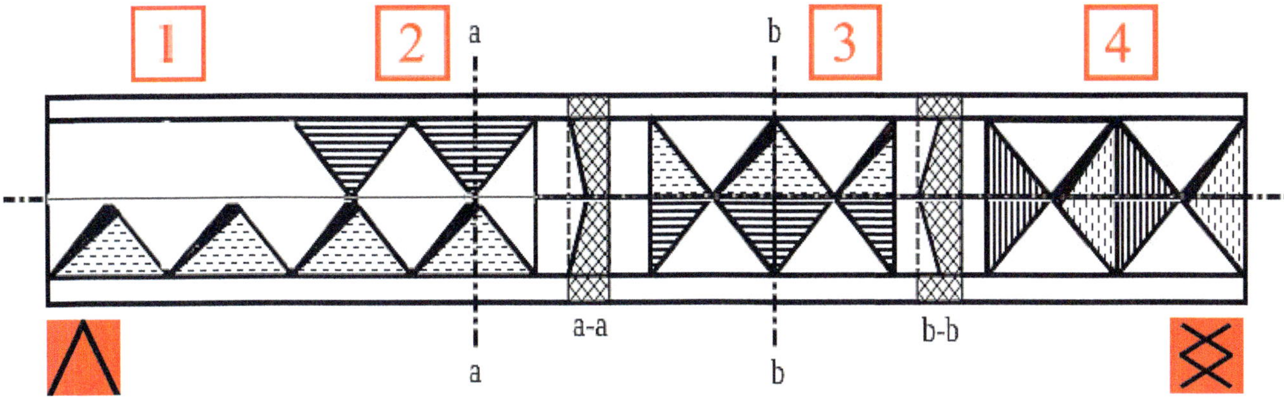

ly arranged. The shaded parts show where the surface of the wood is to be removed.

2 In the second the border is the first pattern reversed and duplicated. The first incision should be cut deep at the apex of the triangle, and very lightly as it reaches the base line (see the section a-a on the dotted line at 2.

3 In the third pattern the diamond is cut into two triangles, the ridge being on the central horizontal line, as in section b-b on the dotted line at 3.

4 Finally the pattern can be simply rotated by 90° at with the central ridge now vertical. This sequence results in a very ancient diamond patterns emerging called the Ing-Freyr rune. This is an ancient pagan symbol of life and virility that crept into early church decoration, especially common in Gothic ornamentation. Runs and patterns are produced by step-and-repeat.

Moving from rectangles and lines and linear progressions, by introducing the circle to the construction, not only do you greatly extend the repertoire, but you also get into the realms of more ancient symbology and hidden meanings. By drawing the two diagonals at 90° on a circle it divides the circle into four sectors, giving the four points of the St Andrew's Cross. From a decorative stand point, this is usually used as a flat motif as it does not lend itself to "excavation". By dividing the circle into five, it produces pentagram (in the USA the "Star of Texas") - a five pointed star, which is based on a pair of superimposed triangles, that are constructed using the basic geometry of a circle. Although the construct pre-dates Christianity, it was used by early

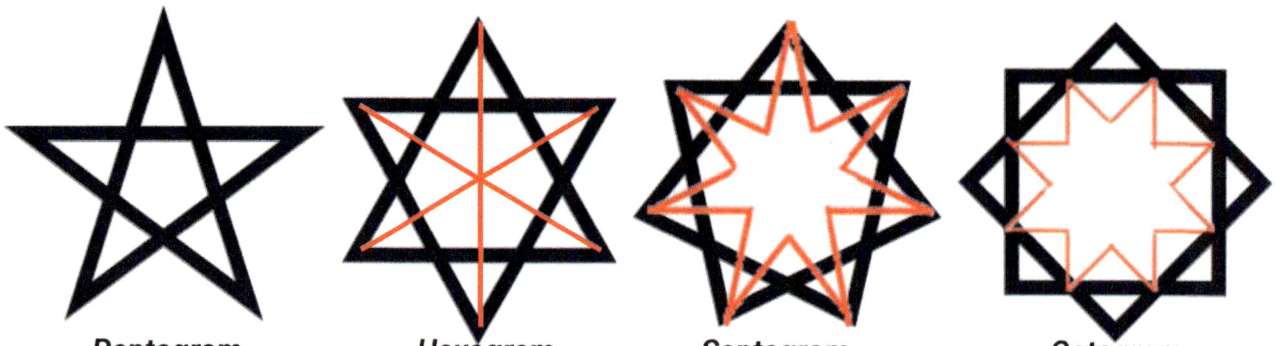

Pentogram *Hexagram* *Septagram* *Octagram*

Christians, It again came to prominence in the Renaissance, where the orientation became critical (point to top: good, to bottom: evil) as it became associated with with Black Magic. Again, decoratively, it is usually used as a flat motif as it does not lend itself to "excavation".

By adding an extra sector, which adds an extra point it becomes the six-point star (the hexagram). Here you are back with the Norse as the Hagall rune. This shape also appears elsewhere; in ancient Hindu symbology as the Jewish "Star of David", in early Christianity, and also in Islam, - all, in one way or another, symbolising life and light. It is made up of a pair of superimposed equilateral triangles and lends itself well to further sub-division for relief carving.

Add another sector and you have the septagram or heptagram is again seen in Judeo-Christian symbology to symbolise the seven days of the creation, hence God himself. It's also known as the Elfin or Fairy star in pagan/witchcraft, where it has magic powers. It is said to be a protective charm that embodies the seven powers of the universe. As it has an odd number of apexes, one construct joins these in a straight sequence that weaves itself under and over, so combines the good-luck of four. with the holy trinity in the "Star of Babylon".

The octagram is the Christian "Star of Redemption" and represents baptism or regeneration. It also symbolises the eight paths in the way of Buddha and the eight Immortals in Chinese culture. In astrology it is the "Celestial Conjunction" or "Wheel of the Year" symbolising the four points of the compass with the four sun-rises and sun-sets of the two solstices.

It is also an old Norse pattern re-generated in the 19th century in Selbu, Norway as possibly the most recognise knitted rose pattern in traditional ski jumpers, so sometimes known as "The Norwegian Rose" or "Selburose"[2]. Each of these basic patterns can be further sub-divided to get more and more complex designs based on

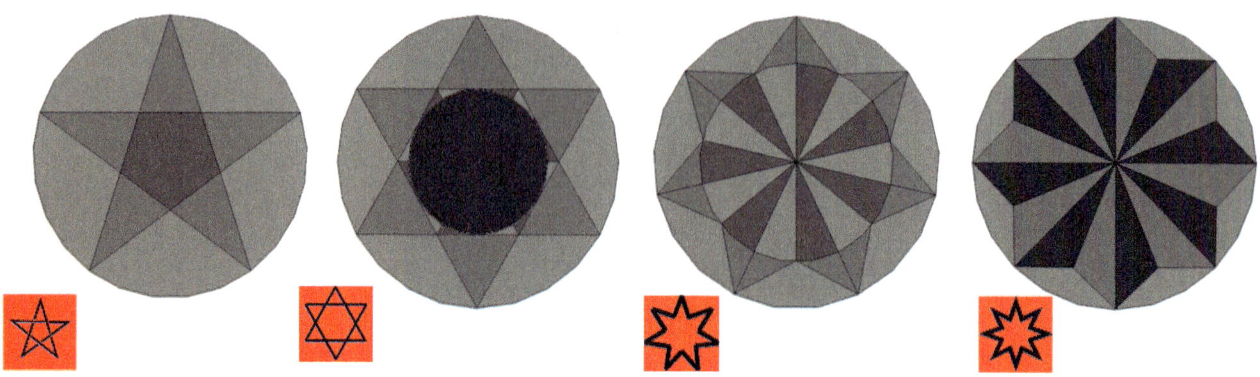

the underlying geometry. All that is needed is a "puzzle-book" mentality to work systematically connecting more and more diagonals. To further complicate the design, small off-sets can be introduced, which will have the effect of providing sub-dividing lines within the pattern itself. This allows yet another layer of visual complexity to the final work. Both the skill of the carver and the ability of the wood to take fine detail need to be kept in mind.

GEOMETRY:

For the traditional geometric construction, only a drawing compass is essential, with a straight-edge or other ruler used to join the points. The geometry required to construct the stars is all about finding the length of the chord that will divide the circle into the required number of segments mathematically. By simply using a compass, no measuring errors are introduced from ruler (miss)-readings following a simple sequence:

Pentagram: Draw the circle and leave the compass set at 'r' bisect the radius to find it's mid-point M, then place the point on M and the pencil on A to get the sector length. With this length A-M fixed, step-&-repeat from A round the circumference, before finally connecting the dots across the centre. Draw a circle and without changing the radius, draw another arc from the apex.

Hexagram: Keep the compass set at the original radius 'r' and place the point at the apex A and draw an arc. From where this cuts the circumference, draw another arc - then step-and-repeat all the way round. Again, get a straight edge and join the dots, to form two superimposed triangles.

Septagram: From where the horizontal diameter intersect the circle draw an arc of radius 'r' cutting the circle twice. Join the two intersections and the new chord-radius is the distance BM, the perpendicular from B to the intersection with the diameter. Set 'r'=BM on the compass and step-and-repeat round the circle, before joining the dots.

Octagram: The circle is divided into eight segments by drawing a pair of 90° diameters, with the second pair rotated 45° from the first - then join the ends.

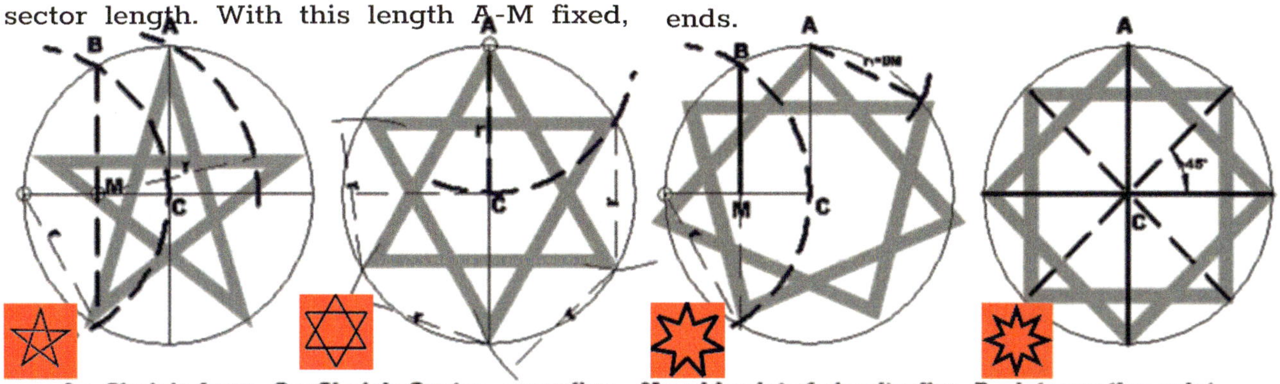

A = Circle's Apex C = Circle's Centre r = radius M= mid-point of chord/radius B = intersection point

SKETCHUP[1]

Sketchup *is a free design program - not strictly Computer Aided Design (CAD) as it does not use a rigorous mathematical model for drawing. This is one time that you can make use of Sketchup's inability to draw a true circle - it just makes a "polygon" of short lines that "looks" like a circle. Described above is the traditional geometric constructs used to find the right radius with which to equally divide the circumference for "step-and-repeat". This can be easily mimicked in Sketchup through using the* ***"Entities"*** *where you can change the number so segments in the circle to one divisible by the required number of points on the star, For example below is for a Pentagram:*

1. Draw the circle of your required dimensions

2. Go into the ***"Entities"*** *pop-up box and change the number of segments to one divisible by the required five points on the star.*

3. Locate the ***"end-point"*** *of each of the fifth segments and join them across the circle with a chord.*

4. In some cases, the program will not leave a point at the top, so you may have to use the ***"rotate tool"*** *to restore it.*

5. To get a subsequent concentric circle with the same number of sectors (for developing your design further), the trick is to generate it separately, to the required (smaller) radius, adjust the segments to suit, then simply move it to become concentric, before inserting the required lines as above.

[1] *Sketchup Free Download: https:https://www.sketchup.com/offline-download*

[1] *Also known as "wolf tooth" in Middle & Eastern Europe*

[2] *https://no.wikipedia.org/wiki/Selburose*

FIG. 12.

"Chip" Carving

1903 Woodcarving Design - Jack George

Chapter Seven - Design & Drawing

If you want something more challenging or rewarding than a simple geometric design, first it will need to be designed & drawn such as with the traditional Acanthus leaf

Acanthus design goes back to antiquity, with its stylised leaves appearing in both ancient Greek and Roman architecture. As such, it was an obvious style for the Renaissance carver to re-invent, bringing it back to life throughout Europe in the 17th and 18th century. In contrast to the pseudo-realistic styles of Grinlin Gibbons in England, acanthus and its later cousin rococo dominated the architectural decorations in the Baroque period in Europe, reaching its zenith in the ornate gilded carvings of Louis XIV's Versailles & Peter the Great's Winter Palace in St Petersburg. The acanthus design also found a home in Norway with its long tradition in the work of the artists of the Gudbransdal and Telemark regions. Here the more traditional gilding, still used in formal settings, was supplemented by the dramatic painting of carvings in the traditional Norwegian ***rosemaling*** style, later developed by Lars Kinsarvik into the Dragon Style "***Dragestil***" re-creating ornamental themes taken from the Viking Age. In the early part of the 20th century the "***Dragon Style***" was taken up by the Norwegian "Art Nouveau" architects, with building designs featuring massive exposed log walls, decoratively carved interiors with steep roofs and large over-hanging eaves, all decorated with Dragon finials, in the style of the old Norwegian Stave Churches.

While the design drawing of the Renaissance acanthus looks deceptively simple, it contains within it all the various aspects of the ancient classical beliefs in symmetry of natural form, complete with a formal structure and geometry of its own, all beautifully documented in the Victorian tome by James Page[1] printed in 1886.

The basic leaf form, shaped like a "***fishing rod***" (mathematically termed a ***Bézier Curve*** if you're looking to use a computer based drawing tool). When the perfect fishing rod can be drawn, the variety of ways of interconnecting the "fishing rod" curves can explored, with the second line, drawn above the first to develop the "leaf" motif, giving plenty of width to the start of the two leaf blade but always tapering away to the notional vanish-

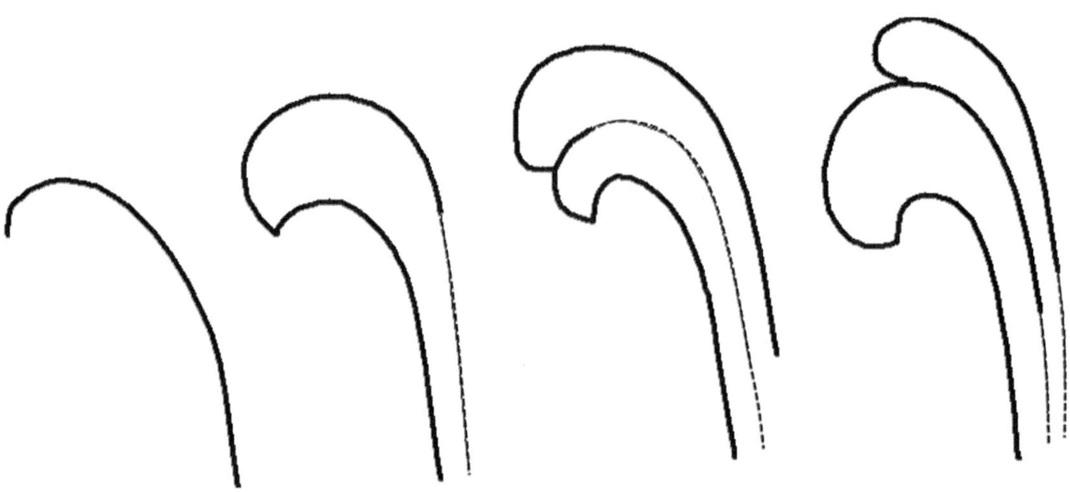

1886 Guide for drawing Acanthus - James Page - Plate 5

a "snout" or nose, a third line can then be developed, to balance the first line, in the formation of the three-blade design. The various rules for the two and three blade combinations of the traditional acanthus design highlight the significance of the shape of the initial line, as it is from this that the shape of all others are developed. The root, together with subsequent stems, is then evenly divided to provide for the required number of shoots and for the development of The actual acanthus leaf shape is then added by drawing from the leaf tip back to the root, or intermediate branches, ensuring an even taper along the spline. This means that the largest "leaf set" is drawn in first, with progressively smaller "sub-sets" added to fill the design. The form and style of combining the individual leaf designs is developed into a coherent patter, using a linear progression of splines, and snail shell "S" curves. This is developed on a ratio of two to three (slightly

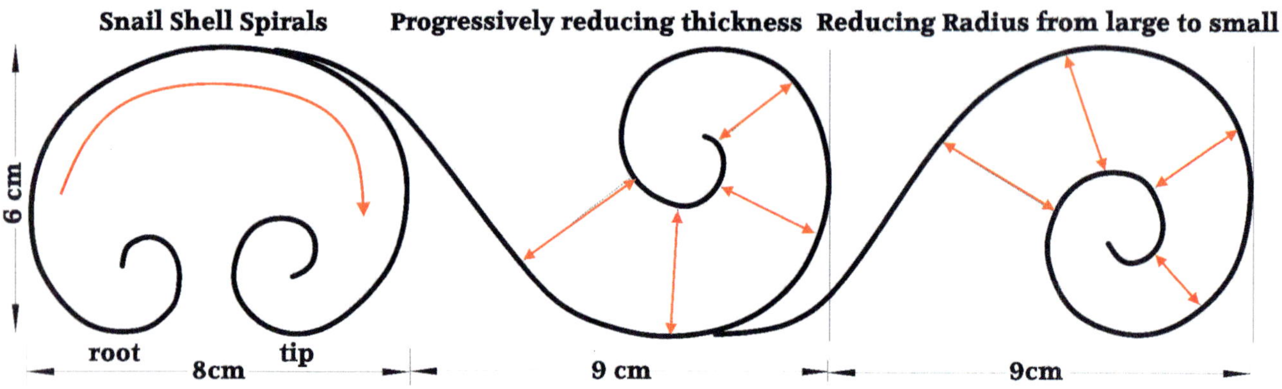

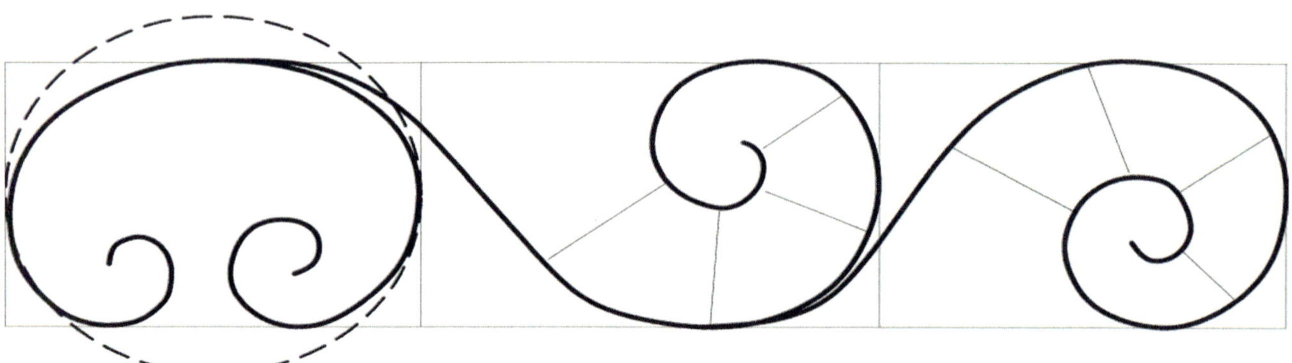

From: A Norwegian Woodcarving Textbook: Fauske, Odd; ISBN-10: 1861518633; ISBN-13: 978-1861518637 (2020); Amazon

truncated for the "root" end) to maintain the progressive taper of the leaf form. The layout is then developed from the "root" end, working upwards to the leaf tip to form the underlying "snail" or "S" shape. A key requirement of a balanced design is to ensure that the spaces left between the leaves are progressively smaller as the size of the accompanying "leaf set" also declines in size. The general guide given for maintaining balance, is for the design to start with a full three-blade leaf, then systematically move through a two-leaf to a one-leaf at the root or stem junction. To ensure that the leaves maintain their full width near their top, the construction or sight-line must go right out to the outer edge of the "S" shape, ensuring a generous curve to the all important "fishing-rod" curve beneath. Through the development of the repeating designs along, the splines of the reversing "S" forms, there is a progressive pattern of declining size. This takes into account the need to fill the spaces sequentially, with each "main" leaf just "kissing" the high point of the end curl of its predecessor, all the while ensuring that the top leaf maintained its thickness throughout the first half of its length. This will ensure that its body fully fills the space available. While working through a design, the small embellishments, that introduce movement to the leaves, are added, enabling full use of the space to be made in the final design. Finally the leaf veins is introduced, with the convention that a single leaf has one vein, a double two and a triple three, with the vein in the top or "main" leaf being placed along the original sight line of the stem, and those for subsidiary leaves placed along their spines. By no means necessary, but as an aid to "visualisation" of the pattern, the leaves can be shaded to show the intended third dimension.

The Acanthus style of carving is used extensively in traditional Norwegian style carving, with many patterns for the decoration of wooden implements and utensils being used over the years.

Acanthus Band: Design Odd Fauske

[1] Guide for Drawing the Acanthus, and Every Description of Ornamental Foliage - Page, James, London. Reprinted 1886 http://onlinebooks.library.upenn.edu/webbin/book/lookupid?key=olbp71221

Acanthus Bargeboard: Design Odd Fauske; carving & photo ©Iain Whittington 2021

Chapter Eight - Simple Techniques

Before there was carving with edge tools,
the ancients were putting simple designs on their artefacts.
Some of those techniques are still in use today.

Incised Ornamentation:

Basic ornamentation of wooden objects has been around for as long as wood has been used by man for implements. The initial use of basic incised decoration developed into simple wood cutting, in time giving rise to the art of chip carving. With the development of metal tools, with a sharp cutting edge, came the ability to whittle wood, which in turn developed into wood carving as we know it.

Needless to say, wood is not the only material that man has taken to decorating, as many a bored person with a sharp knife has turned their hand to personalise the tools of their trade or simply reached for the nearest available material, that the work environment has left to hand, to create a decorative item. Materials varied from wooden handles to animal tusks, horns and other by-products of their daily work, such as whale bone. Probably the most common artefact to survive in a maritime nations, such as UK, is the "*Scrimshaw*" decorated whale ivory or bone from the heyday of the whaling industry in the 19th century. Less well know outside Norway (and the Norwegian-American communities) is that the technique used for Scrimshaw had its origins in the Viking period where one of the better known examples is the decorations on the Viking carvings for the 12th century Lewis Chessmen[1]. This form of incised decoration is still practiced in Norway and more widely by the Sami[2] peoples as a "folk art" throughout the Nordic nations,where it goes under the name of "*Kolrosing*"- a reference to the 19th century sailors' use of coal dust or soot to colour their incised ornamentation.

Kolrosing & Scrimshaw:

The underling technique for both decorations is the incision made by a sharp point, traditionally the "artist's" own work-knife, with the incisions then highlighted by rubbing a contrasting powder into the cut - in the days of steam-ships and open fires - the omnipresent carbon from coal dust or soot

The 12th-century Lewis chessmen in the collection of the National Museum of Scotland (CC BY-SA 4.0)

A Kolrosing "knife"

This can be made easily. The form needed is more like a pen with a sharp tip than a knife, as it needs to be able to glide round curves smoothly. A good source for a suitable start is the proliferation of inexpensive tools from China, where their small carving tools have a pen-like shaft. A suitable "set" for conversion is the three piece collection where you get a straight blade, a skew blade and another tool in a plastic case. The first two can be uses "as is" and the "other" blade can be replaced by a ¼" HSS drill bit sharpened to a 30° tip.

was used. As Kolrosing was also practiced by the Norwegian rural population and Sami people, ground birch bark was more traditionally used for illumination, although the modern by-product of the coffee boom - used espresso grounds - works as well, (or you can even use the synthetic version - instant coffee). This is in effect "***wood engraving***" where the knife point works well for highlighting the required design, but like other forms of traditional incised work, (such as stencil cutting), this has its limitations when following curves. A chip-carving knife was designed to follow curves, so works well and purpose made Kolrosing knives are available from the Internet. A workable Kolrosing knife "kit" can purchased economically from the host of Chinese detail carving knives

available from e-bay. A "Cutting gauge" is ideal for framing lines.

The best woods for etching are those hardwoods that have a light colour and fine grain structure. In Scandinavia birch was

traditionally used for utilitarian items such as small boxes and utensils and is one of the better woods for Kolrosing. However, any fine light, grain wood is suitable, such as lime (basswood) and many fruit woods. Prior to transferring the pattern, the surface of the object should be finished by fine sanding, then sealed, so that it will be impervious to the application of the "*koling*". After sealing, re-sand at 320-400 grit to a super-fine sheen. Sealing is best achieved using clear French Polish, as this will also accept most other finished applied to the completed artwork.

The pattern is then drawn or transferred to the wood and traced with the appropriate

"knife". One benefit of using French Polish as the sealant is that small errors can be "patched" using an artist brush dipped in the French Polish, as a correcting fluid. For geometric patterns I find the best knife is probably the continental chip-carving knife, pulled towards you with care. However, for curved designs and free-hand (such as Norsk Rosemaling patterns) a special "pen" shaped knife is better suited, with the blade upright and pushed slowly away from you, under the control of your free hand with the thumb placed on the rear of the blade. By using only the tip of the blade, it can be controlled round curves while the shaft (or if you prefer, the object) is carefully rotated.

The coloured "*koling*" is mixed with a finishing oil of your choice and best applied as a slurry - rubbed well into the incision, before the surplus is removed with a rag. Leave over-night to harden, then finish with a furniture wax. A similar effect can be achieved through the use of a punched patter to be filled with "koling" for effect.

Chip Carving:

While Kolrosing can provide an elegant decoration, especially suited to curved objects, a more common form of incised work is traditional Chip-Carving. In its simplest form this is based on a triangular cut, with a fourth, deeper incision, made at the apex to allow the "chip" to be released from the

wood. The term "*chip carving*" is thought to have first appeared in 1888 in England, coined by architectural historians, as a transliteration of the German word "*Kerbschnitt*". It is an ancient art form, evident in most cultures where there is a surviving archeological record. Examples vary from Bronze Age artefacts from Europe, right back to Egyptian tomb goods. It holds a special place in Islamic art where the depiction of the human form in art is banned, and was probably taken to Persia (Iran) and Northern India, either through the ancient Greeks (via Alexander the Great) or later by the moguls. The tools required depend on the "scale" of the intended work, as the pattern can be rendered at small scale in hard wood with a knife (the Alpine areas of Europe have developed special knifes for this). It can also be used for architectural work at large scale, usually in soft wood, using a chisel. Simply by alternating the orientation of the chip removed can give four different borders that take shadow to give the effect of relief, amply illustrated in "The School Workshop" handbook[3] published in Vienna in 1895 - see page 63. There have been many different forms of specialist knives developed for chip carving, bur the most popular design (as it gives good control in both straight and curved cuts) is the Alpine style, with a thin straight edged blade that curves downwards to its point, firmly set in an ergonomic styled solid handle. Such knives are often included in sets of basic carving tool in central Europe, where the form is more embedded in local folk-art. Probably the most significant contributor to spreading the genre outside Europe is Wayne Barton[4] whose writings are highly recommended and are more commonly available than the few English translations from German of the other reference works.

[1] https://www.nms.ac.uk/explore-our-collections/stories/scottish-history-and-archaeology/lewis-chess-pieces/
[2] More traditionally known in English as Lapps, although the Sami themselves consider the name Lapp pejorative.
[3] 1895 Die Schulwerkstätte in ihrer verbindung mit dem theoretischen Unterrichte: http://scans.library.utoronto.ca/pdf/4/8/dieschulwerkst00bruhuoft/dieschulwerkst00bruhuoft.pdf
[4] Wayne Barton is the author of seven best selling books published in six countries and a video and all on chip carving. https://chipcarving.com/meet-wayne-barton.html

1895 (Table 19) Die Schulwerkstätte in ihrer verbindung mit dem theoretischen Unterrichte

Swiss Style Stool top: Designed & Carved Iain Whittington

Chapter Nine – Carving Courses

While following written instructions can impart the basic skills, nothing rivals the "hands-on" of a good course.

As with much of the rest of woodworking, carving is a skill that is not best learned from books of videos - at least a basic "hands-on" course is essential. As the making of family furniture had been a long-standing hobby, I decided that it could be enhanced by the application of decorative woodcarving to the repertoire.

With this in mind, I started with a series of evening classes to learn the basics and to confirm that it was a skill I would enjoy. After an a few projects based on the basic skill learned, I started looking round for more training opportunities that could provide two to three weeks tuition in decorative woodcarving, preferably covering both design and technique. I quickly discovered that the majority of the courses run in UK are only of one or two day duration and generally leaning towards the art of carving in the round. There were a few exceptions, such as the education provided as part of the full time courses at City and Guilds of London Art School and at summer schools by Dick Onians,[1] or previously the opportunity for work experience under Michael Painter[2] with the Linford Building Group in Lichfield (unfortunately no longer trading). The larger tool merchants, such as Axminster Tools[3] run short courses in what I would call "*wood sculpture*". I may be wrong, but, after much research, I was forced to conclude that there does not seem to be a short course available in UK to teach *ornamental* or *decorative* woodcarving.

Widening the (web) search to Europe turned up some opportunities in nations with a history of carving:

Austria

The Geisler-Moroder Carving School (*Schnitz- und Bildhauerschule Geisler-Moroder*[4]) in the Austrian Alps

Germany

There are a number of short courses in Germany organised at different locations by by Dictum Gmb[5].

Norway

Here there are a number of courses at the Norwegian Heritage Centre for Rural Culture[6] (*Senter for Bygdekultur*) in the central highlands of the Gudbransdal in Norway.

There are also opportunities to join the Summer Schools at *Raulandsakademiet* in the upland region of Telemark.

USA

In the USA[7] , there are courses at various locations such as the traditional Norwegian carving courses held at Vesterheim[8] (as part of their summer school); also at Norsk Wood Works[9]; There are also Chip Carving courses by Wayne Barton[10] and for Flat Plane (knife) Carving by Prof Harley Refsal[11] all at various locations.

If you are luck enough to live in a local authority area in UK that offers Woodcarving as a part of their Adult Education programme, you may be able to avoid travelling to find instruction, or you could treat the whole thing as a holiday and go abroad. If the latter, the following will give you a "taste" of what you might find.

Carving in the Style of the Austrian Tyrol

The Geisler-Moroder Carving school lies high in the Austrian Alps near the 'woodcarver's village' of Elbigenalp, Tyrol. Armed with schoolboy German, I enrolled on the Austrian Carving course. The Geisler-Moroder Carving School runs a wide variety of courses in the Tyrolean village of Elbigenalp. Moreover, they add some special language courses that combine an Alpine tour with traditional Tyrolean carving, complete with a spouse's programme. Having already done the Tyrolean tour while stationed in Germany with the army, I was taken by the unique opportunity to do their "Ornamentation and Interior Decoration" (***Ornamentik & Verzeirungsschnitzerei***) course. However, not only was the instructor very able to demonstrate, but with much waving of hands and a little school boy German, the services of the 'translator' were seldom called for.

Reporting for class on the first morning, I was greeted by the other four members of the course and the instructing master carver the "***Schnitzermeister***". We were all given a piece of 4" x 2" (100mm x 50mm) local Zirbe pine (Arolla or Alpine Stone Pine) along with the use of a set of 16 Austrian Stubai tools, or 'irons'. Now is the time for any previous experience to be declared and assessed from the practical use of the 'irons' on the piece. I was an enthusiastic learner attending my third course. Hence, lack of German and lack

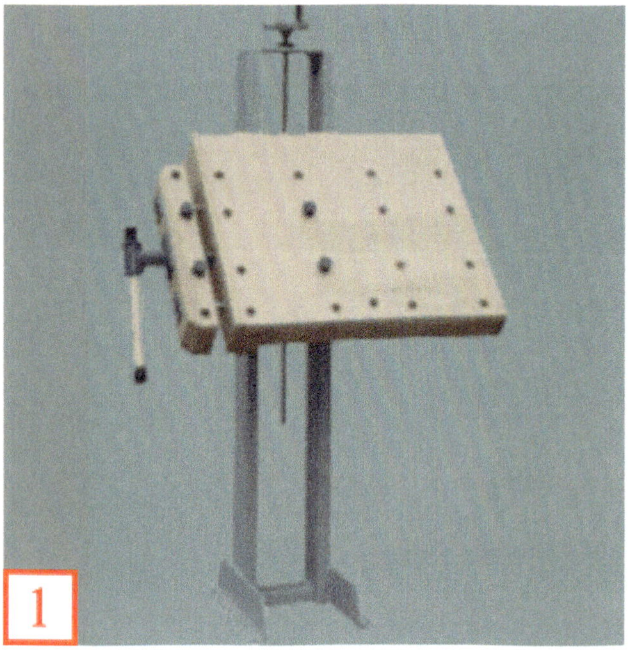

of skill were closely matched, but caused no problem for the course leader. The course covered what one could call 'oversized chip carving' through to traditional Tyrolean low relief carving. If you had ever wondered how the delicate designs of the 'Wayne Barton'[12] school of decoration could be adapted to large furniture and buildings, ask Geisler-Moroder. If you want to see the king sized patterns executed in the way Wayne Barton demonstrates on his video, but using full

sized chisels on a bit of 4" x 2" (100mm x 50mm), watch the Schnitzermeister.

1 Each student was placed on an adjustable work bench and shown how to get the light just right. Although I normally work with the end-vice of a traditional Scandinavian work bench, I found little difficulty in adapting to the Tyrolean bench[13], with the exception that I lost count of the number of times I hit my elbow on the central support column.

2 Day One took us through simple circular patterns to the three dimensions of the Barley Twist, (or 'plats' in German). The layout and techniques were each demonstrated and then given to the students to execute on their own 4" x 2"(100mm x 50mm). The S*chnitzermeister* was always on hand to demonstrate the way out of the current impasse, with much good humour and expertise.

3 Day Two had one graduating to the basic low relief and its design and execution, including hands-on guidance when required. The workshops don't close until 10pm and the Schnitzermeister was often still there after the formal end of instruction to make sure you had enough to keep you going if this was your aim. As my German was not up to making full use of the social life associated with the course, I normally only took meal breaks and made full use of the evenings in the workshop.

4 Day Three, saw the introduction of the router as a labour saving device for outlining and removal of background and pattern tracing. I selected a ceiling panel pattern for my "major work", for which the layout and design was completed by the end of the day,

4

combining all the elements taught so far into a single 2' (600mm x 600mm) square panel of Zirbe pine. Day Four started by putting the router demonstration to good use, setting-in the main pattern with a 'V' bit and raising it to half the background depth to set-in detail work by hand. It was then back to the 'irons' to show what you had learned from the course.

5 The rest of Day Four & Five were spent alternating between the Schnitzermeister demonstrating technique on a portion of your work and repeating the pattern yourself. Critical appraisal was always available and, as confidence grew, any untoward over-confidence was kept in check by the occasional reminder that the high standards of instruction were not being reflected in your work (the Schnitzermeister had again spotted the silly mistake you were trying to hide). As I was making good progress with my ceiling panel, but had not undertaken the less structured form of carving alpine flower decorations, I was re-directed for Day Five to correct this oversight. It was a delight to watch the Schnitzermeister regard the lines traced onto the wood ('Linden', or lime, this time) as only an indication of intent. He then

5

set-to to create free-form flowers. It was less of a delight when he took a small bow and handed the irons back so that I could replicate the piece of art he had just created. Needless to say, this kept me gainfully employed for some time, so much so that I decided to miss out on the lesson in carving Gothic script. All the techniques taught were reinforced by practice. A wide variety of demonstration pieces were taken home as reminders of how to do it. The on-site shop offers a wide range of 'how to do it' books[14] and tools, You can also buy anything else you need to maintain and improve your skills, including a special offer on the set of Stubai irons.

6 The set of 16 Stubai[15] tools provided were comprehensive. In use, one quickly discovered why they come from the manufacturers with a short bevel and rounded wings, as most of them are used on both sides to get the exact dimensions and fine finish required of the traditional Alpine decorative patterns. Each workshop was equipped with a Koch sharpening centre, with an a combination of abrasive and waxed wheels for sharpening and honing. In addition to the carving school, Geisler-Moroder also runs a large technical support works, including a wide range of 'pre-carve' rough-cut figures. You can be sure to get the best from your course, without the labour of roughing out the models, by using the 'pre-carve' service. The pre-carve inventory not only covers traditional and modern figure carving, but includes a range of furniture and decorative pieces from an Alpine chair back, through to Rococo frames, wall hangings and furniture decorations. However, I found enough to do using the bits of local Zirbe and linden, bought from the workshops.

I would not recommend a carving course in Germany as a first course, unless you already had the level of German required to understand fully the instructor or limit your choice to one of the special bi-lingual courses. However, with a little prior carving knowledge and possibly some basic German, the '*show & tell*' technique worked well, with little use being made of the friendly translation available. If you want a course with a difference and either have some basic German or can book a bi-lingual course, the Geisler-Moroder programme is there for the asking. Most of the *Schnitzermeisters*' have some English and there are some courses specifically run for English speakers, so do not be put off' by a lack of German. The Giesler-Moroder office will help in the provision of accommodation, either in their own B&B or in one of the two main hotels in Elbigenalp. I found their B&B to be excellent and sampled the food in all the other hotels as well. You can, of course, obtain details of the current accommodation in Elbigenalp from the Tourist Board Tyrol[16].

6

Carving in the Style of the Norwegian Gudbrandsdal

The course is located in the mountains at the Hjerleid Technical High School at Dovre, near Dombås, at the North end of the Gudbransdal. Hjerleid Technical High School was founded at the end of the 19th century to preserve and teach the art and craft of traditional cabinet making and carving. It was the "home" of the celebrated master carver and teacher, Johan Amrud[17] (1913-1997) It still runs a variety of courses throughout the year, from full-time three-year courses in traditional hand craft, to an annual programme of part-time courses in design, carving, furniture decoration and turning. From this programme, I opted to take a two-week course covering both the design and execution of acanthus style carving. The first week of the course started informally on the Sunday evening, with eight students being given an over-view by the Course Coordinator and introduced to the basic requirements, such as coffee making, by the course tutor. The class assembled in the drawing office on the first day of the course to be introduced to the basics of the acanthus design, followed after lunch by practical work. For the practical work, all students were issued with a set of Swiss[18] tools, all carefully pre-sharpened, with the slightly rounded wings and inside bevel preferred by many ornamental carvers. The practical work started with an introduction covering all the normal aspects such as safety and tool handling, followed by the initial project - a pierced carving for a 250mm (10") door number plate, in local fir.

7 While the design drawing looked deceptively simple, it contained within it all the various aspects of the acanthus design that were the subject of the morning's works. The first afternoon was interspersed with demonstrations from the Instructor of the fundamental concepts of teasing the acanthus shapes out of the wood, allowing the individual to set to with gusto. The Instructor then spent the time moving between the students, giving individual attention to either demonstrate the next step, help when stuck or even cure budding over-confidence by tactfully correcting the errors in shape or interpretation that had mystically crept in between demonstration and execution. The formal instruction finished at around five o'clock, giving time to clear up the workshop & to prepare for the evening meal, which the students enjoyed together at a local hotel. The workshop was available for individuals' use in the evening, although additional informal evening lectures were also provided, covering subjects such as

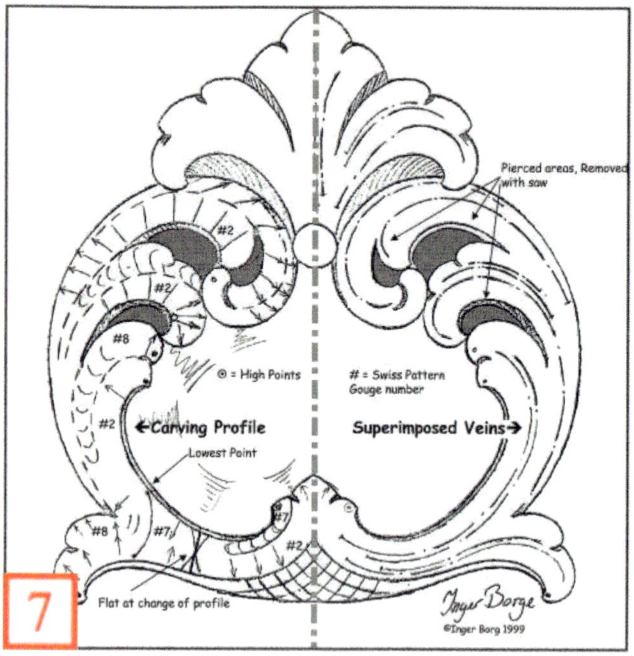

7

timber science and sharpening. This daily routine was maintained throughout the week, with the design work in the mornings and practical carving tuition in the afternoon.

In the design work of the first day, the Instructor introduced the class to the history and style of the acanthus design, with reference to its long tradition in the work of the artists of the Gudbransdal. Students were then given pencil and paper to start, for themselves, drawing the basic leaf form, When the basic leaf form could be drawn without supervision, the variety of ways of inter-connecting the basic curves were explored, The various rules for the two and three blade combinations of the traditional acanthus design were explained and demonstrated, and exercised. The second and third day in the drawing office then went on to teach the form and style of combining the individual leaf designs into a coherent patter, using a linear progression of splines for the development of the symmetry within the individual patterns. By the end of the third morning, the whole class had successfully completed the exercise. Up until this point, The Instructor had been providing careful guidance, together with the required "templates" to guide the class, but having mastered(?) these basic concepts, the fourth morning found the class looking at a large blank sheet of paper and being exhorted to decorate it with a classical "S" pattern of an acanthus design. Needless to say, this kept me gainfully employed, trying to understand my (much too cryptic notes from the earlier lessons) and wondering how much more mileage I could expect from my hard working eraser. The morning went quickly, interspersed with The Instructor's gentle reminders, from basic curves, though pre-planning patterns of declining size, to the need to fill the spaces progressively, with each "main" leaf just "kissing" the high point of the end curl of its predecessor, all the while ensuring that the top leaf maintained its thickness throughout the first half of its length, to ensure that its body fully filled the space available.

8 While working through this design, the small embellishments, that introduce movement to the leaves, were added to the lesson, enabling full use of the space to be made in the final design. On the final morning in the drawing office, the theory of the design of the leaf "nerves" or veins was introduced, and developed However simply the "theory" was explained and practiced,

8

during the time of my short stay at the school, it became apparent that the subject of the placement and interpretation of veins, in the acanthus design, was a major topic in its own right, with interpretation of the rules being as individual as the proponents own handwriting.

9 As the class was of mixed experience, the practical carving, in the afternoons, progressed at different speeds. However, the combination of the morning's work in the drawing office and the afternoon's practical, where all the techniques taught were reinforced by practice, maintained a very

9

10

pleasant balance, while also serving to demonstrate and confirm the more theoretical aspects of the design work. In my case, the initial project was completed before the end of the week, to be supplemented by a clever development of the same basic design, into that of a 430mm (17") long mantle-clock, giving practice in the emphasis to the third dimension of "flat" carving. The second week saw the routine changed to having the whole day spent in the workshop, although the style and format of the instruction remain consistent. With the emphasis now purely on the execution of the design, the variety and scope of the projects was greatly expanded, to enable individuals to work on their own chosen design, either from those made available by the Instructor, or even on work brought with them. Having brought forward the mantle-clock from the previous week, I had the added benefit of seeing how two master carvers brought their own style to the common interpretation of a single theme — there being more than one way to skin any cat!

10 With the second project completed, I then moved onto a final project of my own choice, this time more directly oriented to furniture decoration — with 600mm (24") ornamental shelf bracket. With greater length to the project also came the greater challenge of balancing the depth of the carving within the 25mm (1") depth of the timber. This is where I find the "art" of the decorative carver departs from my limited skills with the third dimension and where I found the Instructor's guidance and expertise to be most helpful. The second Instructor also taught on the school's furniture decoration course, and was happy to be diverted onto this subject during breaks from carving instruction.

11

11 If you have an interest, they also give courses in painting as a furniture decoration, in the traditional Norwegian style of Rosemaling, which can also be applied to their carvings.

The "standard" course package includes the provision of "continental" style breakfast, light lunch and the evening cooked meals for five days, with accommodation in a single room in a student "barrack" block on site for six nights. While the accommodation was somewhat basic, with shared facilities, it was possible to pay extra to be accommodated in an adjacent motel. With arrival on Sunday evening, instruction goes through to Saturday morning, with dispersal before lunch.

While an ability to speak a little Norwegian made my time on the course easier, many Norwegians, including some of the instructors speak excellent English. However, before booking, you do need to check if the scheduled instructor is happy to teach in English. With a little prior carving knowledge, an English speaking teacher, coupled to the inherently "show & tell" style of carving instructions, I can confidently recommend the courses to all comers. When you add in the spectacular scenery of the upper Gudbransdalen, it could most profitably be combined with a holiday to Norway.

Antique Alpine Music Box Chair

[1] Dick Onians: http://www.dickonianssculptor.co.uk/home
[2] http://www.mikepainter.co.uk
[3] https://www.axminster.co.uk/skill-centre/woodcarving-courses
[4] http://www.woodcarvingschool.com/cms/website.php?id=/en/index.htm
[5] https://www.dictum.com/en/woodworking-iaa/ornamental-carving-ku3232001
[6] http://www.hjerleid.no
[7] https://www.finewoodworking.com/2007/01/18/woodworking-schools-directory
[8] https://folkartschool.vesterheim.org/classes/woodworking
[9] https://www.norskwoodworks.com/life-long-learning
[10] https://chipcarving.com/wayne-barton-class-schedule.html
[11] http://www.cca-carvers.org/bio-pages/refsal.html
[12] Alpine School Of Wood Carving, Park Ridge, IL 600688 http://www.chipcarving.com
[13] Tyrolean Workbench: https://www.schnitzeisen.at/werkstattausstattung/werktische-platten/900-metallwerk-und-schnitztisch.html
[14] Chip Carving & Relief Carving – 1987 by Joseph MADER ISBN-13: 978-0020007203: Austrian 2nd edition 1987,
[15] Stubai ZMV GmbH: https://www.stubai.com/en/n-5602-stubai-wood-carving-set-polished-20-pcs/
[16] Tourist Board Tyrol http://www.tyrol.com
[17] Ornamental Woodcarving in the Norwegian Tradition, Johan Amrud, Heart Prairie Press: ISBN10:0962266396.
[18] Pfeil Tools: http://www.pfeiltools.com/en/products/sculping-tools/roll-case-with-12-tools-ro-12.html

Chapter Ten - Computer Graphics

Many people can struggle with design and drawing but there are many good carving pattern books out there. With a computer & scanner these can be made to work for all.

1 Final Product

For this chapter, I have used designs from Lora Irish's book "***Wood Spirits & Green Men** ...a design sourcebook for woodcarvers...*", of which there is a brief résumé at the end of the chapter. Using material from the book and a computer, I will show how adapt some of the book's drawings for a specific Green Man project.

Computer graphics are split into two families - lines or images - (pictures). In "computer-speak" these are ***Vectors*** and ***Rasters*** respectively. In Chapter 6, I have shown how to use a free program called ***Sketchup*** to make line (*vector*) drawings and in this chapter I will be showing how to exploit a pictures (*raster*), to modify it so as to adapt it to different shapes. There are also "traditional" methods of re-scaling images, such a grid plotting, but I am assuming that a computer is available, with a scanner to allow. "Image-capture" and printer to allow "image-output". The processes illustrated can also be used to exploit graphics available from the Internet or from a digital camera. The best results are with a scanner and it will be easier for the subsequent subsequent "*image processing*" if you scan as a "*black & white*" image which will be saved and manipulated as a "*raster*" format image made up of a matrix of dots. Avoid using a camera unless no other method is available, as even with a tripod, it is almost impossible to take a photograph without distortions and the correction of such distortion is not trivial. The easiest way to adapt an image will be with simple photo editing software, which you may already have on your computer. If not, a suitable bit of "freeware" called

Terminology

Computer control information is indicated in the text using the following layouts:

A Menu choices are indicated by enclosing the required sequence in square brackets, for example, as sequence: **[File>Open Recent>File name]** is an indication that you select the "**File menu**" followed by the Sub-Menu "**Open Recent**" followed by the relevant "*file name*".

B Keyboard sequences are illustrated phrases such as "**[Ctrl+Z]**" These indicate that, while holding the **Ctrl** key, also press the key indicated after the plus sign.

These are *"keyboard shortcut"*, originally essential to insert when computer communication was via Teletype and punch-tape, as the Ctrl key warned the computer that a command comes next rather than a letter.

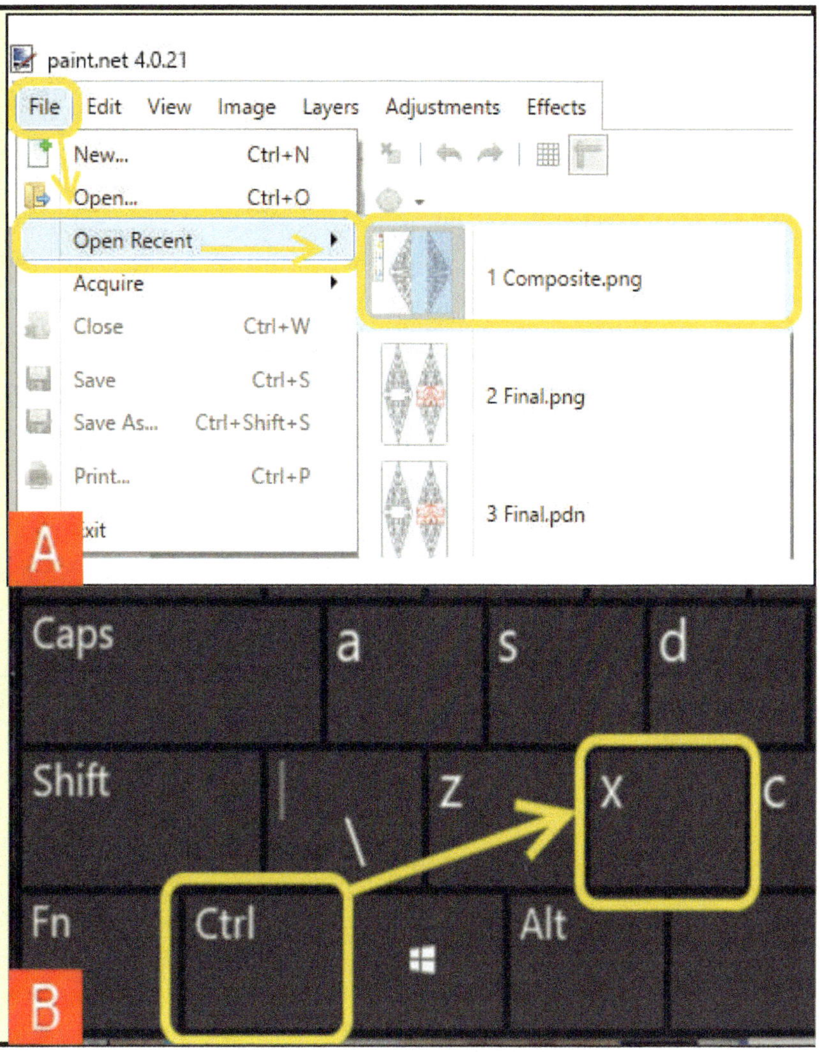

Paint.net[1] can be found from the Internet, where you can read about, download and install the software for free. Although most photo software supports the techniques, my specific tips will be for *Paint.net*.

1 I needed a couple of Greenmen for the two roof bosses/finials on the barge board on our old Linhay (a special form of Devonshire Cow barn), so having worked out the final diamond shape and dimensions I made a scaled image of the outline, I then set about adapting the drawings of the *"Sacred Oak"* (the final products is on the previous page) and the *"Gothic Man"* patterns to suit. Unfortunately, I lack the artistic talent of Laura Irish, but I did work through the period where the "Office Support" (initially comprising the joint efforts of a typing pool, central filing clerks & a graphic section) was progressively replaced by "do-it-(all)-yourself" with your "personal" computer terminal. As a result, amongst new skills I have had to learn have been how to use a computer to prepare high quality graphics. As a result, as this project entailed some manipulation of Laura Irish's original images, I naturally turned to "computer graphics".

2 With the image scanned, (saved) and loaded, it now needs cropped to just the outline of the drawing using ***[Tools>Select>Move>Crop].*** (original shape is the the red lines).

3 It can then be simply resized either by ***Ctrl+R*** or by selecting ***[Image>Resize]*** dialogue box, then check "***By absolute size***" and un-check "***Aspect Ratio***" & finally

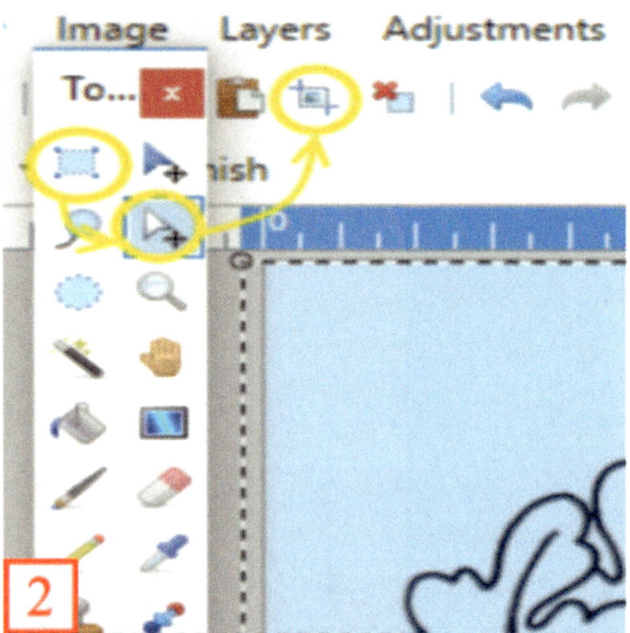

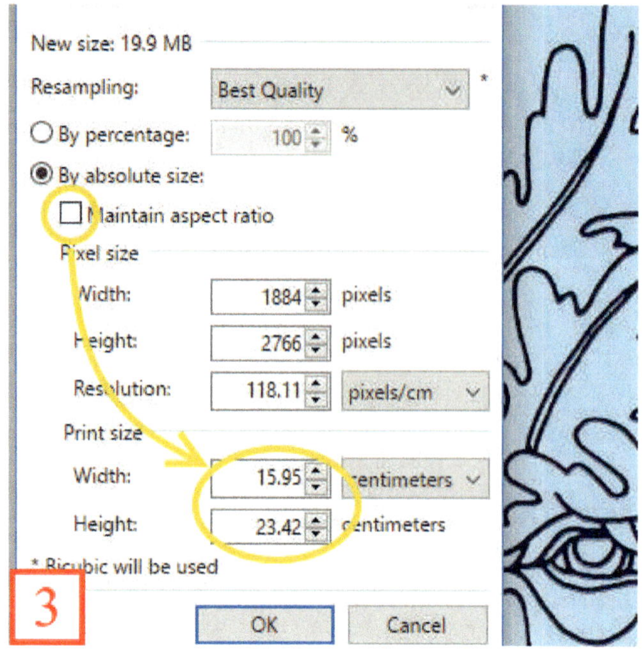

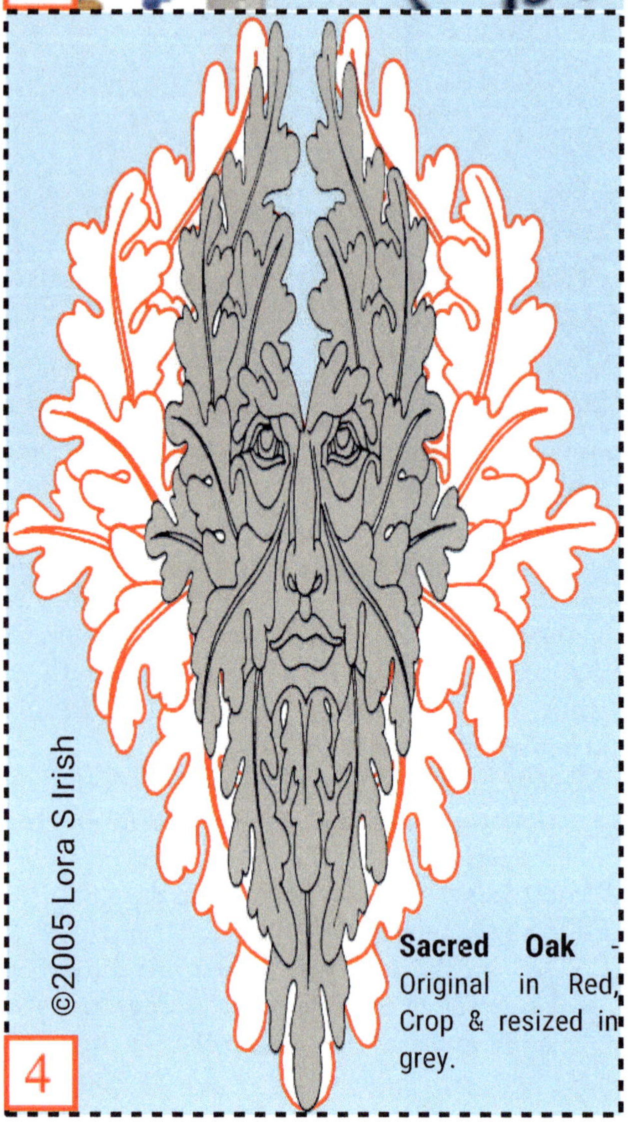

insert the dimensions you require - to reflect the dimensions of your project..

4 The above works for a rectangular project, or in the case of the "*Sacred Oak*" drawing that was already a diamond shape. However, I will also be needing a second design for the finials as an irregular diamond shape

5 The second pattern was developed from a montage of various drawings from the book. This will be achieved by altering

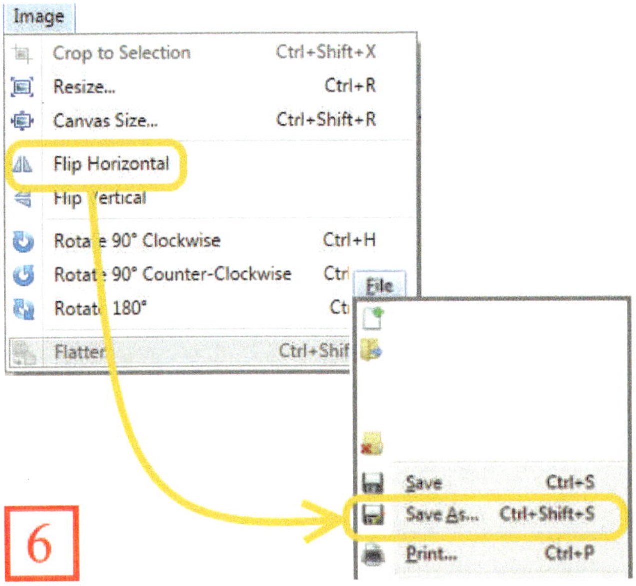

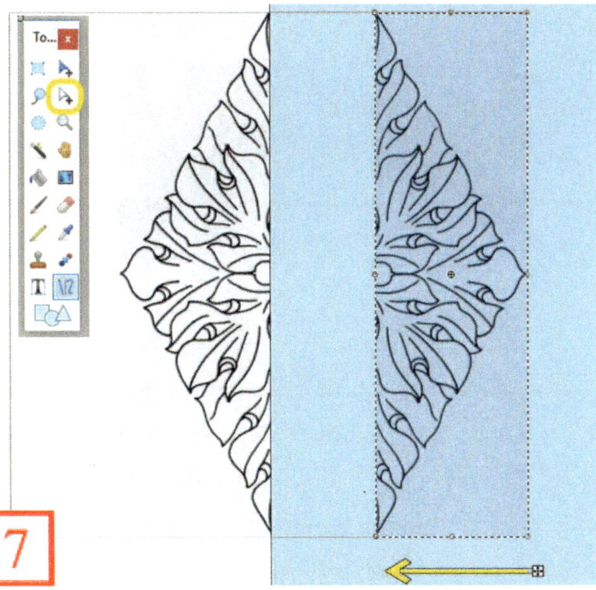

several drawings from the series of "*Gothic Man*" designs in the book. The end product is again the same diamond shape, so my starting point is the "*Gothic Diamond*". Load the image and rotated the drawing through 90° ***[>Image>Rotate 90°]***, then used ***[Select>Cut]*** or ***Ctrl+X*** on the lower half (now left side) to delete the face. Save this image as "RHS".

6 Open a copy before flipping it ***[>Image>Flip]*** & ***[File>Save-As]*** this time named as "LHS".

7 Re-open RHS & add LHS by ***[>layers>import from file>]***. As this is in a separate layer, you can move it to where the pair mate down the centre-line, then use ***Ctrl-M*** to merge the layers together then ***[>File> Save-As = Background]***.

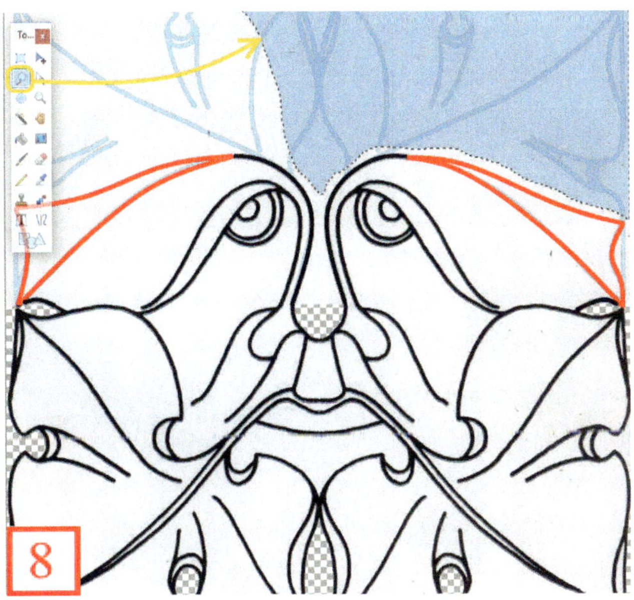

8 I decided that the "*Gothic Square*" face would suit the centre of the revised background, but to use it I had to remove the area above the eyebrows ***[Tools>Lasso>Delete]*** before reinstating the top leaf line by "tweaking" the line tool as a curve shape (with the little handles) to suit the lower part from the original (I've selected a red line for the curve to highlight the altered linework). Save this modified face file.

9 Then take the background image again and stretching it to the desired size (as with the "Sacred Oak" on page above, before superimposing the modified "face" onto the outline by loading it as a new layer

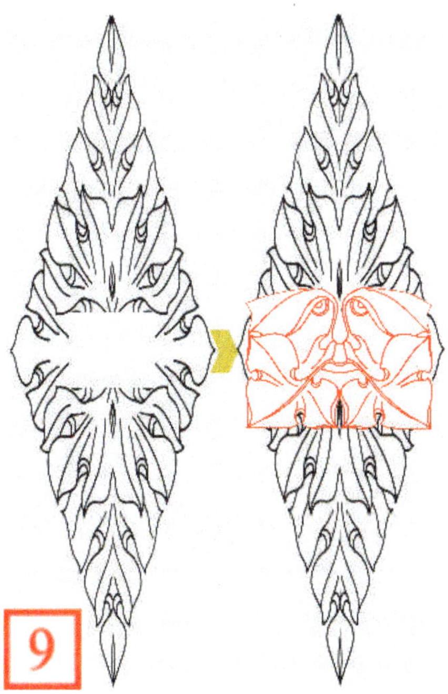

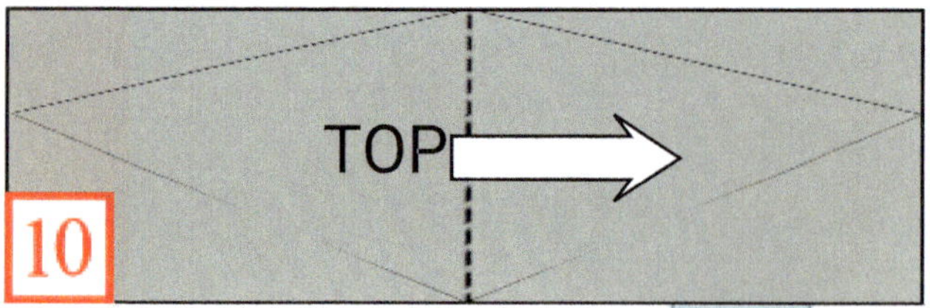

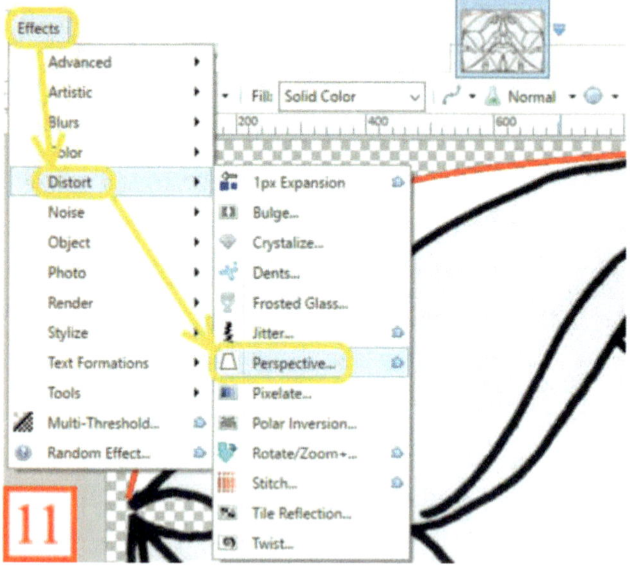

over the outline file *[>layers>import from file>]*. Now you only have to save & reload the final image into MSPaint to print it onto two pages as before.

10 Both the previous examples were for a symmetrical diamond shape. However, my project was actually an asymmetric lozenge (acute-rhombus) - that is made up of two unequal triangles. The basic designs above can be easily cut in half to give two triangles, with each half being re-sized (as on page above), but the superimposition of the amended Gothic Square face will not look right.

11 To get the face to fit the distorted triangle, it will need warped, to change its perspective. Before using the *Perspective Tool*[2] it is advisable to increase the canvas size as warping the image may loose linework outside the visible are. Place the image of the required shape as a "layer" behind the pattern as a guide, using **[>Layers>Import from File]**.

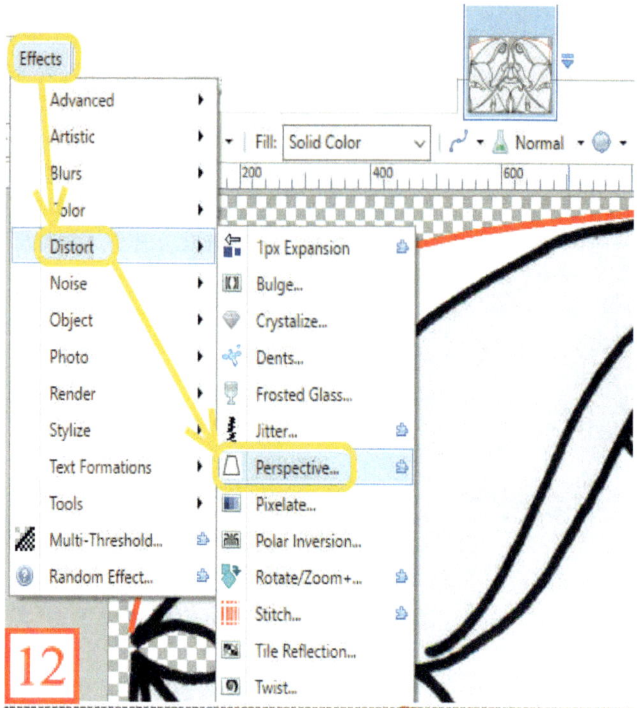

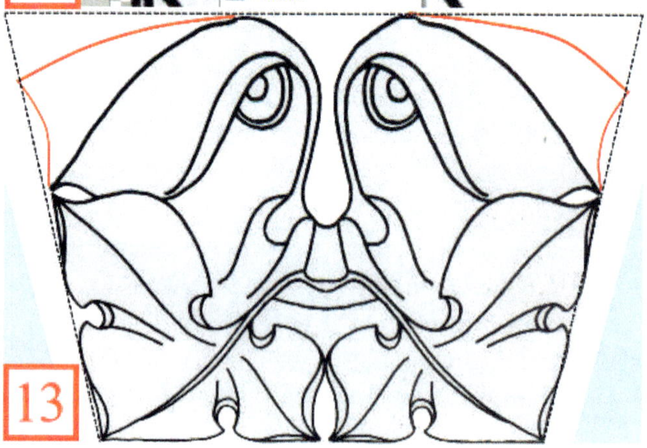

12 Activate the Perspective tool **[Effects>Distort>Perspective]**.

13 Adjust the top and/or bottom size to suite the required width of end product. The warped face can then be saved, to be combined with the line work for the lower triangle to produce the final pattern in the same way as on page above and then printed on two sheets through MS-Paint.

[1] *Paint.net Download https://www.getpaint.net/index.html*
[2] *Guide to using Perspective Tool: https://forums.getpaint.net/topic/16197-perspective-effect-v20-update-030510/*

PRINTING

Many basic printers will now refuse to print an enlarged image across two pages, but the much maligned old "Classic" MS-Paint® program can. This is pre-installed on many Windows Computers. To open Paint, type "paint" in the search box on the task bar and then select it from the list of results.

A Open the image you've saved from Paint.net in MS-Paint and Select: ***Print>Page Setup>*** then:

B ***Orientation>Margins>Scaling*** to *Portrait>Zero margins* & in Scaling select ***"Fit to"> "1 by 2 page(s)"*** & Click OK

C Print the image from MSPaint, and make sure to select ***"All Pages"***

D Trim and stick onto your blank.

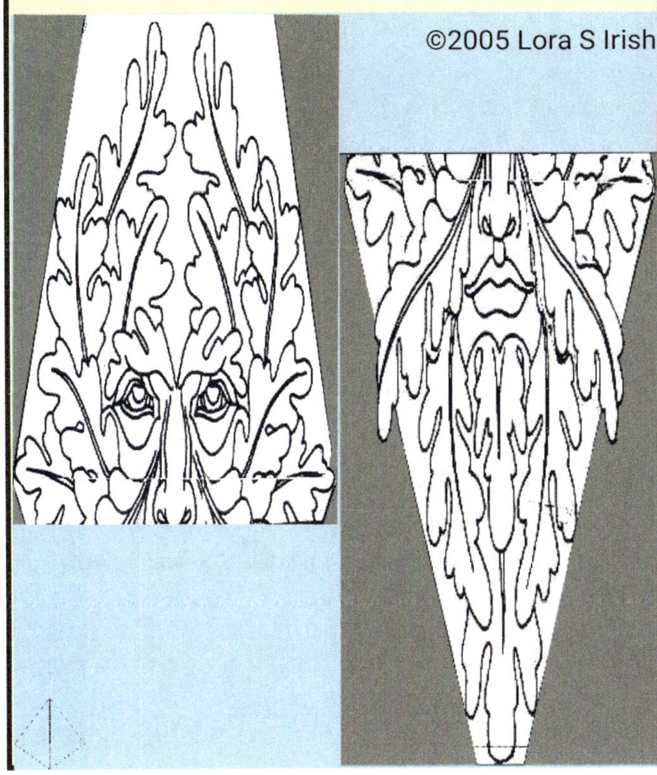

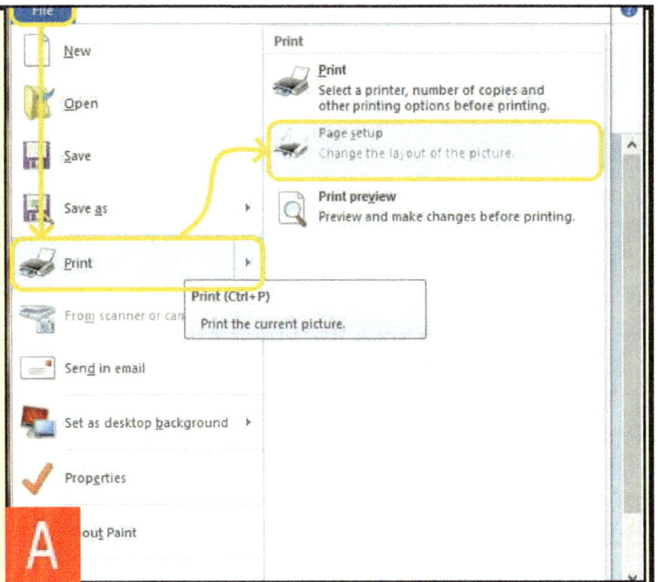

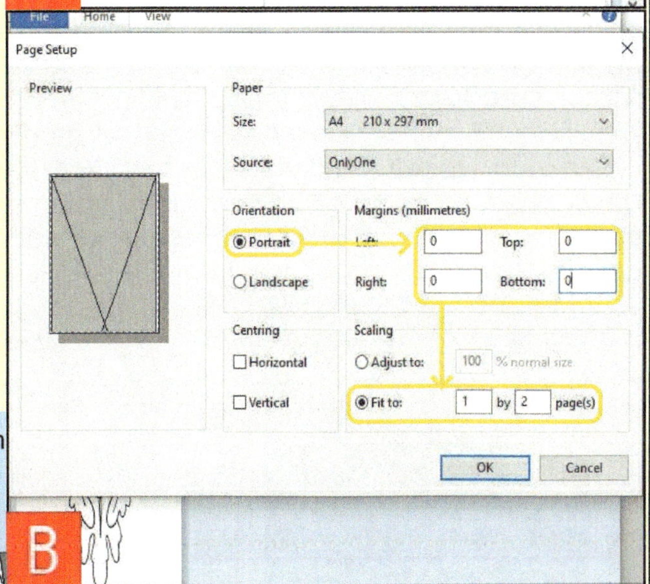

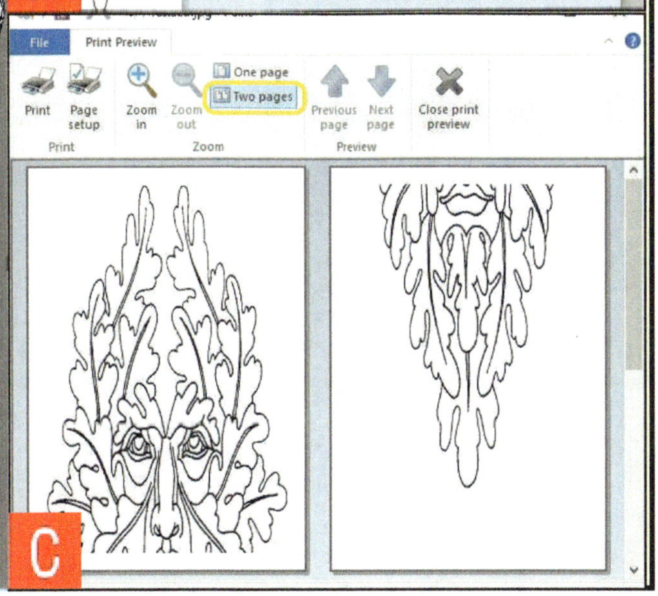

BOOK NOTE

When reading the book "**Wood Spirits & Green Men** *...a design sourcebook for woodcarvers...*" by Laura Irish, bear in mind that the clue is in the title. What the book is not is a "how-to" book for carving *Wood-spirits* and *Green-men*, although it does give a slight nod in that direction with the contributions by Shawn Cipa (*wood-spirits*) and Chris Pye (*green-men*). The book starts with Lora Irish's personal views on the evolution of the green-man into the wood-spirit, which is amply illustrated with her own artwork, before launching straight into Chris Pye's chapter on the carving of the traditional style "**Man of Ewyas**" that forms the image on the book's cover (below left) - all this amply illustrated by Lora Irish's line drawings and ample clear photographs of Chris Pye's work-in-progress. This is followed by Shawn Cipa's chapter on a *Wood-spirit* carved on a walking stick (below centre & on the cover's top left corner) - using the same format of Lora Irish's line drawings and plenty of clear photographs of work-in-progress. This chapter concludes with a compendium of variations on the walking-stick theme by Lora Irish. There then follows an impressive gallery of Clive Hick's photographs (sample at right hand below) of the many and varied Green-men from his extensive travels in UK and Europe, including a local Devon example from South Tawton. The final part of the book is a comprehensive collection of evolving designs for both *Green-men* and *Wood-spirits* beautifully drawn by Lora Irish. The book concludes with a short bibliography. In all, It's a very well illustrated book full of Lora Irish's excellent and inspirational line-work but possibly more for a devotee of *Wood-Spirits* (in the North American style) rather than the follower of the traditional European *Green-man*. Hopefully this chapter has illustrated how Lora Irish's book and drawings live up to the subtitle, as a source book for inspiration and guidance for those, like me that lack artistic ability. She has written numerous books and supporting her books, there is also a pattern download service on her website[1]

©2005 Chris Pye

Man of Ewyas - Chris Pye

©2005 Drawing Lora S Irish

Will o'the Wisp - Shawn Cipa

©2005 Clive Hicks

South Tawton Church - Clive Hicks

[1] *Laura Irish's Pattern Link https://www.lsirish.com/epatterns/*

COPYRIGHT ©

Copyright laws apply in most places to protect "intellectual property". While being a legal minefield, Copyright will apply to most imagery that you may want to use. In general terms you can only exploit an image with the permission of the copyright owner, especially if it results in "commercial gain". The usual exceptions include personal (non-profit) use for research, education, criticism or review and the reporting of current events. The rule-of-thumb is that if you make money from exploiting it, you need permission and must make acknowledgement to the rights holder (as I have gained for the images used here). For example, all the original drawings from "Wood Spirits & Green Men ...a design sourcebook for woodcarver..." *are shown as* ***©2005 by Laura***

WOOD SPIRITS
AND
GREEN MEN
A DESIGN SOURCEBOOK FOR WOODCARVERS AND OTHER ARTISTS
Lora S. Irish with Chris Pye and Shawn Cipa
Gallery Photographs by Clive Hicks

Chapter Eleven - Tool Miscellanies

There are a number of less common tools out there of varying value and utility - Some are listed here.

One "problem" with Wood Carving is that encourages the "*tool squirrel*" instinct. This is often combined with miscellaneous gifts from friends and relatives. The following information is gleaned from some years of the above and is given as a record of my experience with tools that originated from many and varied sources.

For some time, outsourcing to companies in Asia has been common by most of the large tool manufacturers. For example, Indian companies, such as Anant have been selling good 'clones' of Record and Stanley products for many years and even working as their outsourced sub-contractors. In a similar way Mike Davies has teamed up with Record Tools to re-launch their woodcarving range, although the tools are no longer made in Sheffield. In the immediate post-war era, "*made in Hong Kong*" became synonymous with cloning of western style products. Latterly, the rapid advances made in production capacity in East Asia has brought Korean and Chinese products into the mass market. While much of this import market is dominated by ruthless price competition, some surprising "traditional" tools have also come to the West from Asia, some are from the lateral-thinking that has re-purposing common industrial metal working materials, such as High-Speed-Steel (HSS), re purposed for woodworking, now offered as plane blades and chisels. Others are through re-introducing materials, such as laminated steel, mostly lost in the West due to short sighted economies. Research, engineering and production standards in these countries are often highly developed, but frequently under-utilised by the Western tendering process as UK purchasing decisions are conservative and very price sensitive.

The tools covered here are all items that I've purchased and used over the years and the following information relates to my experience of testing and reviewing this variety of alternative products:

1 Korean carving tools that are a modern re-invention that are probably based on their 19th Century predecessors, but now made from a modern "knife" steel.

2 The traditional Chinese carving tools, are still hand made from forge-welded laminated steel in the southern Chinese city of Donyang which has been one of the major centres of wood carving in China since the Tang Dynasty (618-907AD). It is quoted that "***...there the best blacksmiths still use the centuries old traditional methods with these tools. The larger carving gouges have conical sockets to keep the handle from splitting when struck with the traditional iron mallet. The large carving gouges are made of double layered steel and have a cutting edge whose harness is over (RC60). The smaller detail carving tools are made of a single layer of carbon steel (C60) with the harness of (RC58)....***".

3 I have found an old "Bent paring" chisel of mine, of unknown providence, to be an invaluable tool for gently shaving a shape in tight spaces. When adding it to the list of "***Recommended tools***" in Chapter 1, I went looking for a source of current production and found the nearest production tool to be the Ashley Iles N°33xl, as this differed from my original pattern, I approached them and they made a "special" for me to test.

4 Old tools from Addis Bros. That I "inherited" from a kind friend who was having a clear-out.

1

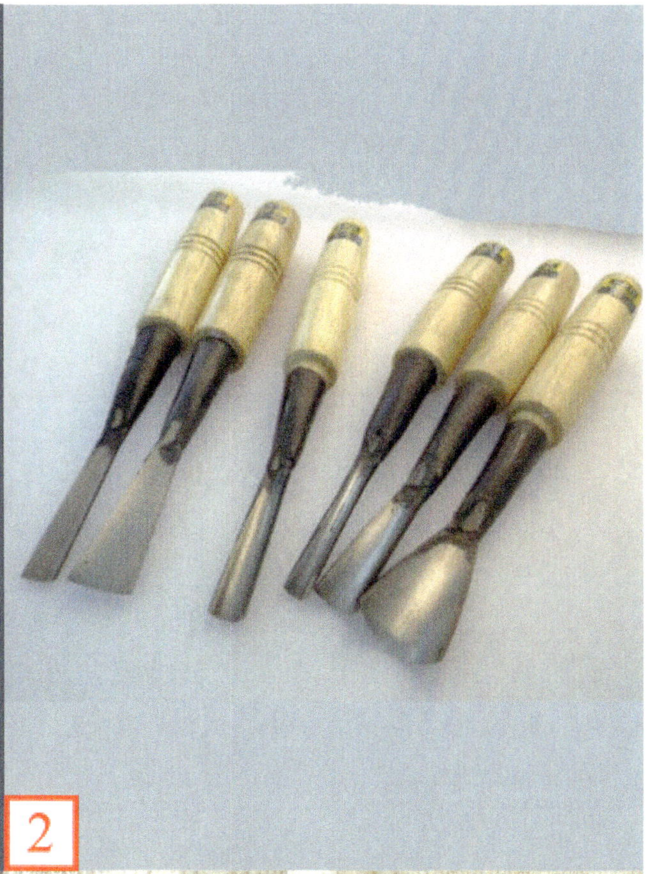

2

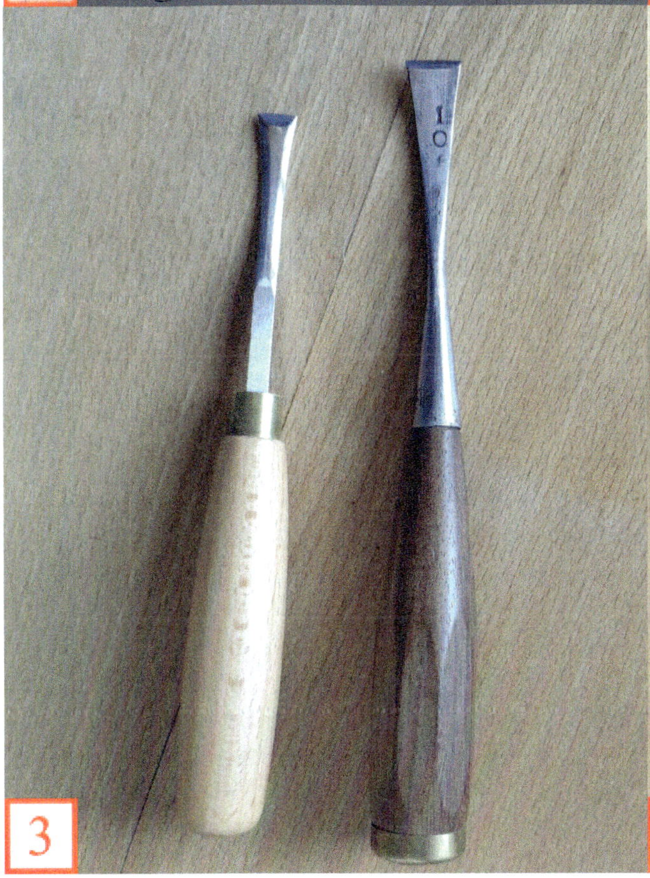

3

4

Tools from East Asia

Korean architectural dragon carving

East Asia, or in the old Latin "*The "Orient*" - (where the sun rises) - is the source of a certain style of carving tool not commonly seen in the western cultures. The history of tool-making is possibly a bi-product of warfare and religion. The swordsmiths' creations were for warfare and drove the development of steel and tools. This, together with religion (often the victor's), drove their application to monumental sculpture and carving as a means of cultural dominance.

Chinese swordsmiths probably imported the technology for laminated steels from the Tamil Wootz Steel in India[1] to improve their best sword steel and evolved a variety of techniques for laminated blade in the 5th Century.

Korean metalworking had, by the 6th Century, seen this technology migrated to them. The the ancient Korean ***Baekje*** metalworkers and sculptors are credited with passing their skills and ideas on to Japan when the Korean King, sent Buddhist missionaries to Japan, together with the necessary artisans to build a "new" Buddhist infrastructure therein the mid-6th Century[2].

Contemporary records indicate that metalworking and the art of sword manufacturing, were still in a rudimentary state in Japan at the time of the Baekje's technology transfer from the Korean Peninsula, The "new" skill-transfer included iron smelting (with the import of the high-carbon iron ore from Korea) with metalwork manufacture and steel working. These methods and techniques, as well as their updates, continued to be transmitted from China, via Korea, to Japan until Japanese connections with the

Asian mainland were largely closed off by Japan's ***Sakoku*** period (200 years from mid-17th century), when Japanese metalworking diverged, resulting in their evolution of their unique ***katana*** or Samurai sword. The early 17th Century saw the end of the ***Sengoku*** period of the War Lords in Japan resulting in a sharp decline in the requirement for the ***katana***, so the highly skilled swordsmiths had to turn their hand to normal blacksmithing, so transferring their technology to other edge tools[3].

Not only in Japan but also in many of the East Asian cultures, for various reasons, the skill of the swordsmiths has been deprecated at some period of their history, resulting in the transfer of their work, skill and technology to the regular blacksmiths for the making of hand tools.

The steel used for traditional Japanese laminated tools is possibly the best understood in the West due to its history being so well recorded although[4] there has been an increase interest in the history of swordsmiths globally, resulting in a spin-off into metallurgy history.

Developments in both China and Japan include the introduction of High Speed Steel-(HSS) into their range of chisels, this is a tough steel that resists abrasion and chipping (so suitable for restoration and conservation tasks). However, it is unable to take the fine edge of the traditional carbon steels. Although I have not seen HSS used for carving tools, I have successfully used HSS chisels for restoration work where the ancient oak in our house is good at killing a tool edge as it is like hammering it into steel.

The traditional Japanese tools were early to market in UK, but the high cost of their quality handmade items were beyond most budgets. To combat this, some tools manufacturers adapted the old techniques to mass production leading, to a reduction in price at the expense of ultimate quality. Both styles are widely available, although there are still limited UK sources for Japanese carving tools.

Traditional Chinese tools tool have been available to craftsmen through Hong Kong for some time, with the Hong Kong based exporter Mujingfang[5] (木井坊) or Woodwell Tools (www.mujingfang.com) taking its catalogue of traditional hand tools to the international market in 1982, (although I suspect they have been in the import export business for tools since the 1920's when European manufacturers' started to sell Western tools into Hong Kong and Shanghai). Their traditional wooden hand planes gained a cult following in the West and some other hand tools such as their chisels then followed into western catalogues, with traditional Chinese tools quite widely available on the Internet, You do need to be careful about the fine details as to what is being offered, as quality can vary more widely than the prices would indicate. While there are a few specialist companies in North America that supply Chinese carving tools and plane blade (for Bailey transplants), possibly the most reliable and long running source of traditional Mujingfang tools is Dictum in Germany[6]. On the other hand, Korean tools remain more of an enigma.

[1]2016; A Profile of the Steel Industry: Global Reinvention for a New Economy; Warrian, Peter; Business Expert Press; ISBN ISBN-10: 1631573837
[2] http://www.baekje-heritage.or.kr/html/en/historic/historic_010101.html
[3] https://www.japanvisitor.com/japanese-culture/samurai-sword
[4] https://www.tf.uni-kiel.de/matwis/amat/iss/kap_c/articles/wadsworth_laminated_steel.pdf
[5]WoodWell Tools http://www.mujingfang.com/t/eng/default.asp
[6] https://www.dictum.com/en/tools-b

1: Korean Carving Chisels

Korea has a long history of wood carving, both as "sculpture" and in "calligraphy" (a specialist for of chip-carving to represent the Hangul alphabet[1]) - where Hangul is one of the oldest written languages recorded for posterity in the ***Tripitaka Koreana*** carved onto 81,258 wooden printing blocks in the 13th century.

Korea also had a highly developed metalworking culture capable of producing high quality laminated blades, a skill unfortunately lost under the suppression of the Korean identity during the period of occupation 1910-1945. The ancient ***Baekje*** metalworkers and sculptors passed on these skills and ideas to Japan in the mid-6th century when. Some of the historic work by these craftsmen including the Hōryūji Temple still remain today, where much of the original woodwork and carving was by Korean craftsmen.

Modern steel manufacture started under the Japanese occupation, but these plants fell into the Soviet Zone in 1945, now in North Korea (DPRK). More recently, in the post-occupation (post-war) period South Korea (ROK) was left as an impoverished agrarian economy that lacked capital, technology, manpower and natural resources, so President Park Chung-hee's vision to transform this agrarian Korea into an industrial nation seemed implausible[2]. However, the investment and drive put into this new steel industry drove their modern economy and enabled Korea to be a world leader in "clean steel" production.

After the liberation of Korea in 1945, ceremonial swords were once again manufactured both in southern and northern Korea and by the 1960's, sword-making had revived and was again a vibrant and increasingly secure industry; however, due to the depredations and systematic destruction by the Japanese during the Japanese occupation of Korea, some traditions and techniques were lost and were either completely unrecoverable or have yet to be recovered. Traditional woodworking skills have been retained in the post-war programme of temple construction and restoration, that involves a huge amount of wood working. Unfortunately, the allied role of the blacksmith in the making of old-style laminated carving tools does not seem to have fared as well as in Japan, possibly indicating that high quality modern tools are available[3].

I can find little information about modern wood carving/wood sculpture in Korea and very little information is available in English about the current range of Korean carving tools. What I have been able to establish, from Internet searches, is that there are possibly three main grades of modern carving tools, represented by the following manufacturers, each aiming for a different domestic market. In addition, some of the manufacturers have two styles - first the "Sculpture" tools, with a hooped handle for striking and then the "Carving knives" with a shorter blade and a longer, thin handle solely designed for hand use. The former seem to come in "standard" sets of ten, the latter in sets of twelve.

1 At the bottom end of the market there are basic grade tools for the amateur that are used domestically in "art" classes, that are made under brand names

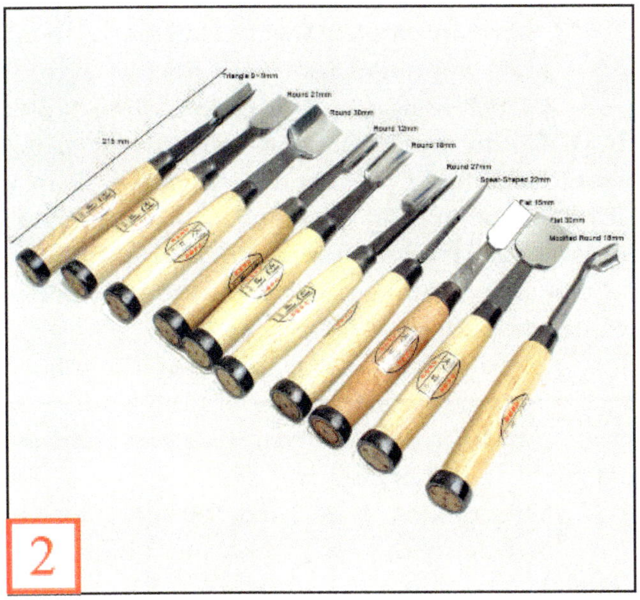

2

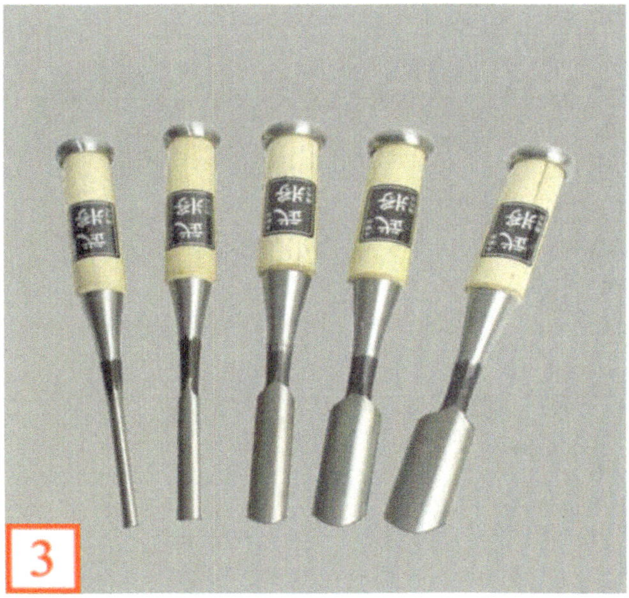

3

such as "SMATO" and "Goldfinch" "*Geumhwa/Kumhwa*" ( ).

2 In the mid-market (20% price increase) there is the basic craftsman tools by "*Chonbi*" (4

3 At the top end (30% price increase) there are tools for the professional by "Iron Horse" (

4 Unfortunately, the only samples I have been able to buy off the Internet are of the "basic" Geumhwa tools, which can be obtained from eBay for upwards of £10 each (half the price of a tool from UK). The tools are provided accurately ground (including a traditional "hollow back" to the straight blades that is clearly artificially cross-ground, with a black paint finish to emulate hand forged tools.

5 With a bit of paint stripper to enable a close inspection of the *Geumhwa blades,* indicates that they are a single (non-laminated) steel blade that has actually been forged (some budget "sets" are stamped from sheet steel). Final shaping of things like the tang have been ground, not forged.

4

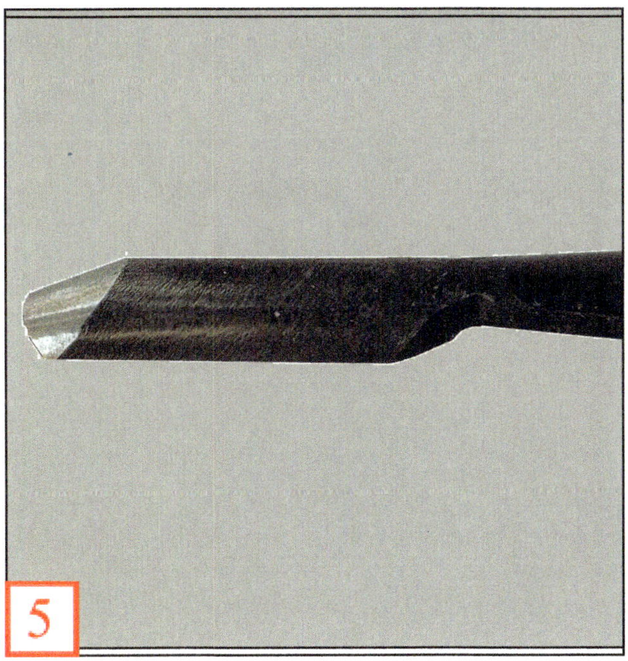

5

6

7

8

6 My simple Rockwell Hardness "cone test" suggests that the steel is harder than the standard hi-carbon steel[5] used in UK and more in line with the "spring steel"[6] quoted by Flexcut®. It takes only a little bit of honing and polishing to provide an excellent edge finish, that I found was sharp and durable, well up to the challenges of carving English Oak.

7 The high quality finish of the blade, with a mirror finish on the inside, is much "cleaner" than I have found on any UK or EU blade.

8 This makes them especially well suited to a finishing cut, when used inverted.

9 In use, the curved front profile of the blades automatically provides a useful "slicing" movement when cutting paring timber, which I found most useful. The handle hoops of the Sculpture tools need the same attention as other similar tools and I found the length and shape of the thin handles on the hand-work set to be very good at getting close to the work without snagging.

10 These "basic" Korean tools are well made and provide an excellent budget alternative to the "cheap & nasty" offerings found elsewhere on the Internet. It is regrettable that I have been unable to source the higher quality tools to compare, as even

9

at a price increase of up to 50% over these basic tools, they could offer serious competition to the low end "quality" tools from European manufacturers. From the Internet they come as sculpting tool sets (Picture 1 above on page 87) and detail tools sets (here in Picture 10), although I have also seen the occasional offer of both individual tools and small sets of three or four.

10

Available Profiles[1]

As far as I have been able to establish, the available profiles are shown below:

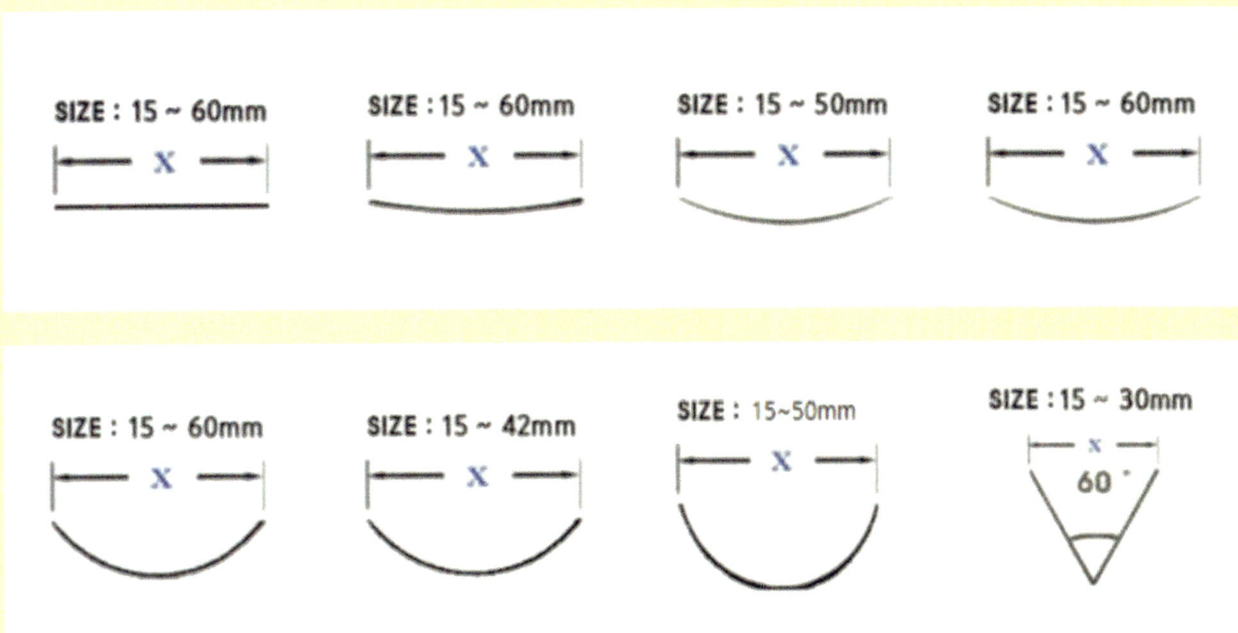

[1] http://www.chonbi.co.kr/main.php?m1=28&m2=34&m3=46

[1] The Hangul language was promulgated with carved blocks in the 15th Century by King Sejong the Great
[2] Korean POSCO http://www.koreatimes.co.kr/www/nation/2019/12/291_69759.html
[3] With thanks to Dr J E Hoare, Centre of Korean Studies SOAS, London WC1H 0XG
[4] Chonbi Tools:http://www.chonbi.co.kr/main.php?userAgent=PC
[5] High-Carbon Steel - C155 in Europe and 1055 in the USA
[6] Spring Steel - C100 in Europe and 1095 in the USA

2: Traditional Chinese Tools

As in Japan, the traditional blacksmiths in China can still turn their hand to laminated steel. At the industrial level, the Chinese have also been thinking latterly and have found another more modern steel to adapt to traditional hand tools - High Speed Steel - HSS (T1). No self respecting turner these days buys turning tools made from the "normal" high-carbon Tool Steel (O1) - which has a HRC56 that is still the "standard" for most UK chisels and plane blade. HSS (T1) has long since taken over the turning tool market. HSS is harder, generally above HRC60, but still takes a good edge and, critically for the amateur, does not lose its temper when one "blues" the edge on a grinder. The down side is that it is more expensive, more brittle and it lacks the flexibility to withstand the frequent blow of a mallet or the abuse of being used as a lever to get the last bit out of a mortice. Lateral thinking, in the Chinese traditional tool making industry, has literally blended the two - with a HSS cutting edge simply brazed to a mild steel shank to produce a "combo blade". This does not look pretty, but it certainly works and has been adapted for use in a number of their traditional tools, from chisels to planes and still costs less than the expensive A2 Tool Steel (HRC62) used in "premi-

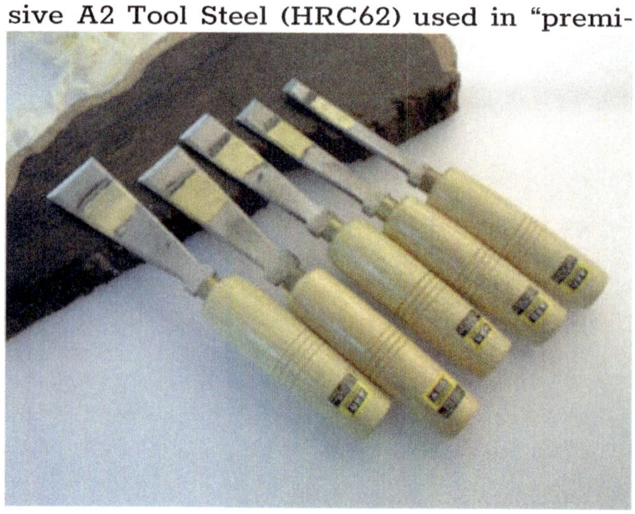

The traditional Chinese craftsman starts to shape his timber with a side axe (a shape that is well suited to a laminated steel tool, as the main cutting edge can be made of hard steel, supported by the soft steel head). After initial stock preparation with the side axe, the traditional Chinese carpenter would pick up the long "Hong Kong" pattern Jack Plane, with a blade set at 45° and with a conventional chip-breaker attached via a screw to the blade - much in line with the setup of the metal Bailey planes. These Jack Planes are traditionally used for preparation of hard woods but can be easily transferred to use on European and North American softwoods. They can come in two widths, several lengths and with many different woods offered in the body. To add to the variations, the Hong Kong planes can come with a variety of different blades, from normal steel, through a "HSS Combo" blade, while the top end planes have a laminated steel blade and are usually offered in the traditional Chinese Rosewood. When the work has progressed through different lengths of Jack Plane, the Chinese woodworker will move onto the high-angle "polishing" plane, which is the pattern for the well known Australian HNT Gordon planes[1]. These feature a solid HSS blade set at 60° degrees for (or if the blade is reversed, can be used at 90° as a scraper plane). Polishing Planes come in several lengths, from 120mm (4¾") to 230mm (9") and are exceptionally adept on hard woods, such as European and North American Oak.

Both the jack and Polishing Planes feature a removable cross-handle, as they are "normally" pushed in the western style, rather than pulled in the Japanese style - although they are amenable to either. Then finally there are the Taiwanese planes. If you consider the Hong Kong Jack Plane to be something of a hybrid western plane, then the Taiwanese planes could be considered as a hybrid Japanese plane, with a short HSS blade set at 45°, which is well suited to hardwoods — but still used either on the push or pull stroke. There are also a wide range of all the "special" planes you would expect; from rebate planes, to "hollows & rounds" to chamfer planes and spoke-shaves — all usually only available with a normal steel blade. With the wide range of planes available and the multiple variations within the planes, you need to careful that you know at what you are looking. A top quality traditional Chinese rosewood plane can cost twice the price of similar planes in other woods, including some of the lesser "ebonies". The better planes will have a brass or copper mouth insert. Added to that are the variations in blade dimensions and steels; blades vary from conventional 2mm - 3mm tool steels, through 2.5mm "HSS-Combo" blades to high quality 3mm fully laminated blades (which may be too thick for transplant into the conventional Bailey planes. By comparison the Western Bailey variants have an O1 steel blade with a thickness of 2mm - 2.5mm depending on age and manufacturer - although the new "quality" planes usually have 3mm A2 Steel.

The possible down-side of these Chinese excellent planes is the need to learn how to adjust a wooden plane, while the up-side is the possibility of a quality product that will take a fine shaving, straight out of the box. These traditional planes are made for the domestic market and are in a different league from the mass produced "Bailey" planes that Chinese factories turn out for the DIY sheds.

CHISELS

Taking a look at Chisels, where the "Chinese standard" is for a "fish-tail" shape. The smaller sizes are fitted to the handle with a conventional tang, but the larger sizes are fitted with a socket (which gives greater strength to the larger sizes for heavy blows such as needed in working hardwoods). A set

of five HSS fishtail Chinese "Cabinet Maker's" chisels will set you back a similar price to a comparable set of budget chisels made from "normal" O1 Tool Steel, while a similar set of large HSS tipped wide socket style chisels will add 10% to the price, with little other competition in the budget market. On the down side, the "HSS Combo" blades do not look pretty and neither type of chisel will fit easily in the normal "Eclipse" honing guide (but most of the tool catalogues offer alternatives that have been extensively reviewed). On the up side, once sharpened, HSS holds an edge well and last much longer between honing than their European style brethren. From personal experience (with restoration of old oak), the socket chisels will happily take considerable abuse.

CARVING GOUGES

The southern Chinese city of Dongyang 东阳

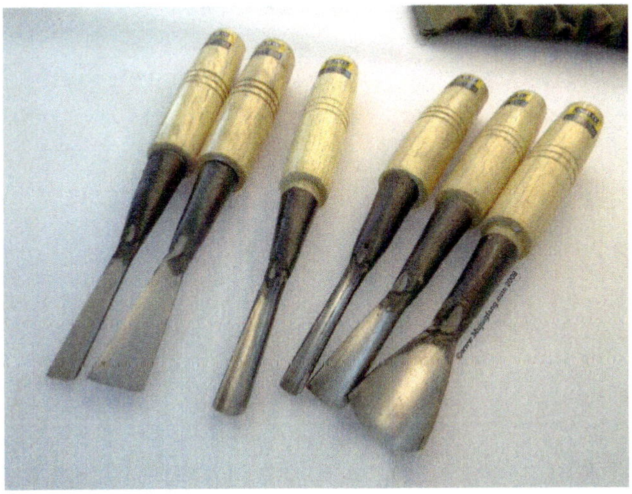

has been one of the major centres of wood carving in China since the Tang Dynasty (618 – 907AD)[2]. Their carving gouges, again available only as "fish-tail" are usually in some sort of set. These are offered as either detail carving tools (with tangs) or as larger laminated sculpting tools, with socket handles. In addition, there is a unique range of long handled (laminated) socket gouges for timber framers and architectural (and ice) carvers. Either way, the individual tool price represents a 25%-30% saving on similar European style sets, while a "complete set" without handles was priced attractively when I reviewed them some years ago[3]. On the down side, the range is limited and the finish can be a bit rough, but this is again off-set by superior edge holding and the ability of the larger socket style tools to take the abuse of architectural carving and wood sculpting. The traditional Chinese Sculpture (Carving) tool have been available to craftsmen through Mujingfang[4] (木井坊) for some time. Originally Hong Kong based, this exporter took its catalogue of traditional hand tools to the international market in 1982, (although I suspect they have been in the import-export business for tools since the 1920's when European manufacturers' started to sell Western tools into Hong Kong and Shanghai). Their traditional wooden hand planes gained a cult following in the West and some other hand tools such as their chisels then followed into western catalogues - now on their websites. A range of their tools are available from a few tools sites in EU and US.

The traditional Chinese chisel handle is made from oak and does not have a handle-hoop, but is still struck with a metal hammer. Their artisan "chippy" hammer is shaped like a side axe (雕花斧 transliterates from Chinese as "striking axe"[5]) and the chisel is struck with the broad side (I suspect this is a descendant of the Carpenters' side-axe,

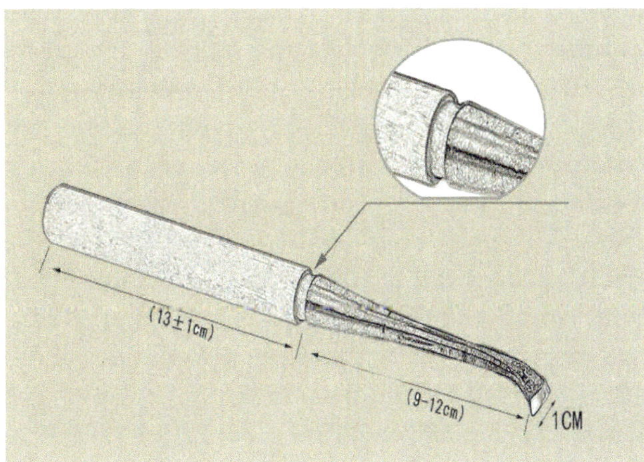

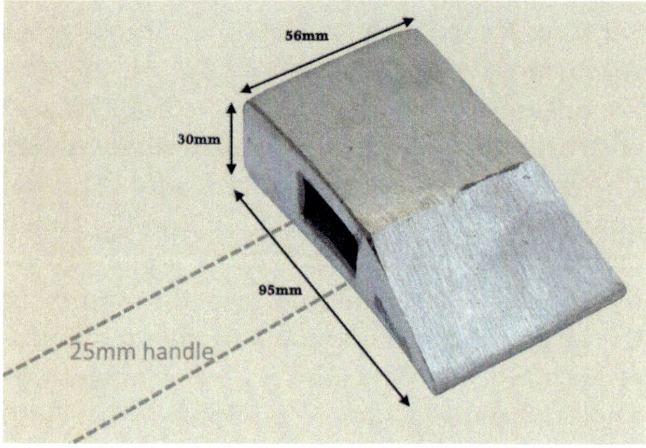

which was a common tradesman's tool for rough cutting and hammering until the 20th Century). In China the axe has a more expensive laminated blade, so I assume a cheaper lump-metal hammer has evolved for the "master" as rough cutting with a side-axe was delegated to the apprentices.

The reason that these traditional chisels are of interest is that they potentially offer a significant saving compared to the "set" of 8 UK chisels (See Chapter 3) that will currently cost £180-£200 for professional quality tools from Henry Taylor or Pfeil (£20-£25 each). Only the smaller "standard" (ie amateur) tools from Narex would be less from £15-20 each or approximately £120. Also of note is "complete set" of 20 Flexcut retails at £200.

By comparison if you search for "***Assorted Lot Wood Carving Tools***" on the Internet, you will be offered a "complete set" of 62 Traditional Donyang blades by the likes of the Song music Instrument Co. Ltd[6]. These now cost about £120 rising to £200 with handles. When I bought my blades[7] the price in Europe for a "full set" of 36" was about £60 from DICTUM Fine Tools in Germany[8] for "naked" blades so was a good price from a secure source - by comparison, just the set of detail tools now cost about £60!. On the basis of the blades I reviewed I feel sure that you would probably at least cover the "recommended eight" from a set of 62 from China as my Dictum set of 36 only really fell short on the N°7 x 7mm, for which the N°6 x 5mm supplied will probably substitute. With the prices from China having doubled in the intervening period, the cost/benefit of these tools is no longer as clear cut and possibly more of a gamble especially with the spectre of possible import duties as well,

CHISEL CONSTRUCTION

Unlike their Japanese cousins, the "striking" chisels are a of a socket construction, with a mild steel socket forming approximately at a 4½° cone that is 40mm long with a 15-18mm diameter. The westernised handle used by Mujingfang (Chinese oak) is about 150mm (6") long and 25mm (1") thick with a tapered end (to suit the socket), with a wide shoulders to cover the hard rim of the blade. If hit with the broad side of a metal "Striking Axe" it will slowly mushroom. There's also a wide range available in the USA from MASTERCARVER®, including a useful basic set of 10 at $100[9]

ANCIENT & MODERN BLADES

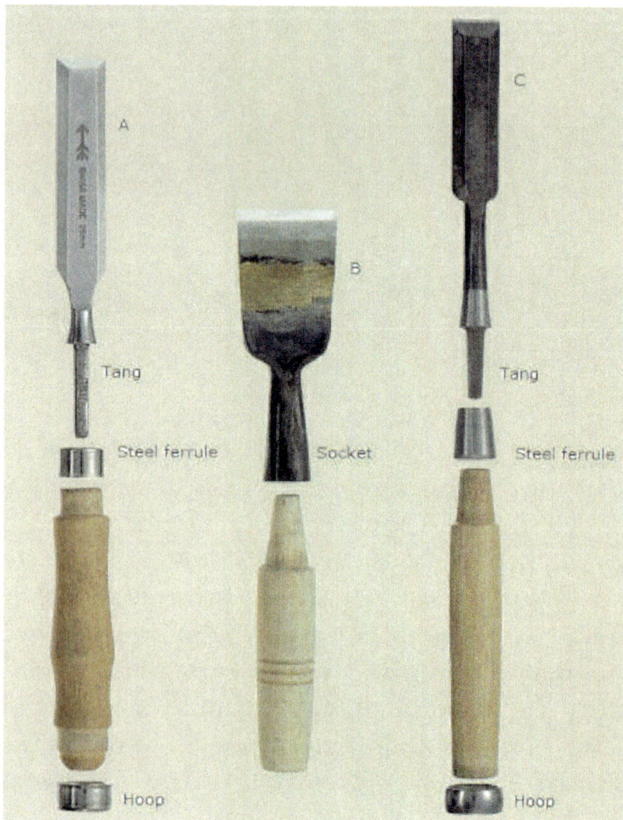

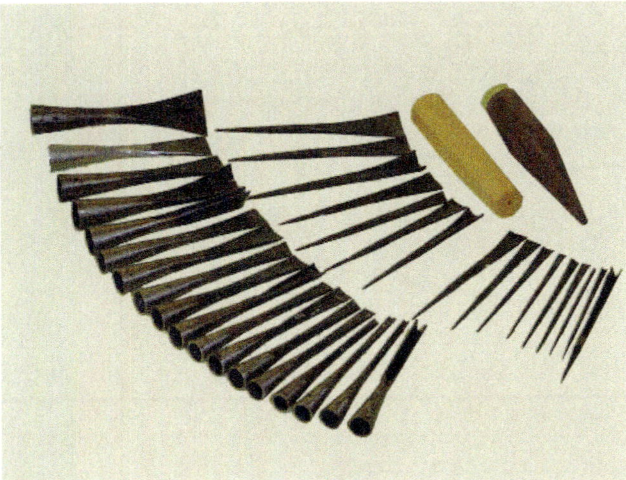

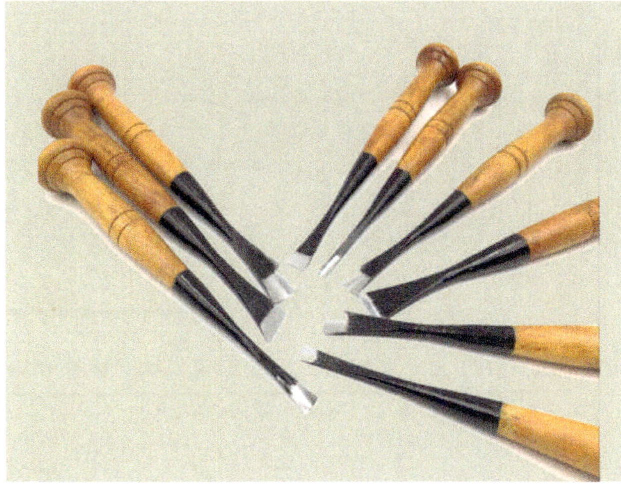

As an amateur carver, justifying the expense of Japanese laminated tools is difficult, so there is an attraction to a set traditional Chinese laminated carving blades. From what I have been able to establish, the socket & shaft are made form Chinese #45 steel (medium carbon) with the laminated edge from Chinese #60 (high carbon spring steel), that is forge welded by hand to the medium carbon steel backing. However, I have also see evidence of a move to some use of #65Mn alloy steel (a Chinese Standard Manganese spring steel grade) in some newer - non-laminated socket blades as well as a move to offered with affordable sets of (apparently) well finished tools, mainly from on-line Luthiers' suppliers[10].

THE CHOICE OF HANDLES

To get the equivalent combined full set of 62 of these tools with handles is about £80-£100 more, so there is still a strong incentive to "handle" them yourself. As a guide, The Mujingfang handle is on the left, with a shouldered socket, the (rosewood) cone deign I used is next, then two handles for tangs, a European style octagonal and a UK round with ferrule. Purchasing a single "replacement" handle is upwards of £5, but some reductions can be found for bulk purchases. All-in-all, the expense of buying in handles quickly exceed the premium required for buying the set-with-handles.

Making a handle without a lathe is not complicated, especially if you start with suitable hardwood dowel, such as beech or oak. "Ringing" dowel is reasonably straight forward, using a clamped block or even just tape on a tennon-saw to set the depth, then

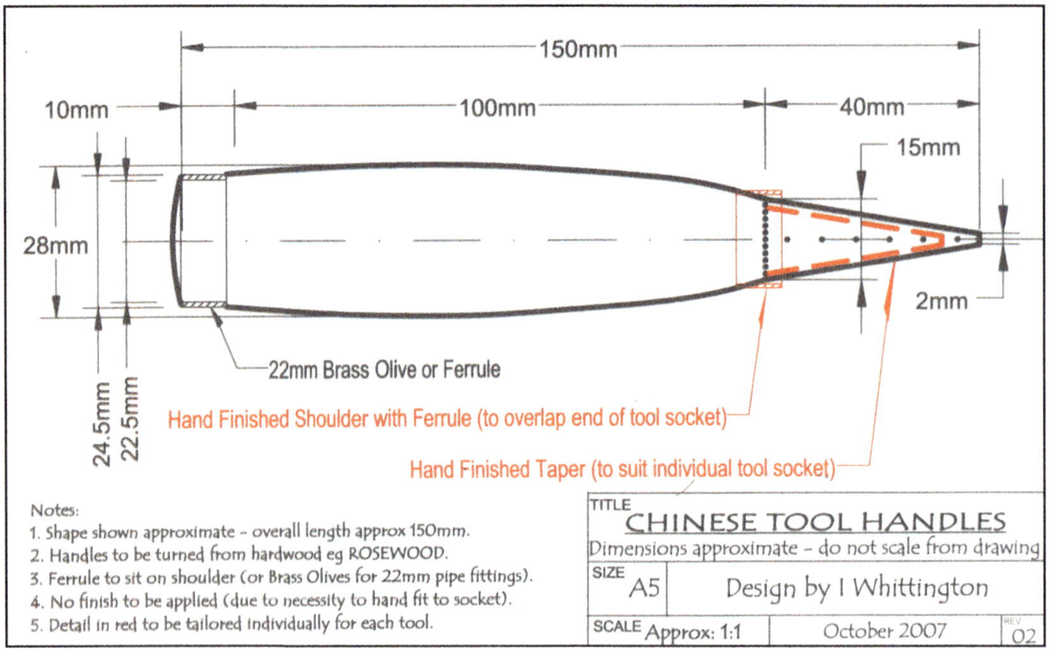

"pruning" back to the line with a knife or chisel.

The brass (rather than copper) "olives" from a plumbers' compression joints come in various sizes, the smaller 10mm(⅜") & 15mm(½") suit as a ferrule on smaller handles and the larger 22mm(¾") as the "striking ring" on socket handles. Either can be seated with epoxy if the "ringing" is less than perfect. A "socket cone" can either be whittled with a knife, rasp or machined with a disk sander. Either way, the progress measured by frequently offering-up the socket for trial fitting. If you need further inspiration, there are many on-line articles on handle making without a lathe.

When I originally tested these tools from DICTUM, bearing in mind that the mixture of sizes and shapes in a "set" will not suit all, my conclusion was that the experiment was a success. What should not have been a surprise was that the two sets were so com-

plementary. Perhaps too many straight blades with the laminated skews being effectively "handed" all one way and, for ornamental carving, although the selection through N°3-6 worked well, especially the range of N°5s, but with only a single N°6 and no N°7s at all, there was a significant "hole". I felt that both sets could to trade "surplus" straight irons for N°7s. The "V" tools were excellent, but no veiner. With the finished laminated tools working out then at £4.50 each, I had derived a lot of satisfaction from taking them from the blacksmith's rough irons to useful and practical tools at a very keen price. Their combination of edge-holding and fish-tail shape, added significantly to my existing tools. In addition, the tendency of N°3 detail tools to "relax" their profile away from the centre to more of a N°2½, made them into excellent finishing tools, and earned them a place in my list of recommended tool at pg 9 There were some problems, but, as these were easily overcome by a combination of some re-design and DICTUM's excellent after-sales support, these did to detract from the quality/price equation. I would still recommend them to the keen amateur, as an inexpensive way of greatly extending the scope of an existing set of ironware — particularly if purchased in conjunction with the "detail" set — as the two sets are really so complementary. As for the "detail" tools then at averaging at the time at £1.25 each - a budget price with ease of preparation, they remain well ahead of the "generic" small starter sets available and well up to the blade quality expected of the well known manufacturers. The DICTUM set now cost over £50 so roughly speaking you need to get 3 or more useful tools from their set to rival even the Narex tool price - which I found I did. On that basis, I still highly recommended them to any amateur who is capable of adding a handle then sharpening their own tools, even as a "starter set". As they lend themselves to easy adaptation, they will be of use to many professionals as well. The sets still represent good value, even if some of them are irrelevant to your needs — and can you ever have too many tools anyway? Based on material costs only, you are not going to get this sort of quality at such a low price elsewhere. Unfortunately, the price has since nearly doubled — so the cost/benefit is now less clear cut.

I did enjoy working the set up to a good level and still routinely use many of the tools as the resulting tools are generally useful — I often find I reach for the "surplus" straight fishtail for carpentry work. At the time of the review I suggested that I should have kept the handle designs simpler, so I could have made them myself - which is still the case - see below Page - 99:

1 *https://hntgordon.com.au*

2 *Dongyang Carving https://mymodernmet.com/dongyang-wood-carving/*

3 *WC #101 - Mar-Apr 2008 Chinese CarvingTools*

4 *WoodWell Tools http://www.mujingfang.com/t/eng/default.asp*

5 *Striking Axe (Hammer) http://www.mujingfang.com/t/eng/itemdetails.asp?id=MJF4038&SpecialOffer=&rec=13&sql=select+%2A+from+Item_e1+WHERE+Status<>%27Hidden%27+and+ItemClass1%3D%27Woodworking+Tools+Series%27+and+ItemClass2%3D%27Carving+Tools+and+Chisels%27*

6 *Song Musical Instrument Shop: https://www.ebay.com/str/songmusicalinstrumentshop or https://www.ebay.com/str/charmingsongviolinstore*

7 *2008 WC #101 - Mar-Apr 2008 Chinese CarvingTools Pt 1 & WC #102 May-Jun 2008 - Chinese CarvingTools Pt II*

8 *Chinese Blades from Germany: https://www.dictum.com/en/carving-sculpting-tools-baca/sculpting-blades-18-piece-set-700971*

9 *https://www.woodcarverssupply.com/10-TOOL-BASIC-SET-ROLL/productinfo/401004/*

10 Search for *"9pcs Great ASSORTED LOT WOOD CARVING TOOLS,Chisel"*

Simple Handles for DICTUM™ SCULPTING SET

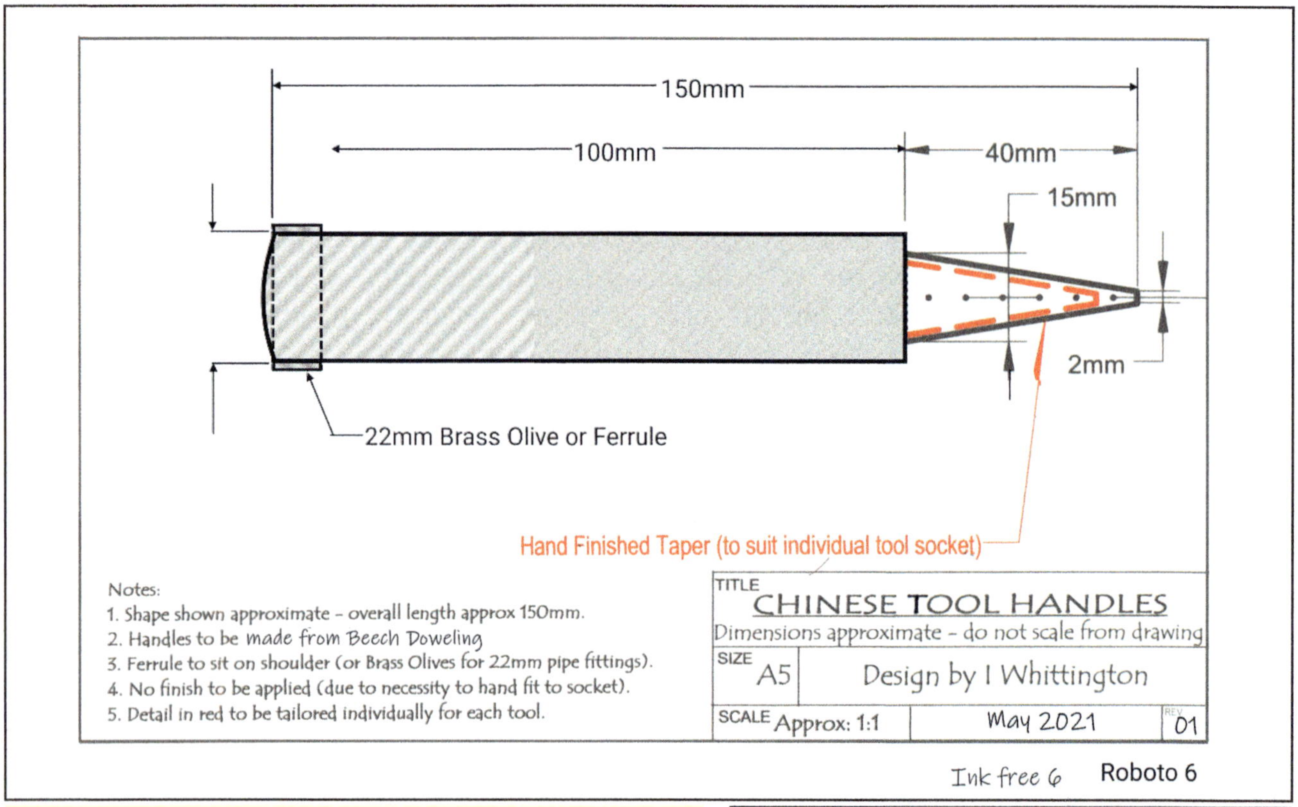

Materials:

The Socket chisels require a handle of greater than the 15mm diameter of the socket opening, for which Beech Dowel at 22mmØ is ideal. A 300mm length will provide two handles at about £1 each. If you want a ferrule to reinforce this, a packet of 22mm brass pipe olives[1] will set you back about 60p each, so materials for a handle are significantly less than the £5 starting price for a “bought” handle.
For the detail tools, an 15mmØ Beech Dowel can be used , which can be paired with a 15mm olive for the “sharp end’ ferrule.

Tools:

It is perfectly possible to use a single “edge tool” such as a knife to fashion these handles. However, if you are making a few of these, you will find a (fine tooth) hard tip saw, a battery drill, rasp and files useful, all of which could be expected to be fond in an amateur’s workshop.

Socket taped handle:

To leave "room for error" put a taper on both ends of the 300mm x 22mm dowel and split it into two handles last thing. Check the depth of the tool socket that you are working with - probably in the region of 35-40mm - and mark this on the dowel end by placing a knife blade at this distance and rolling the dowel back & forth until the blade has scored right round the dowel.

A With the dowel firmly secured, take a knife, draw-knife or rasp to start tapering from this line to the rip in "pencil sharpening" mode.

B When you have enough waste removed, test fit the blade frequently as you refine the cone with a file until a tight fit is achieved.

C When both end are ready for a blade, cut the length in two, slide the 22mm olive over the end and slide the dowel into a pipe fitting then tighten the fitting to "seat" the olive. Place the blade on the other end and with the sharp-end uppermost, strike the blunt-end sharply on the bench, to seat blade.

D If required, a bevel can be added to the shoulder above the socket with a file or sanding block.

A

B

C

D

3: Carver's Paring Chisel by Ashley Iles

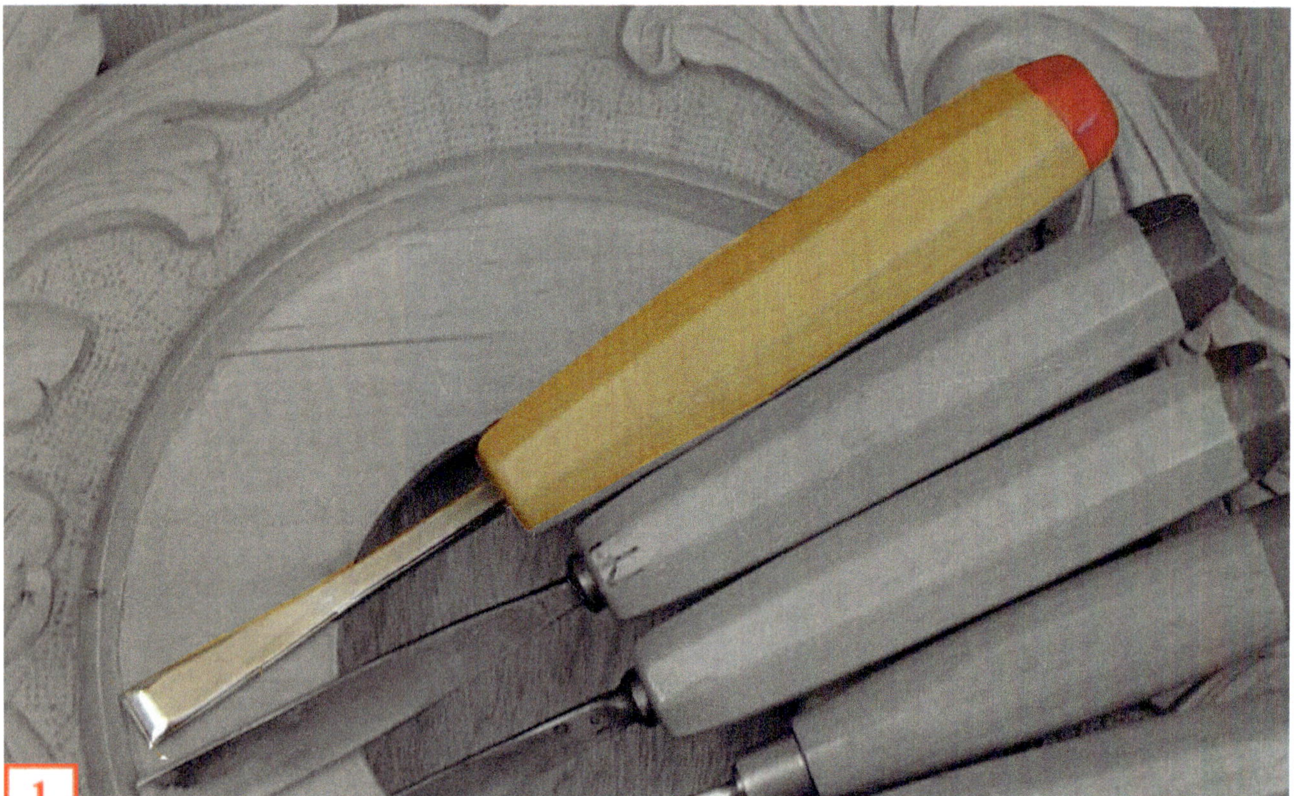

1 In my list of tools, I included one of my own favourites a Carver's Paring Chisel - (*aka: Single Angle Dog-leg chisel*).

1 It's a bent 12mm (½") bevel-up fishtail that combines the utility of a skew with that of a grounding chisel, not to mention a very versatile shaping tool for paring convex surfaces. The origins of the one I have are lost in the mists of when I was living in Norway and, even with the resources of the Internet, When I was writing an article on basic carving tools[1]I was unable to locate one to recommend as a purchase.

2 However, Barry Iles[2] came to the rescue with a prototype that he kindly provided for testing. It arrived in the post in standard Ashley Iles packaging complete with blade protection.

3 When unpacked and compared to the original the overall shape is well within acceptable parameters, perhaps with a more pronounced fish-tail. The first one lacked the side bevels that make the tool so versatile in a tight spot, but these were added to a replacement.

4 Ashley Iles tools always come nicely ground and capable of work straight from the factory, but all tools benefit from finishing. This was no exception, especially as it's designed for use bevel up, for which a mirror finish on the underside is preferable - a quick few minutes with a whetstone and it's ready to try.

5 The tool worked a treat, it pared beautifully, right up to the edge with no snagging when undercutting. I used it to carve the convex surround for an oak panel decoration, which was not a long test, but as expected, it retained its newly polished cutting edge perfectly.

6 This was a prototype, but there is a "cousin" in the catalogue - all it lacks are the side bevels, that are easily added: Ashley Iles ***Angle Dog-leg Chisel (Sweep 51)*** 15mm c£30[3]

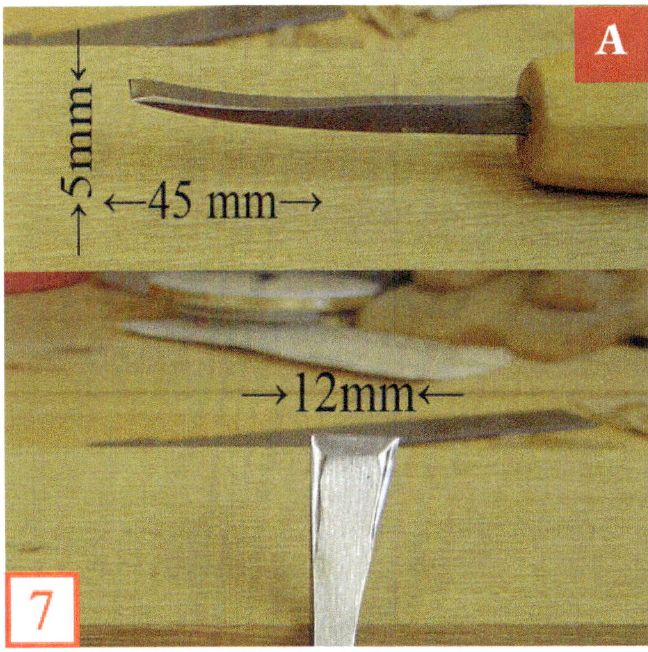

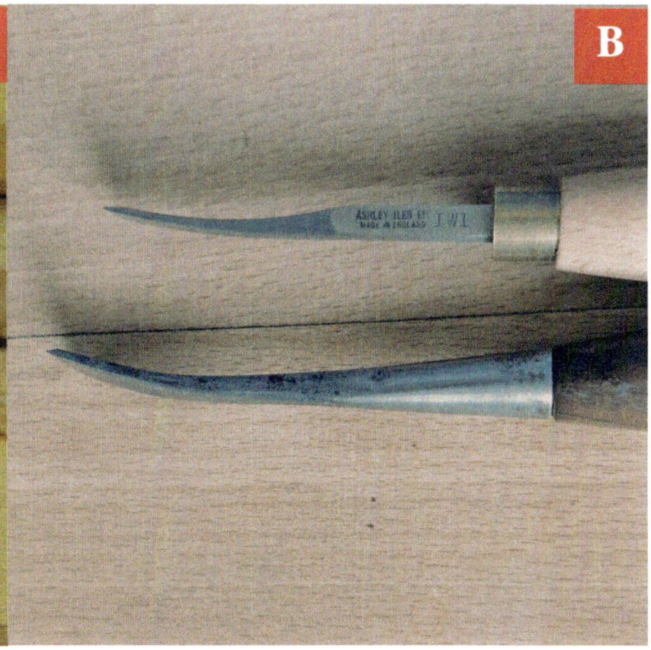

7 If you have gone down the road of tying the Chinese tools (See Pg 91), you may find that you have a surplus fish-tail N°1 that can be easily adapted at little additional cost.

A. As it's already a fish-tail, "all" you need is a competent metalworker to bend the final 45mm (1¾") and re-temper it.

B As I live in a rural Devon, the local blacksmith obliged for the price of a pint of cider.

[1]Basic Carving Tools 2014 WC 140 Sep-Oct 2014- Whittington, Iain.
[2] Barry Iles: http://www.ashleyiles.co.uk/about_ashley_iles.html
[3] Angle Dog-leg Chisel (Sweep 51) :www.ashleyilestoolstore.co.uk/carving-tools/carving-gouges-chisels/special/single-angle-dog-leg-chisel-sweep-51

4: Old Tools

Old tools are another source for carvers. Tool for use vary in price from £15, for tools of limited utility, to over £30 for unusual, but useful profiles. I had the good fortune to be donated a collection by a family friend that has enabled me to get a "feel" for old tools. By many standards, the majority of my tools qualify as "old tools" as they mostly date from the 20thC. However, for this "test" I'm targeting the 19thC tools by Addis.

1

1 The batch that I received were mostly "esoteric" small profiles of limited use, but there were a few "common use" profiles to be able to stack up against their modern cousins. The majority of the tools were J.*B. ADDIS & SON* over "*10 PRIZE MEDAL*" imprint on the reverse of the blade, so probably ***Ward & Payne*** tools from late 19th to early 20thC. There are a few (possibly) earlier ***S.J.ADDIS***[1] "***Cast Steel/England***" with sweep numbers, so these are also probably Ward & Payne tools from the 1890s or later. There are only two Addis tools with Beech handles, which I assume are early 20thC, There are a few "miscellaneous" manufacturers, that also show more variation in handle styles, mostly above delicate blades. These blades from the period were marketed globally by ***Ward & Payne***, appearing in mail order catalogues, marketed throughout the English speaking world, hence marked with sweep numbers.

2

2 Apart from the beech handle most of these tools are similar in size. The Addis is of this period (far right) is typically un-polished (forge-black), much as a current Henry Taylor (HT) tool to its left, They are "full size", unlike the "amateur" tools on the far left (from HT & Narex).

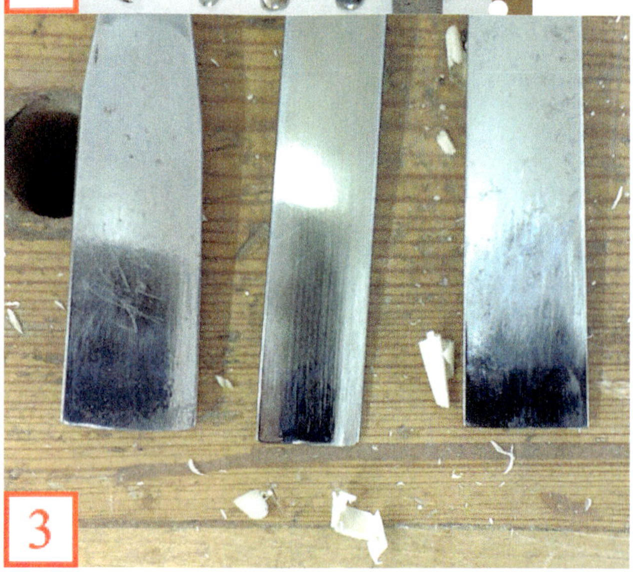

3

3 The "working edge" of the tool will have been finished by the craftsman, but higher up the inside of the blade

was well finished (now with some rust pitting), unlike the 1990's HT[2] tool in the centre of Fig 3, where the finish was inferior to a similar tool from the 1980's (to its left).

4 The finish on the inside only matters if you used the tool inverted, where the ridges on the later tool will transfer to the wood (as will any patina left by rust pitting on the old tool). The earlier 1980's tool - far left in Fig 3 - is the shorter HT "amateur" style which has always been supplied with a polished finish, which may also have resulted in the better finish on the inside of the blade.

5 Does it matter? As a guide, when using a slip-stone, the time taken to remove the ridges on the 1990's blade, exceeded that required for the rust pitting on the 19th Century blade by a factor of two. A hand-held grinder such as the Dremel, would be a better choice for fettling the (replaceable) modern tool, but I was loath to use such an aid for restoring the the old Addis. As a foot-note, the Addis blade thickness is also similar to the modern HT tools at ~1.2mm-1.5mm.

In conclusion, I didn't feel that the 19^{th}C Addis tools were significantly different from the 20^{th}C HT tools, so I doubt that the premium price is worth it for a "using" tool. The time needed for "restoration" varied, but generally speaking was of a similar range as "setting up" a modern hand-forged tool like the 20^{th}C HT series, which also take some time. It is the need for this "setting up" time that has probably increased the popularity of the better European tools that are supplied polished and finished at a similar price point.

4

5

[1] *The Addis Family, the Herring Brothers, and Ward & Payne; MARCH 22, 2018 / CHRISTOPHER STORB :https://cstorb.com/2018/03/22/the-addis-family-the-herring-brothers-and-ward-payne/*

[2] *The history of Henry Taylor Tools is not well documented. It has changed ownership several times since I first bough tools, with three changes since the mid-1990's, the most recent in 2017 and I have no recent experience of their tools. For example, although their catalogue shows tools with a traditional (black) finish, they now also produce tools with a polished finish on contract to DICTUM in Germany:https://www.dictum.com/en/carving-sculpting-tools-baca/dictum-carving-tools-6-piece-set-in-cotton-tool-roll-701536*

PART II PROJECTS

Projects

Project One - Kolrosing a Wooden Plane

This project is typical of the use of Kolrosing to turn a craftsman's hand tools into an individual item of beauty.
The pattern is based on a traditional acanthus design, superimposed on the wooden body of a N°3 transition plane.

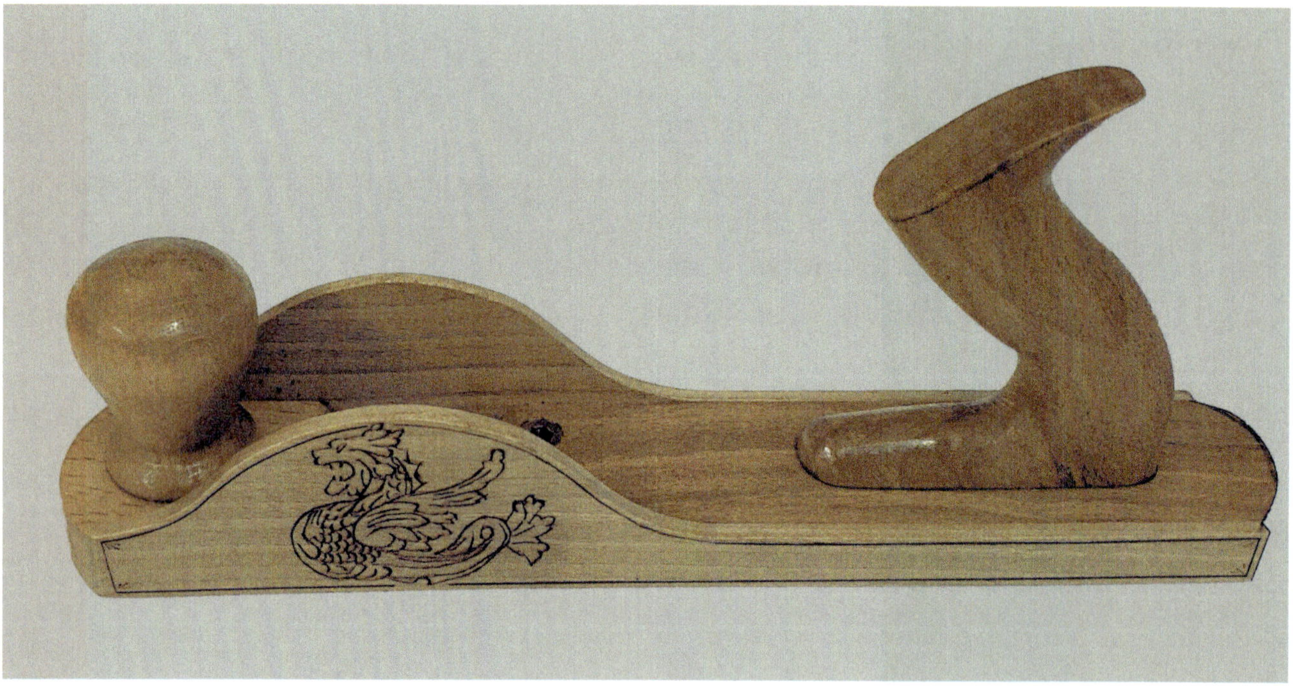

This dragon pattern, derived from a folio published in London at the end of the Victorian era[1] is in a pamphlet that includes a series of traditional drawings pattern that you could find anywhere in Europe, especially in the repertoire of the Victorian revivalists. It has been adapted to be a symmetrical pattern to fit the wooden side profile of the transition plane, with a mirror image for the other side. The original pamphlet gives guidance on how to adapt the "dragon" to be either an eagle or a lion (see extract at the end of the chapter), but I have gone with the original version as a Dragon.

Initially, I had envisaged some additional decoration along the sides of a pattern of leaves, using the "Design for Advanced Panel" from Fig 47 on Page 80 of the pamphlet, but came to the conclusion that the "wings" were too fussy for the side of the wooden plane. As a result, I had to do some re-design work, first deleting the "grape" pattern on the left hand side, then taking the flower off the top of the right hand side. You may well ask why I did not start from scratch, well, by using the remainder of the right hand side, I would ensure that it remained in proposition the the central Dragon. The remaining pattern was cropped to the height of the dragon, before being re-scaled to the size of the project. Finally he remaining leaf pattern from the right hand side was duplicated and flipped to make up the replacement left hand side. To do this, I referred to Chapter 10 and moved to the computer.

1 Having scanned & saved the design, the first task is to adjust its size to that required for the project. This is achieved by adjusting the **Canvas Size,** so

FIG. 47.—DESIGN FOR ADVANCED PANEL.

that the Dragon is at the bottom-centre of the re-sized image.

[Image>Canvas Size>By%>Anchor/Bottom]

2 Then use the rectangle select tool to capture the repositioned image to re-size it to the full width of the project by ***[Image>Re-Size>Print Size]*** and insert the relevant project dimension for "*Print Size*". At this point re-save the part image, to which to add the left hand leaf pattern, shown in red on the next page.

3 A To get the red part of the image. re-load the Part-Image so that you can copy the Acanthus scroll of the right hand side as a separate image.

[LasoSelectTool>Free-hand select>Copy]

3 B Paste the partial image into it & save the new image as RHS.

4 Re-open RHS as a new image so that it can be 'Flipped' for the Left hand side, then re-save it as LHS. ***[Ctrl-***

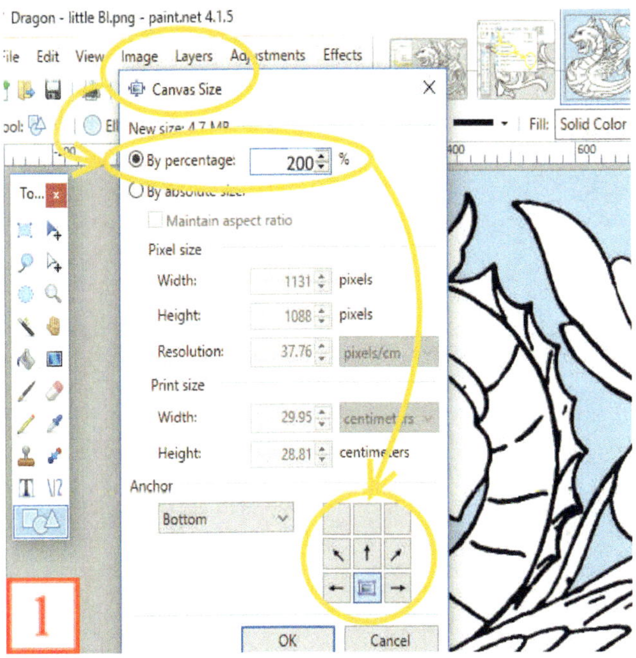

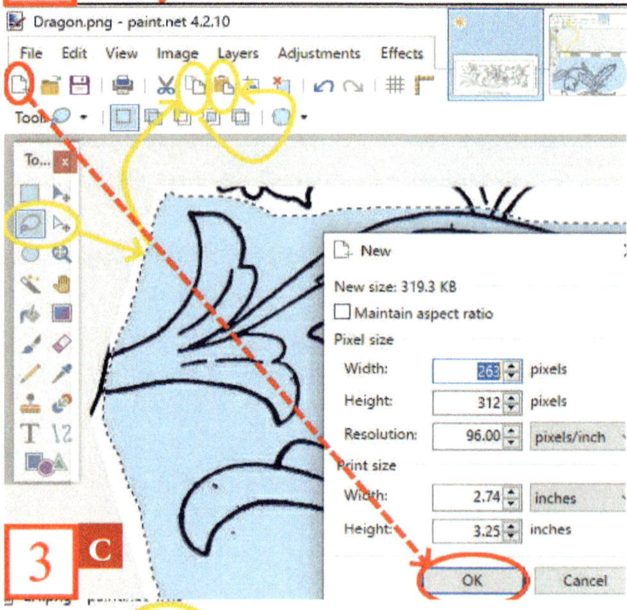

A>Image>Flip Horizontal]. You now have all the components for the final image montage.

5 A To make the final montage, start again with opening the Dragon: *[file>open>RHS]* as a new image so that it can be re-sized to the final project dimensions, but this time anchored at the bottom Left.

5 B Add a new layer: *[Layer>import from File]* and import/position RHS,

5 C Add a new layer again *[Layer>iimport from File]* then import/position LHS and save the final montage image as a JPG, accepting the

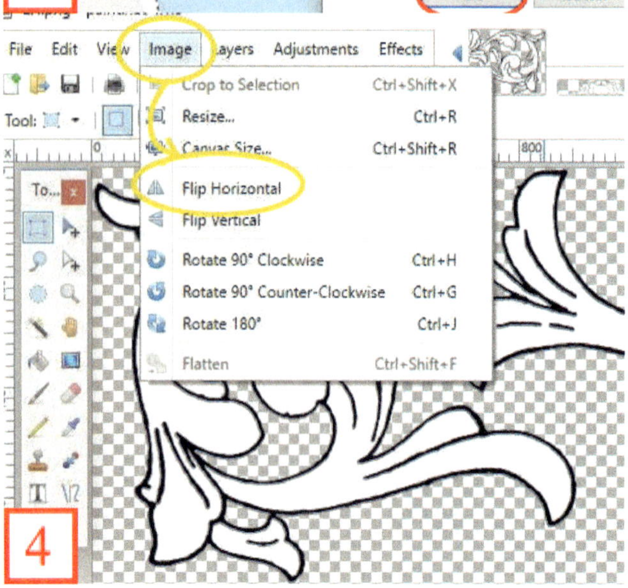

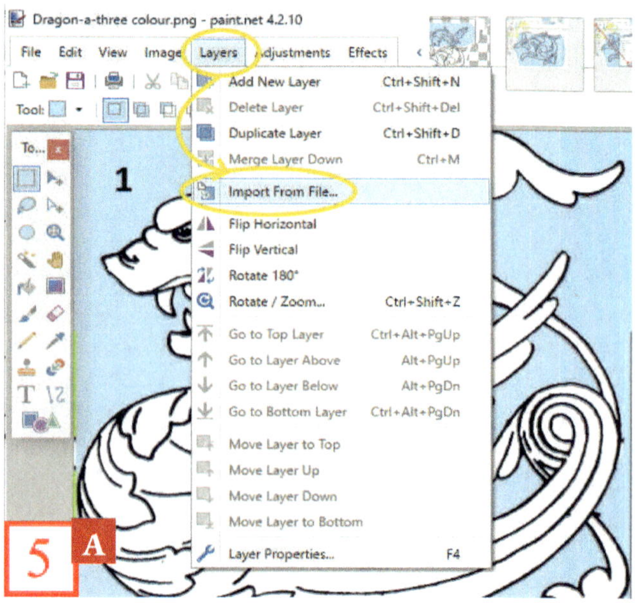

prompt to "*Flatten*" the image layers into one & save.

5 D With all the computer graphics concluded you can now .print the pattern and get started on the Kolrosing.

6 To get started, take the intended item & finish it with a very fine abrasive. Wipe it clean with Mentholated Spirits (Denatured Alcohol) and seal the surface, (I used a coat of clear French Polish). Using some carbon paper (I find "*Hand Copy"* (blue) Carbon Paper"works best), transfer the pattern to the blank. At this stage it became apparent that the full pattern would be too "busy" for the plane, so in the end, only the dragon was used, with the leaves discarded.

7 With your chosen scribing tool and etch the line-work into the wood by pushing the tip round the pattern. I found the "scales" on this to be rather small to scribe in this way, so resorted to tapping a suitable micro-gouge into them rather than trying to rotate the knife in such a confined location.

8 When you are finished, take your chosen "Koling Powder", mix it with a little oil then rub it into the incised line-work, using a gentle, circular movement.

9 Wipe the surplus off with a rag moistened with a finish oil. This which will help the colour flow round the lines. Finally, leave the work overnight to let the oil set, before finishing with a thin coat of clear wax polish.

TIP:

Laser printers "heat-fuse" the "Ink" (toner) to the paper, so as an alternative to Carbon Paper, if you print the image in reverse, then trim it to size, you can use a hot iron on the back (blank) side of the laser printer copy to re-activate the toner and transfer it to the blank.

84 **ELEMENTARY WOODCARVING.**

With regard to the dragon, the photograph shows the method of treatment. It is, of course, quite an imaginative creation. No " dragon" as depicted in this design was ever in existence; but although imaginative in its present form, it is really based upon a combination of natural animal forms.

It possesses a head that might be a development of *either* an eagle or a lion : eagle's wings, no feet or legs, and a fish's tail. The body is scaled, the scales extending each in the form of an entire ring around the neck and body. An alternative method of treating the body with smaller scales is shown in Fig. 49, as also an alternative treatment of the wings. It will be observed that the artificial leaf, which has been a feature of the designs used in this series enters largely into

FIG. 49.-PORTION OF FIG. 47, SHOWING ALTERNATIVE TREATMENT OF SCALES.

the composition of the dragon. Its breast is covered with these leaves springing from a line that is coincident with the outline of the bird; they form its beard, also its ears, and their influence is observable in the treatment of the tail, and in Fig. 49 the wings are composed of leaves instead of feathers

" The Woodworker " Series, No. 7.

LONDON: ISSUED FROM THE OFFICE OF "THE WOODWORKER".

[1] *Pg 84: " The Woodworker " Series, No. 7: London - Issued from the Office of "the Woodworker" :http://docshare01.docshare.tips/files/12543/125435982.pdf*

Project Two – Chip Carved Panel

This project is designed to supplement the more common chip-carving instructions (that use a knife) by demonstrating the use of chisels for a larger scale project.

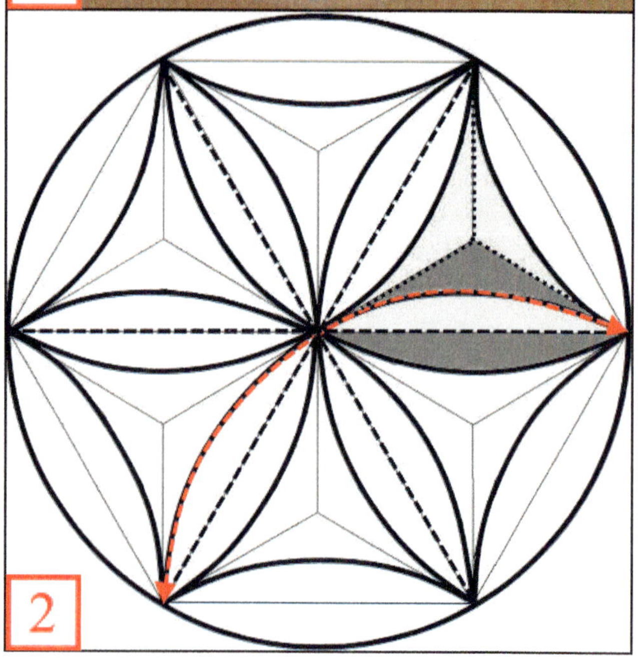

The majority of self-instruction books on chip-carving are based on the use of a chip-carving knife for the production of intricate designs in hard wood or for fine furnishings. However, larger scale chip-carving is also used for architectural designs such as decorating structures and more simply for adding decoration to out-door utensils. Using a larger scale patterns makes work with chisels more appropriate to the scale of project than a knife, and is not often included in English Language books on chip-carving. The tools used are the N°1 straight chisel (although a chippy's chisel is will work) and a shallow gouge. In addition a skew chisel or knife can be useful in tight corners. The choice of material will be limited by the design criteria of the structure or object to be decorated and is most often one of the slow growing native pines in the areas of Europe where this practice is common. In UK, this form of decoration was more common in the medieval period than now, where the the prevailing timber decorated in this style was native oak, probably carved while "green" so still relatively soft. This project is designed for demonstrating the use of chisels to decorate an item of external furniture. In this case, it is simply the end panel of a planter, which will be constructed of tanalised soft wood - not a good choice for carving[1].

1 The design used is based on a ***hexagram*** (a six point star - see Chapter 6).

2 This is enhanced by simple step & repeat by drawing an arc from each

[1] *If available, Larch is better to carve & also rot resistant.*

apex through the centre in turn, resulting in six “leaves”. The fields between are triangulated for a tri-corn cut.

3 The design is drawn off-centre on the oblong end-piece, with one full-circle and one part-circle making up the design.

4 The carving is made up basically of two parts, first the leaf patterns, then second the tri-corn pattern, both of which are simply duplicate around the circle using “*step and repeat*”.

A The leaf-pattern starts with a stop-cut along a centre-line using a N°1, which is best started full depth at the middle and worked outwards, with the last cut being angled up towards the apex.

B The leaf is then cut in, towards this line using a gouge of the matching radius, in this case a N°3. Use a slicing cut, taking into account the grain direction, which is going to change as you move round the circle. The gouge should pop out the chips cleanly where they intersect with the stop-cut.

Tip:

Using a N°1, has the benefit over a chippy’s chisel as it makes an even sided “knife” cut (top illustration) rather than a wedge shaped cut (bottom), that will allow the chip to break-out evenly along the centre-line when cut from either side. If you only have a carpenter’s chisel, the same effect can be achieved by running the chisel back along the line with the blade reversed.

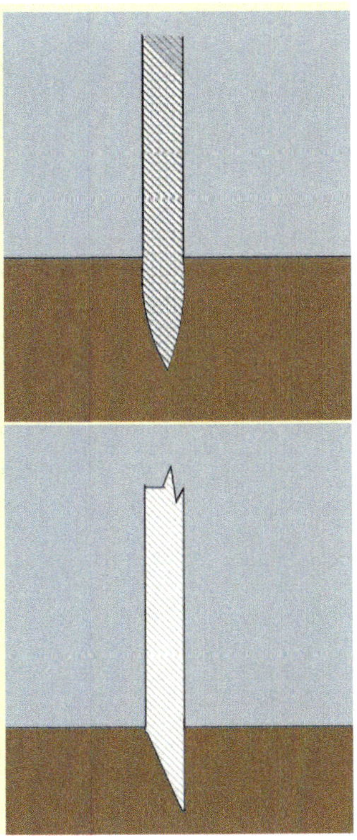

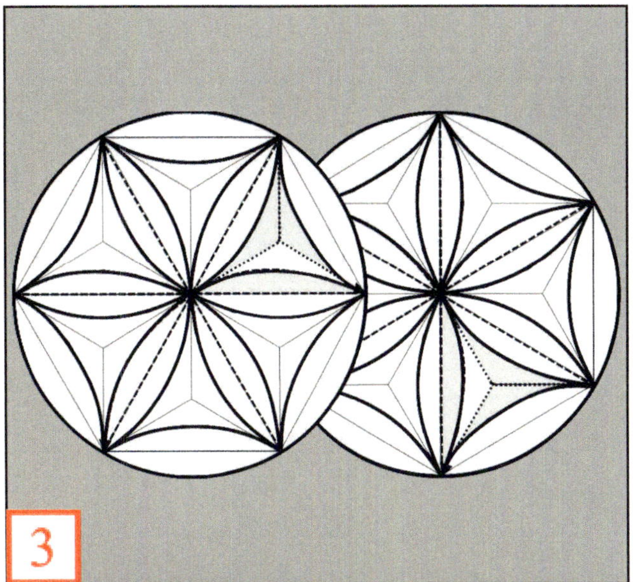

5

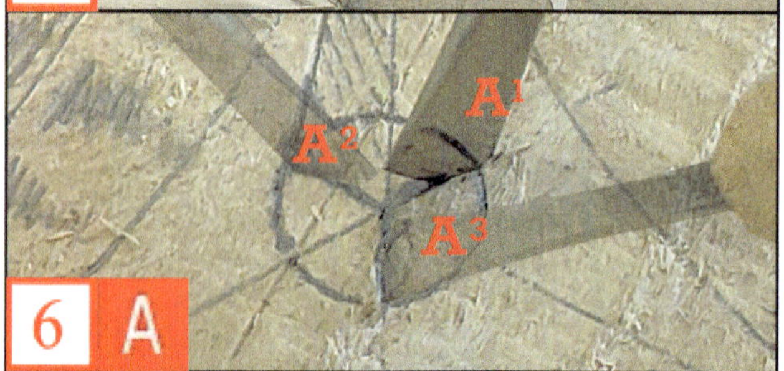

6 A

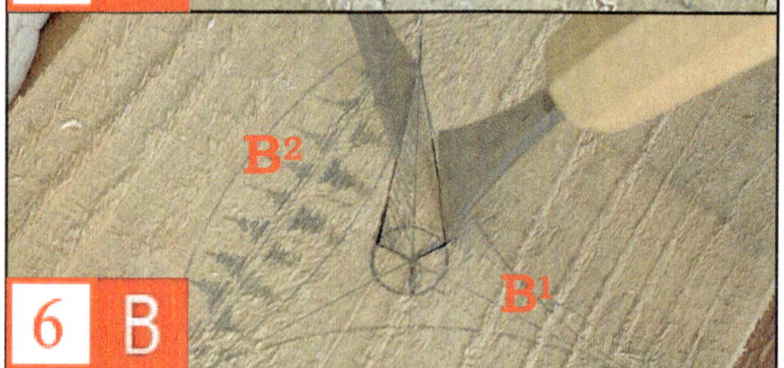

6 B

6 C

6 D

5 If it does not pop out, the stop-cut may simply not be deep enough, so in need of a second attempt. Repeat the use of the N°3 slicing back towards the first cut, taking into account the change of grain direction as you rotate the direction of cut. It is probable that you will need to reinforce the centre-line from time to time, to make sure that the gouge is removing clean chips each time.

6 The Tri-corn pattern sits in the space between the leaves, with its internal shape made up of a series of straight cuts, that dove-tail into the curved edge of the adjacent leaves. The tri-corn is made up of three separate cuts, to produce each triangular chip, the whole being repeated three times at each of the 120° rotations, ultimately revealing a three pointed star or "***Isotoxal***", which in Christianity symbolises the Holy Trinity. The best tool for this work is either a small skew or a knife blade:

A The initial cut is a simple stab at the "blunt" end, most efficiently repeated at all three "points of the compass" consecutively.

B The second is again a stop-cut, this time along the hypotenuse[2] using the heel of the skew to make a deep incision at the blunt end, then rocking it towards the apex, so a graduated depth is achieved.

C The final cut is at an angle taking a slice from apex to base, to pop out a clean chip.

[2]*Hypotenuse: The longest side of a right-angled triangle.*

7

D. When two adjacent chips have been cleared, return with the reversed N°3 and carefully pare the rim of the adjacent leaf

7 In the end there will be a smooth transition between leaf and tri-corn.

8 Finally, run a groove round the outside & apply a suitable finishing product. - In this case a Creosote preservative.

8

Project Three - Carving a Horse

This is a project to show the use of combining a carving knife with other tools to produce a traditional Norwegian handle.

The horse was such a significant asset to agriculture and warfare in the pre-industrial world, it is no surprise that it is a common theme for woodcarving. It not only provides scope for decorative work, but its shape also lends itself to toys, such as the famous Swedish Dala Horse (***Dalahäst***)[1], which started life as a toy in the 19th century but has since grown into a Swedish folk art icon. The same basic same shape that make a sturdy child's toy also works well for handles, as the curved belly provides a comfortable grip, while the solid legs can attach to a variety of utensils

1 This project is designed to bring together a variety of carving tools and skills in a single carving, that will provide a template for any number of ornate handles.

2 This style is modelled on the ancient Norwegian Viking horse, whose descendants can still be found in the West of Norway in the Fjord Horse (***Fjordhest***[2]. These are a stocky all-rounder working through until the late 20th century in harness, pulling carts, ploughs and sleighs, so it's no surprise that they were also put too use pulling doors and lids. There are a number of variations on the patter available in Odd Fauske's book - see bibliography on page 217. While the basic shape can be achieved with the use of the straight blades of carving knifes, I have chosen a pattern where some

1

[1]*Swedish Dala Horse: https://en.wikipedia.org/wiki/Dalecarlian_horse: Photo: Stefanstopko, CC BY-SA 4.0 https://commons.wikimedia.org/wiki/File:Rotes_Dalapferd*
[2]*Norwegian Fjord Horse: https://en.wikipedia.org/wiki/Fjord_horse*

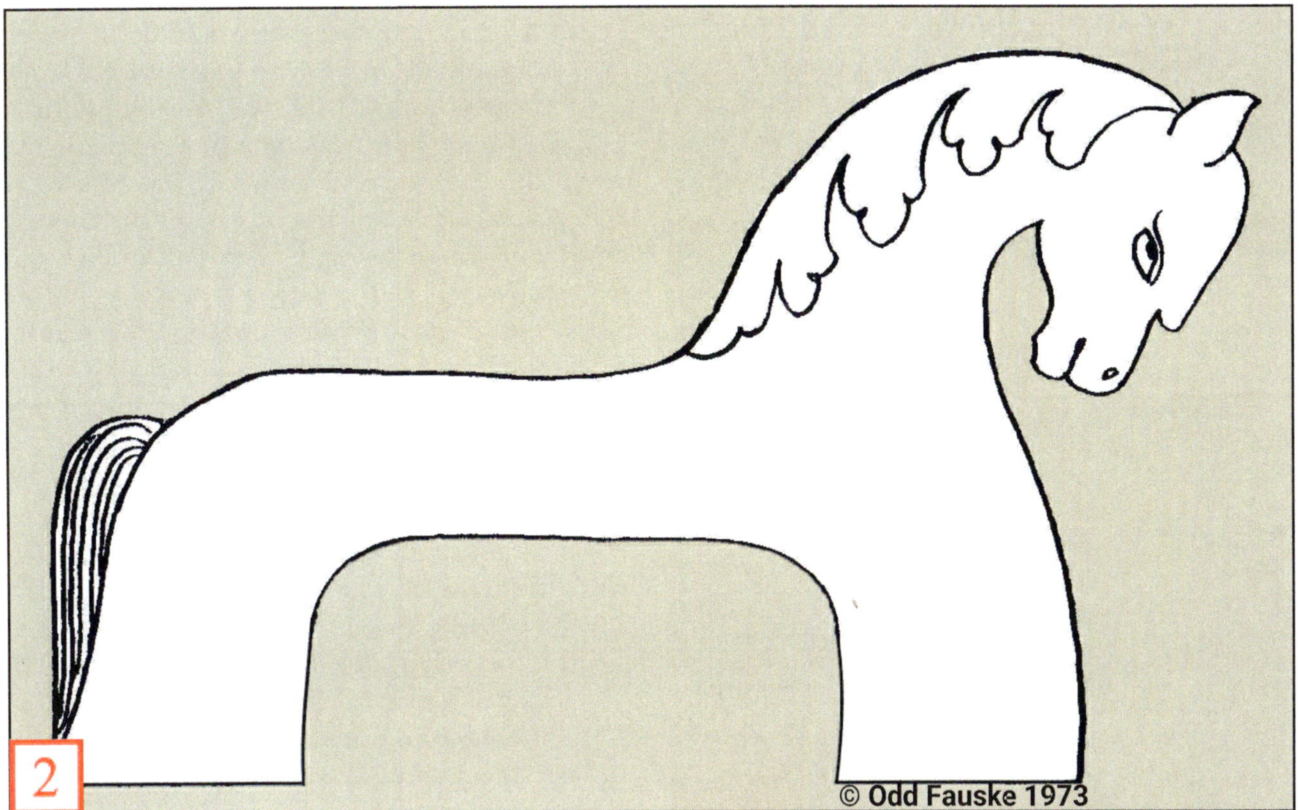

2

of the ornamentation will need the use of carving gouges:

A as it's intended us us as a handle, the cross-section has been modified to include tenons under its' hoofs.

3 With the patter re-sized to suit the intended purpose, stick it down on the timber and drill out the under-belly area needed for the hand-grip.

2 A

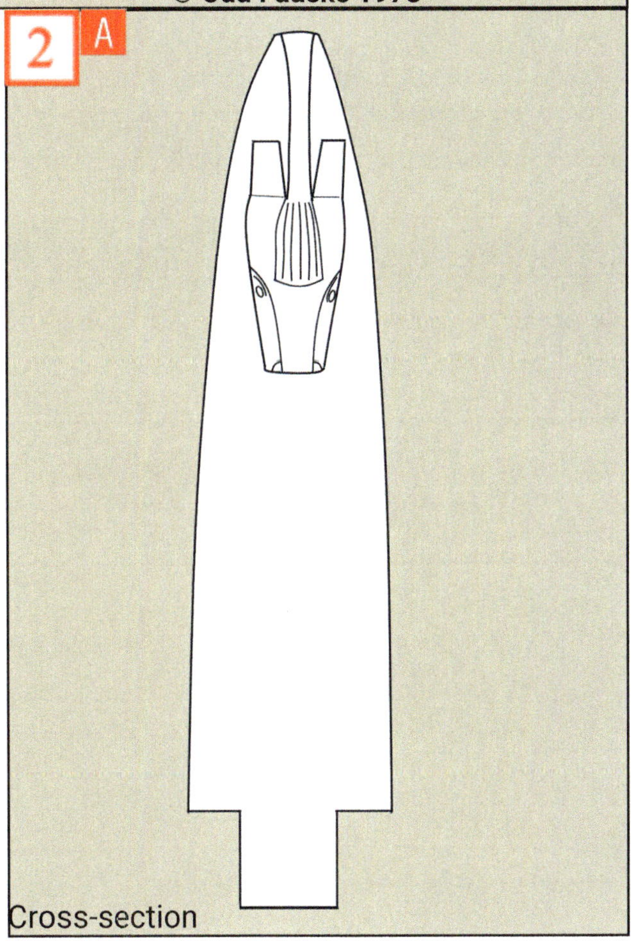

4

5

6

7

4 As this is to work as a handle, it needs a tenon cut under the base, with a view to making a "hidden" fixing, with a pegged-tenon joint. It's worth remembering to do this before roughing out the blank, as it is easier to hold when still as a "block". One way would be with a saw (bandsaw, or a tenon saw), but I chose to use a rebate plane, as I find it gives a tighter fit. A useful by-product of cutting the tenon early is that is provides a holding point that won't dame any work-in-progress.

5 After cutting out the horse profile on a bandsaw, the under-belly will need to be cleaned up either with a knife, or with a series of rasps and files, to leave a suitably tactile finish for a hand-grip.

6 Roughing the figure can start with slimming down the neck which can be achieved in a number of ways, but here I show the use of a Scandinavian twin-handles knife which is used like a Drawknife, but is less expensive to purchase.

7 Changing from the two-handles blade to a short-blade knife, the neck is then roughly tapered neck into the shoulder towards the rump, using a series of deep cuts with the necessary changes in direction to accommodate the grain.

8 When the required profile has be achieved, swap to a long blade knife for the fine finishing, if necessary, using gentle pressure on the back of the blade to guide and fine tune the careful paring of the finished surface.

8

9 The same techniques are repeated to shape both sides of the neck and body, tapering in the profile of the under-body "grip" along the way - using multiple opposing shallow slicing-cuts with the long blade knife. This constant change of direction will accommodate the difference in how the grain runs under the belly.

10 Having carved the neck and both sides of main body, attention turns to the two ends, starting with the tail. If you are using only a knife, you will have to whittle carefully away to form the round shape where the tail leaves the body. However, this can be achieved is much more easily with a carving tool - here a wide N°7. It will need a couple of cuts, first a stab to get the depth, then a complimentary rotating cut, to establish the shape round shape where the tail joins the body.

11 With the base established, the wide taper of the tail-plume can be outlined with a couple of cuts with a fine back-saw, carefully mating with the width of the tail's base.

12 Again, the shape of the tail-plume can be established through careful whittling, but resorting to the inside of a small N°7 gives a suitable profile for the convex curve that joins the fan shape of the tail plume.

13 The end of the tail flips up in a smooth curves that is an ideal shape for the carving knife to join smoothly the two together.

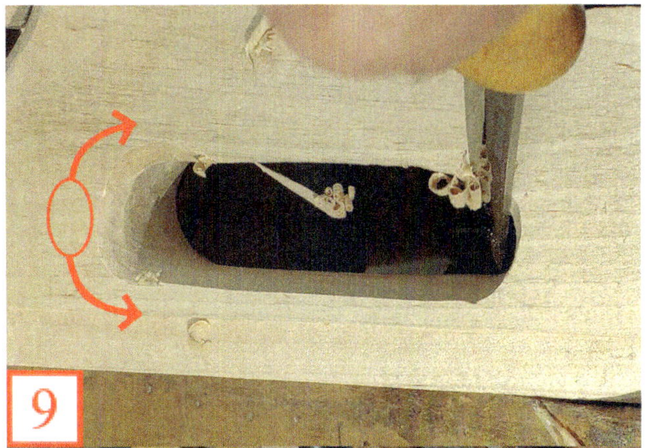

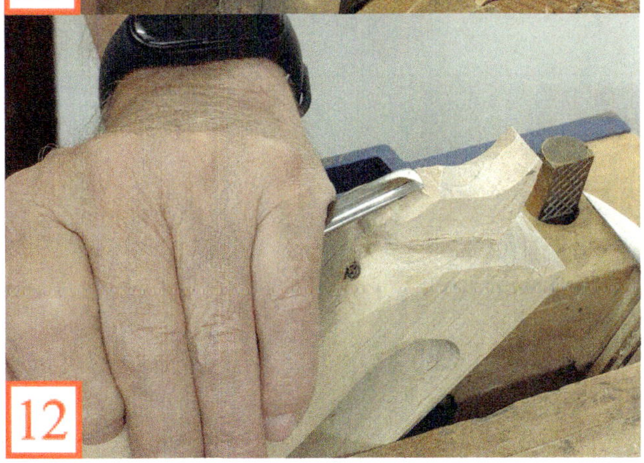

14

15

16

17

14 The front of the animal is carefully carved again using the same combination of the short blade for rough-cutting followed by the long blade for gentle paring to the final finish.

15 This design has a has an stylised acanthus pattern for the mane, to symbolise the careful presentation of the horse's mane for an event such as a wedding. This can be carved using a short blade, such as a chip-carving knife, but is again more easily rendered using delicate carving tools.

16 While the outline and under-cutting of these delicate shapes benefits from the use of carving tools, the confined space still leaves room for the knife blade for the paring of the top surface of the acanthus pattern, enabling a suitable tilt to the surface to align better with the neck-line.

17 While the use of only the knife only requires the model to be hand-held, the introduction of the carving tools calls for a firmer grip. This is one of the times that the make-shift "third hand" of a small vice mounted on scrap timber, enables the carving to be presented in various angles by clamping the mount in the bench vice - see page 39.

18 With the mane finished, that leaves the fore-lock to complete, which uses a similar technique to the tail, where the small fan shape is cut into the horse's face by reducing the forehead above the eye ridge. As with the tail, this takes a number of wedge shaped cuts and a lot of patience.

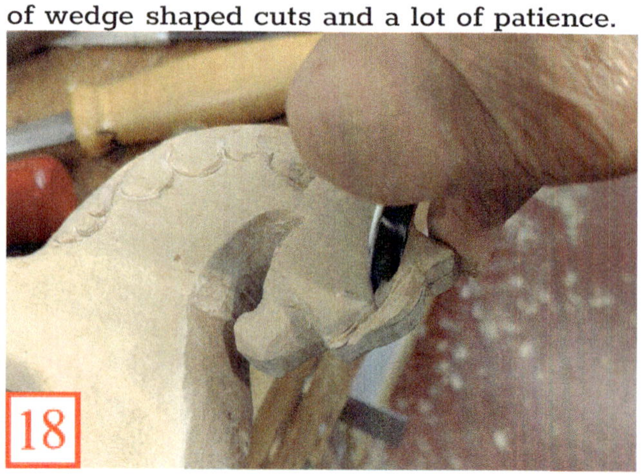
18

19 With the figure complete some basic carpentry remains to prepare the "home" rebate for its mounting, which was simply drilled out then squared with an appropriate chisel.

20 Detailing of the "hair" on the mane and tail is the final task, for which I used a N°11 veiner, although the same effect can be archived with a couple of strokes of a knife point to pop out a smooth groove.

NORWEGIAN FJORD HORSE[1]

As with many carvings that have their roots in Folk History, this handle will be based on a native horse breed - in this case, the Fjord Horse of Western Norway (fjording)[2]*. This is an ancient breed, going back to Viking times*[3]*, that until the end of the 20th century was a common site on farms in Western Norway as they are one of those gentle, "all purpose" horses that could be used as draught horse and also for riding. As with many native breeds, they are less common working in their original environment having been replaced by mechanisation. A striking breed that has attracted a strong following in modern competitions having travelled to many nations round the world. Still fondly remembered in traditional Norwegian woodcarvings, where is is a traditional handle for their Mangle Board.*

[1] *History of Norsk fjordheste https://www.horsejournals.com/popular/breed-profiles/norwegian-fjord-horse-all-ages*
[2] *Photo By Philippe CHAUVET - Own work, CC BY-SA 2.5, https://commons.wikimedia.org/w/index.php?curid=1898781*
[3] *Oak horse carving from the Gokstad Viking ship: G. H. Gustafson (1911), Public domain, via Wikimedia Commons*

Project Four – Simple End Piece

You don't need many carving tools to be able to add a bit of character or to be able to undertake a furniture repair "in keeping" with the original.

This small project is for the carving of an acanthus style feature at the end of a piece of timber. This can be adapted in many ways either for original use, or for repair and restoration, such as to provide a replacement for a carved end piece for a cupboard crown moulding. It can also be modified for use in a leg-bracket repair. The basic carving can be achieved using a basic set of gouges and a bit of patience. The timber you select will be dependent on the intended final use, but in this case, I have used oak (as it will be the "ends" for an oak porch seat). The pattern is a simple single-leaf acanthus and a bit "chunky" as it is destined for oak in a much trafficked and exposed exterior setting, where too much finesse will render it a hostage to the ravages of fate and the Devon weather, It also keeps it simple as a "starter" project.

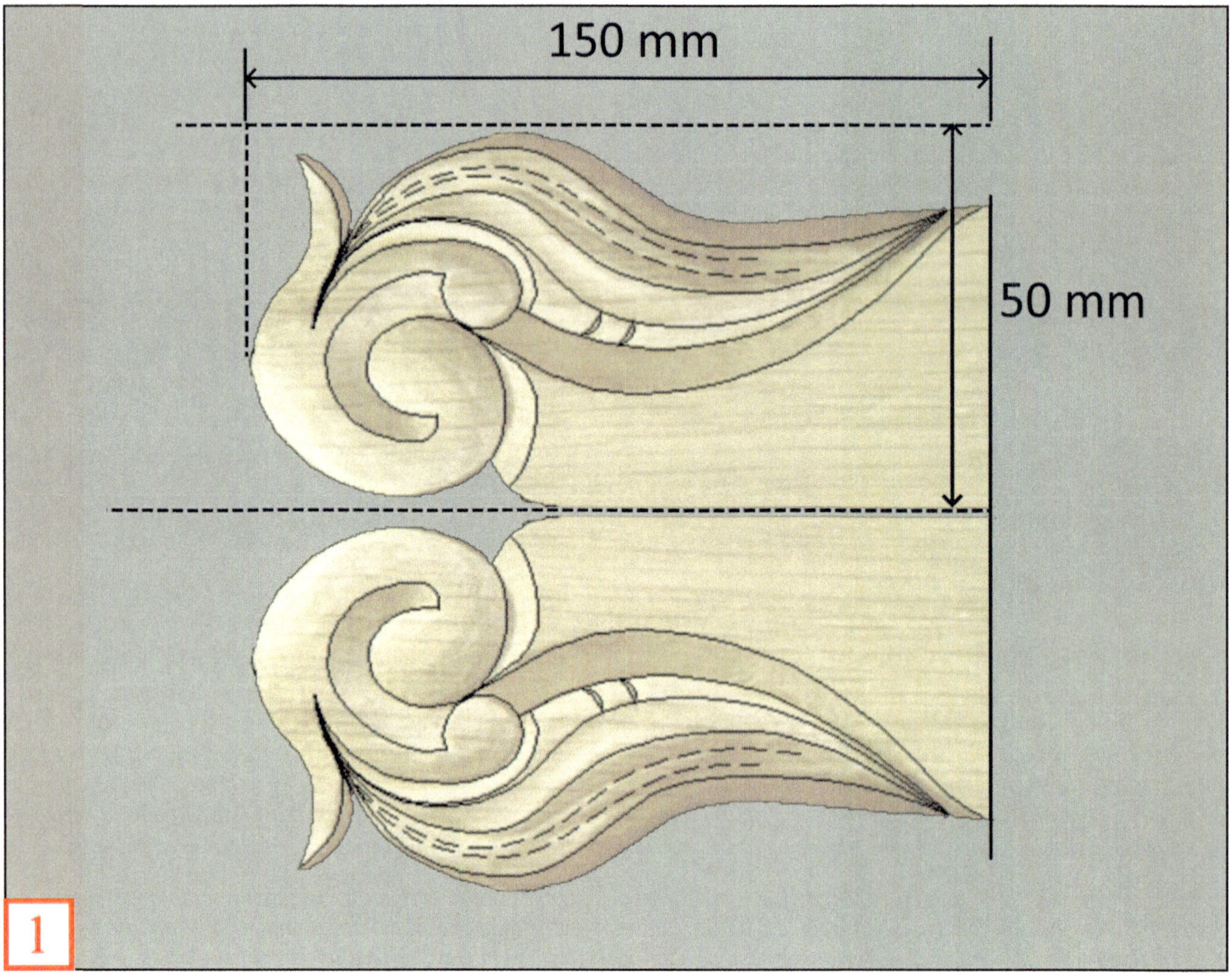

1

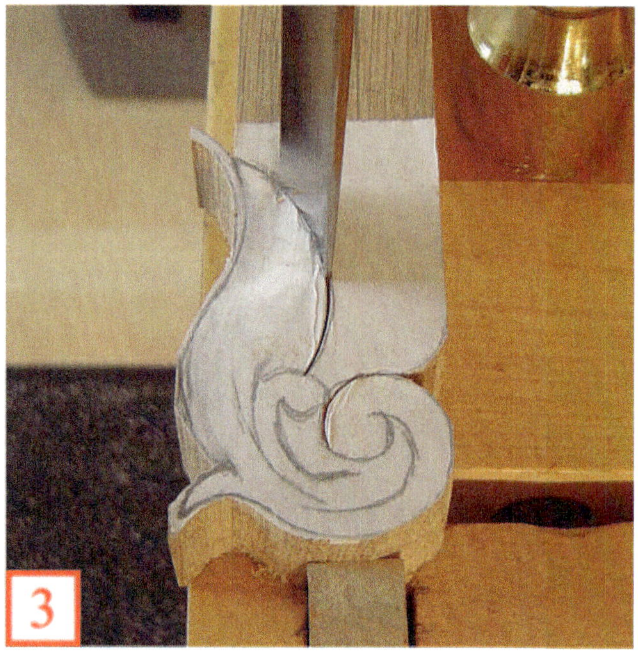

1 The line-work I used is at Page 130 (not to scale), but displays the dimensions I used for my project - you can modify the size to suit your needs, but should try to keep the "aspect ration" of 2:1 unaltered where possible, as you may have resize it to suit your own project and then either trace it, or scale it on a computer to suit). In my case, it was printed out to size on a laser printer. To keep it simple, I just stick the pattern to the timber using a regular paper glue-stick (which may require you to periodically sketch some line-work back in with a pencil as you carve the paper away). The other ways that work are copying or printing the pattern onto tracing paper and then transferring the image to the timber with carbon paper - and I have even had success with ironing a mirror-image from

the laser printer straight onto fine grain timber such as lime or birch.

2 With the pattern in place, the outline can be cut-out using a fine blade on a small band-saw (a fret-saw or a coping-saw are alternatives for the manual toolbox). Don't forget to make a series of relief cuts (at bottom of picture) to allow the waste to pop out - final cut-out shown at the top of the picture.

3 With the outside shape now cut out, (leaving it clear as to where the carving is required), it's time to start setting-in the carving itself. To stop the carving suffering from unwanted chips, the whole of the outside edge is "set in" (see box) With a few tools and a bit of dexterity, a smooth curve can be setting-in using the rocking motion of a slicing cut, progressing along the curve from N°3>N°7.

4 Select the curved gouge that is nearest to the shape of the patter (here a large N°5) and make a series of stop cuts to clear the edge of the pattern itself.

5 With the edge of the pattern now clear, use the same tool to slide a series of chips out along these edge to define clearly the shape and scope of the pattern. The initial result is above, in compare with the end product.

6 With the outline now defined a start can be made on the detail. Unusually for a relief carving, this pattern has a third

"Setting-in" is the process of initially outlining the carving pattern with a series of vertical cuts that also serve as a stop cut to later work - so that the surround will not accidentally chip out when you carve close to the edge of the patter. Start by finding the tool that has the profile that most closely matches the curve of the pattern. For this vertical cut to be fully effective, you need to have a tool that has been sharpened with its cutting edge square (at a right angle) to the shaft. The process can be simplified if a 'V' tool is first round round the pattern to provide a groove in which to place the edge

9

10

11

dimension, so the start is actually on the edge. Secure the carving on its side and make a good stop-cut at the shoulder, before taking a N°5 to bring the side well down, reinstating the stop cut periodically, so as not to split the end grain - (you can see in the background the shape you are after). The knuckle of the edge pattern will need to be rounded with a straight chisel or rasp, before you can lay the piece on its side again.

7 With the edge now defined, the transition between the two faces can be defined with a groove, excised with a N°7, but it will need to be worked down from both ends because of the change in grain round the knuckle.

8 The other edges of the pattern can now be rounded over with a reversed N°5, finally returning to round the inside edge of the knuckle in the same way (at bottom), taking care to change the direction of attack to always cut with the grain. The shape is developed through a series of levels each bordering the one above, with progressively a shallower gouge.

9 To finish take a N°5 and run the final top groove from the knuckle to the end. The inside edge of this groove defines the watershed for the patter, with all to the inside now to be progressively taken down below this line in a series of convex cuts, which can

12

13

14

be either reverse gouge or gentle paring with a straight blade to the the finished convex shape.

10 In this case it the outside edge is shaped with a reversed Nº3 which will leave a slight convex shape.

11 Closer to the knuckle, where there is no space for the gouge, a shallow convex shape is carefully pared with a back-bent fishtail - a favourite of mine in tight places.

12 With the top "wing" of the carving now complete, attention can switch to the "snail-shell" that supports it, starting at the "ear" with a short stroke of a Nº5. Then reverse the tool to pare a smooth round outer ovolo edge. As this is at the end of the piece, you can't get far round it without a grain change, so you need to swap direction & come back at it from the other end as well. You can see in the background that the far side of the "snail- shell" has been defined through the removal of a slice (stab cut with a Nº5 at the circumference, with an adjoining slicing cut to remove a smooth chip).

13 It will still take several small slices to complete a smooth round roll-over of the edge. This will have to be repeated the other side of the knuckle, taking the ovolo shape all the way into the centre of the

15

16

17

18

"snail-shell", again with several change of direction/grain en-route.

14 As this is a three dimensional carving, it needs to be again turned on its side to have the knuckle edge rounded, either with a straight chisel or with a rasp and file to complete the smooth outline of the "snail shell" feature.

15 You need to take into account with furniture ornamentation the potential for damage. Here, where we are using a coarse grained timber, the slender "ear" needs to be cut back for strength using a small N°5 to run it carefully into the finished convex ovolo curve of the snail-shell.

16 The outside edge of the wing was defined with a groove along the edge - a feature that is now developed with a further gentler groove on the inside slope, using a N°5.

17 Often to give a low relief carving some added depth and texture, small decorative effects are added - here a couple of "ears" on the long curve, made from a vertical stab cut and an a subsequent slicing cut below, to ease out a clean chip.

18 The other common decoration is decorative "veining" made with either a 'V'-tool or a "veiner", to giver highlights on the longer curved surface - with the overall effects visible on the completed carving.

19 When you have finish, you should have a matching pair, in my case, for use as bench-ends. In my porch, where they've naturally aged with the bench seat.

19

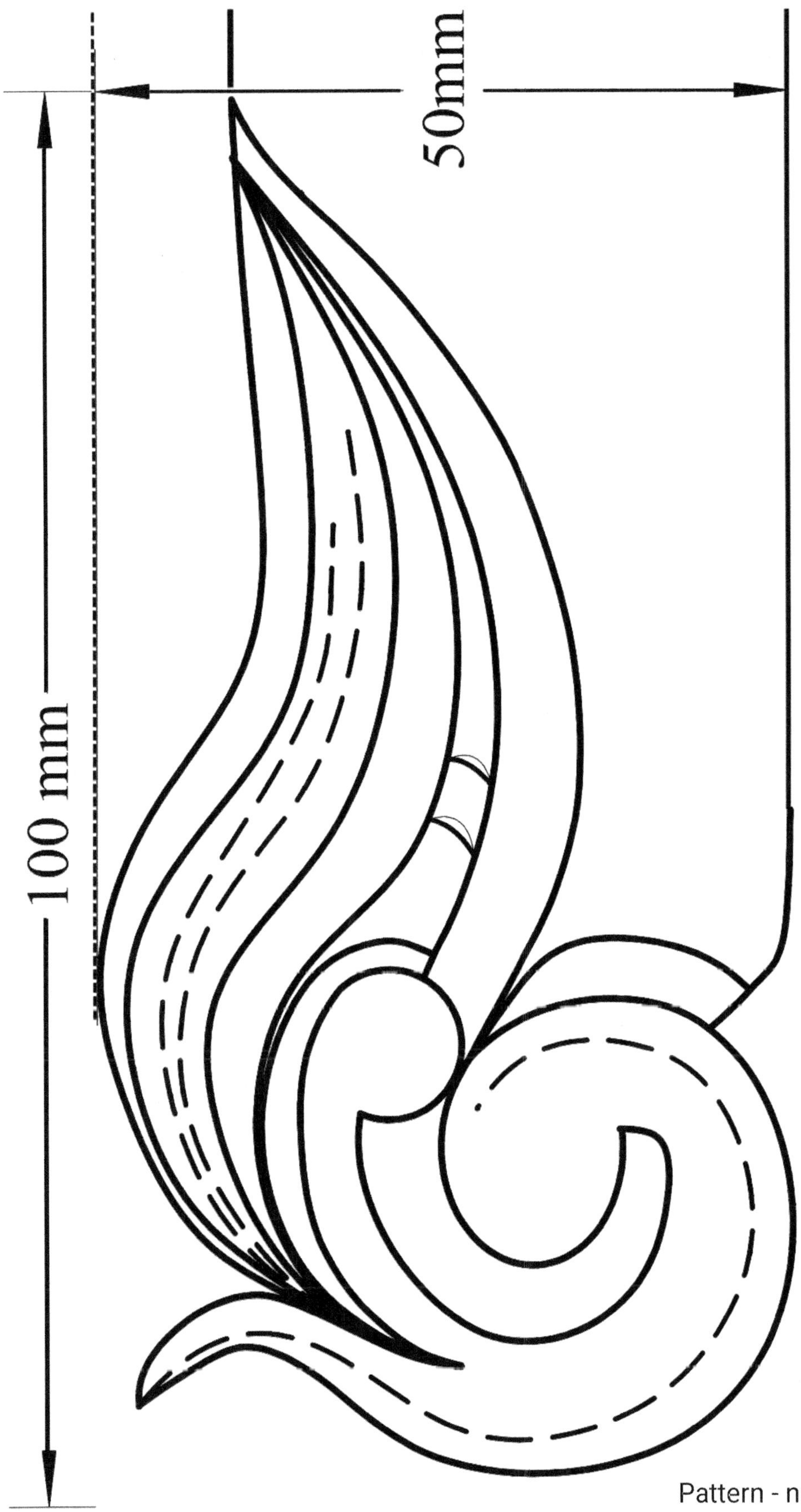

Pattern - not to scale

Design Adapted to a Knife Handle

Knife Handle

A The basic scroll pattern on page 130 can be adapted for many different purposes. For example, by leaving the "ear" off the end, you get a traditional 18^{th}C style "pistol grip" knife handle.

B The ball is cut into the end using a large Nº5 as before.

C To give a comfortable grip for the little finger, it is run into the end using a small Nº5.

D Turning the small Nº5 over, the ball end is gently rounded over on the bottom edge, with the same being repeated on the top edge.

E The underside profile is then run out towards the (sharp) end, still with the Nº5.

F The sharp top edge is smoothed by running a carving knife along the length of the groove in the handle..

G The underside is then given a similar treatment, or both sides can be shaped at the same time using a wide gouge.

H Select a saw with a kerf of a similar thickness to your blade and cut a suitable slot in the handle.

I Then all that remains is to drill the handle, insert suitable copper rivets and peen the end for a tight fit. Ideally, finish with a coat of oil and buff to a light sheen.

Project Five - Bread Board

The amateur carver has traditionally taken to household items as a source for inspiration, such as the simple decoration of this cutting board for bread.

This breadboard is the sort of household "implement" that a young man might carve to impress the light of his life, to show off his potential around the homestead. I have used one of the traditional Norwegian carving timbers — birch — for the board, although I have also successfully used the slightly harder sycamore or others from the maple family, which require a bit more effort too carve as they are harder timbers, but make more durable boards.

1 To keep the drawing process easy, I chose to use a piece of timber that was the same width as my computer's A4 printer — in this case 210mm x 297mm (say 8"x 12") - otherwise scale this design to suite your chosen timber, which should have a thickness of between 19-25mm (¾-1"). Print out your design, mark the centre-line of your board on the side that was closest to the heart of the tree and carefully attach your design to the timber, using spray mount adhesive or white PVA woodworking adhesive. The A4 sized template is on page,and is also available in Odd Fauske's book from Amazon[1]

2 As a cutting board is a common household item, my design has been kept simple, but if you are more adventurous, there are many traditional designs available such as the various more complex

[1] *A Norwegian Woodcarving Textbook: Fauske, Odd; ISBN-13: 978-1861518637 (2020); Amazon*

1

Note on Tools

A medium N°3 & N°5, with a small N°7 and a veiner or 'V' Tool are all that are essential for this board. A large N°5 or N°6 for the broad sweeps will make life easier and quicker, plus a couple of medium to small fishtailed N°3 & N°5 will provide crisp detail work more quickly . Any flat blade or rasp will cut back the reverse profile, I found the largest N°1 from the Chinese tool set ideal, but you can also use a hand plane for speed.

designs by Else Bigton that can be obtained from on the Internet[2].

3 To start, bore the central ring with a closely fitting Forstner bit, or use a coping saw to cut the hole accurately. Then you should trim your timber to the required, shape with a band-saw, before marking the top edge of the board in three equal parts with a pencil line (the back third being later removed). Throughout the carving of this design, you should repeat the carving on one side with the same portion on the other. This not only keeps the carving balanced, but also enables the experience of

[2] 1 *Treskjærer kunsten:Bigton, Else.J. & Odden, Phillip; ISBN-10: 8200417549;ISBN-13: 978-8200417545 (1996); Universitetsforlaget: www.norskwoodworks.com*

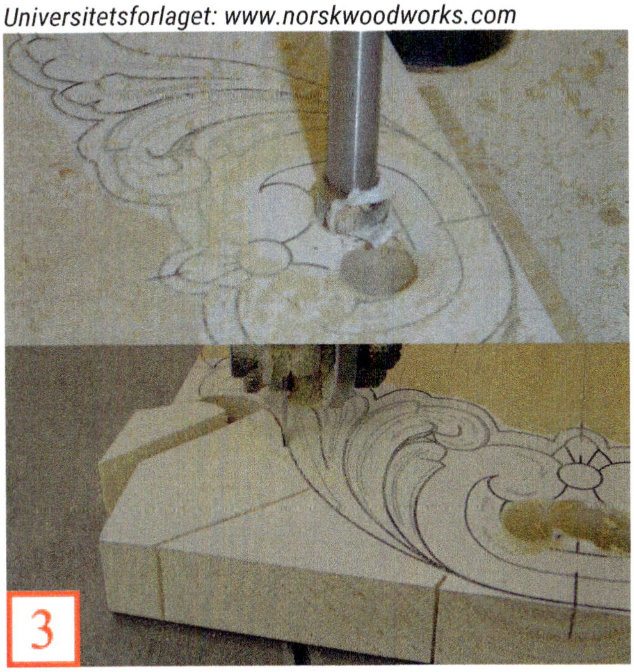

3

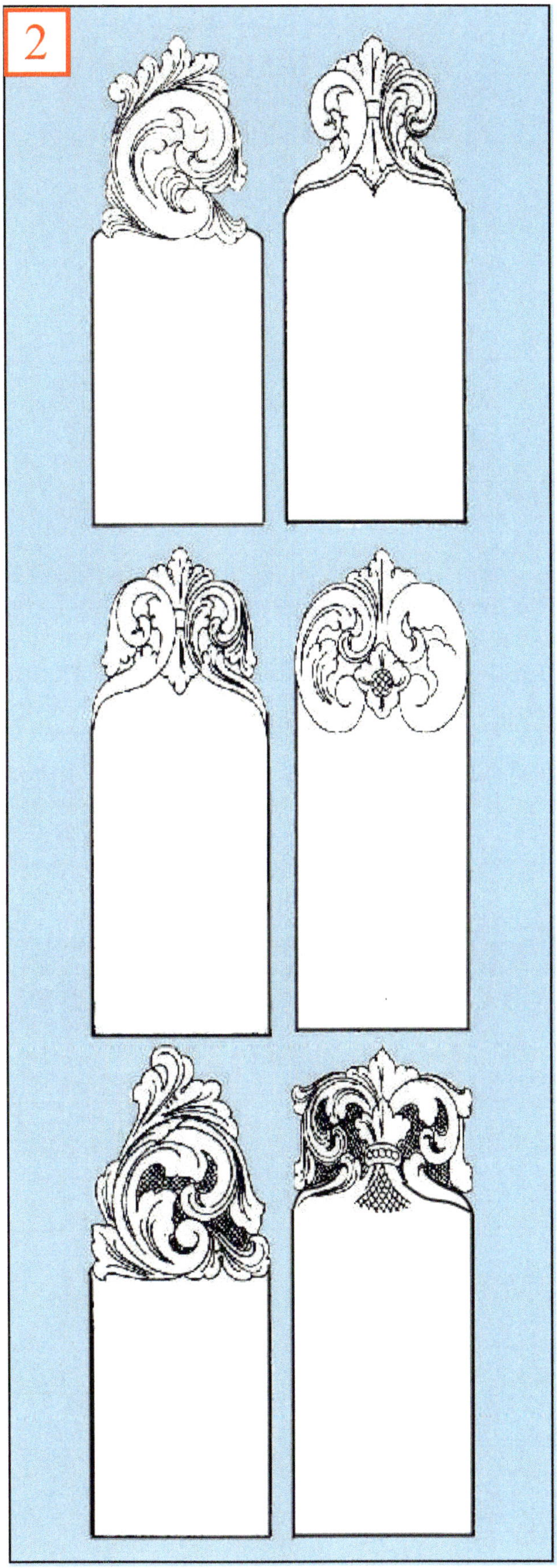

2

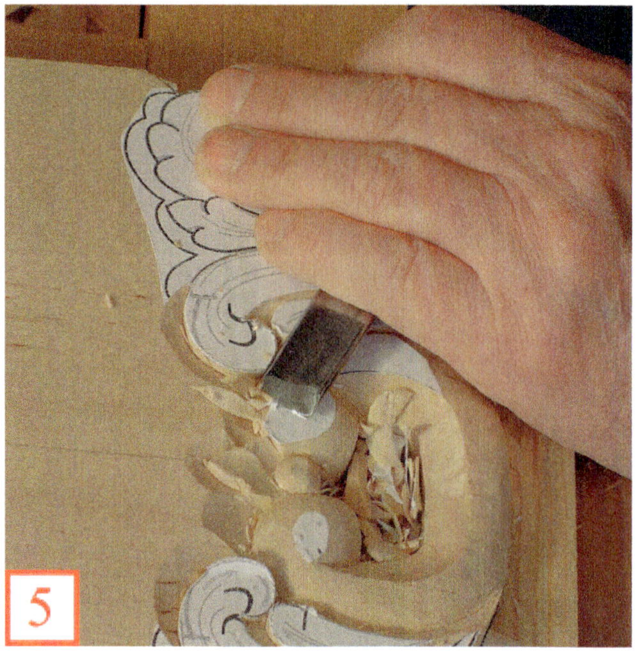

the first part to be applied immediately to the other side. Bear in mind that the curves of the design elements are intended to "fit" the various gouges — for example; N°7 for the small central ball; N°5 for the shape of the ball-end and to give a smooth transition from the N°3 through N°5 to N°7 for the acanthus leaves. The main outline of the design should now be set-in (to stop wayward slips and chips from causing later frustrations).

4 Start with the inside of the ball and use the N°5 to make a rotating stop-cut at

shape and you have the ball-end rounded away from a tiny circle of paper pattern remaining atop.

6 The same process is adopted to shape the first leaf, which lies as a convex shape over the outside of the inner ring, but with the inside surface scooped out with the N°7. Moving out to the second larger leaf, the "eyelets" need established by first taking the N°7 to make an upright rotating-cut towards the centre of the leaf, the second rotating-cut is then made with the tool at an angle away from the first cut, but with the cutting edge starting a fraction out from the line and rotating to finish on the inside point of the first cut. This should cleanly slice out a small crescent shape notch.

7 The outside edge of this leaf will be shaped convex as before, with the inner side carefully established with the sweep of the N°5 in a slicing cut towards the ball-end. As you establish the inside shape, it should be worked together with the convex outer edge as before, so that the whole is slightly undercutting at the inner edge, but has a smooth join on the ridge line and finally a transition to the convex shape on the outer edge. As you shape the outside edge of the round -end, make sure to re-mark the "eye-

7

8

let" as necessary. The third dimension needs worked into this shape, in a similar way to the development of the central ring, with the root of the second leaf taking its turn to issue below the root of the inner leaf, then rising to end above it, with a round-end that just retains a small pinhead of paper pattern.

8 When satisfied with the join of the root to the ring, then move the board onto its edge, griped at 45° in a vice and reinstate the two equidistant pencil lines on the carved edge. With a straight blade or rasp, starting at the tip of the outer leaf and working to the top (back) edge of the ring,,Now waste away the back edge of the board and round it into the top of the ring with a reversed N°5.

9 Now take the small N°5 the right way up, and carve the convex shape of three leaf blades from the tip towards the root — the first at 45° to the front face, following the paper pattern — the second at

9

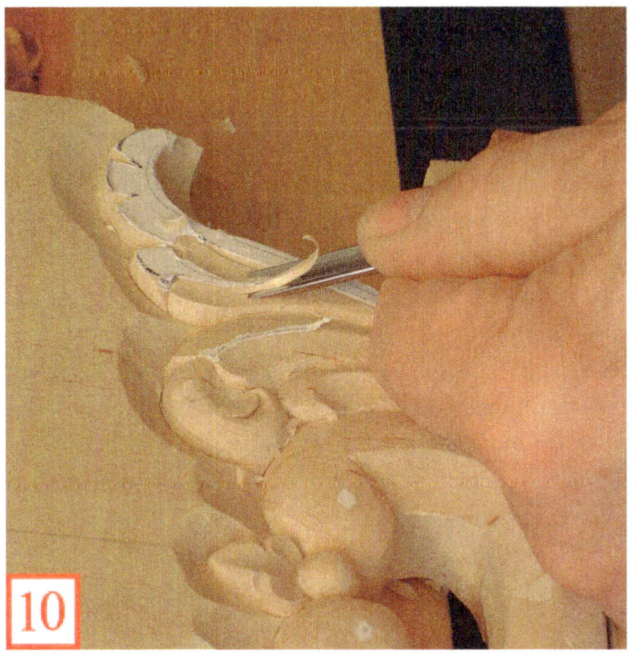

10

45° to the back face — the last along the middle of the edge of the board between the straight lines. While the board is in the vice, shape the back of the top edge with a file or a straight edge tool, before (optionally) returning it to the bench to carve the "back edge" of the central ring onto the reverse side. This can either be simply outlined with a "V"-tool, or taken to more shape by the use of a N°5&7.

10 The final main leaf, with its superimposed subsidiary, has its root below the others, issuing from where the first pencil line (on the top edge) meets the ring. Care needs to be taken with this leaf to allow for the small subsidiary leaf to rise above the inside of the main leaf, with its crest remaining close to the highest elevation of the carving. The technique here for the subsidiary leaf is a mirror image of that used on the first leaf, starting with the "eyelets" before carving the outer blades towards them with the convex side of the N°7; slightly higher on the inner edge, but overlying the main leaf outside it. The central blade is then superimposed along the spine, again with the N°7, before its tip is turned down by the reverse of the small N°5. The main leaf is again a mirror image of the second leaf, but ending without the round-end. First establish the convex end of the leaf to shape the bottom curve — reinstating "eyelet" as necessary,,then work back towards the root.

11 On the outside edge of the board, take the rounded shape of the root as far up as you can to meet the ring, with the inside of the large N°5.

12 When you are happy with the overall effect, the last bit of carving is to put in the leaf veins with a "V"-tool before finally adding the carvers mark and date.

We all aim to carve but once, however,,mere mortals will now need to cleaned up the carving, for example; taking care to leave clean cuts all along the base between,of the carving and the cutting-board; or carefully smoothing the ball-ends with the reverse of a gouge; removing the last "blob" of pattern paper; or even going round all the leaf ends with the reverse side of a N°3 or small N°5 to clean them up with a small chamfer.

To finish the board, I sand it smooth,before adding three coats of food friendly oil, such as walnut oil. Remember to enjoy the carving, as this is a kitchen utensil, so do not get too wound up about slight imperfections as you are about to cut onto it with a kitchen knife. If you want to improve on your initial labours, why not just turn the board end-to-end and carve the whole thing again and this time you will have a double ended cheese board?

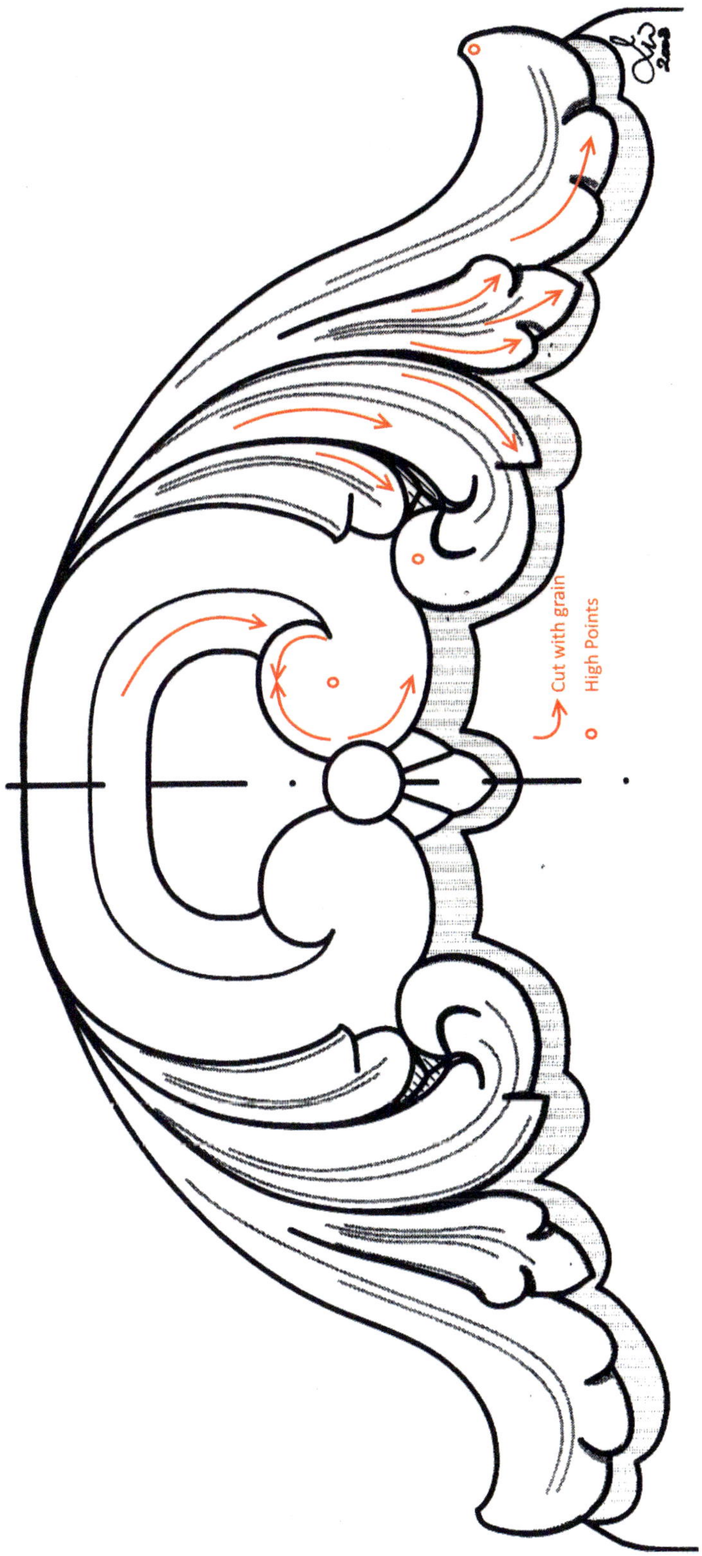

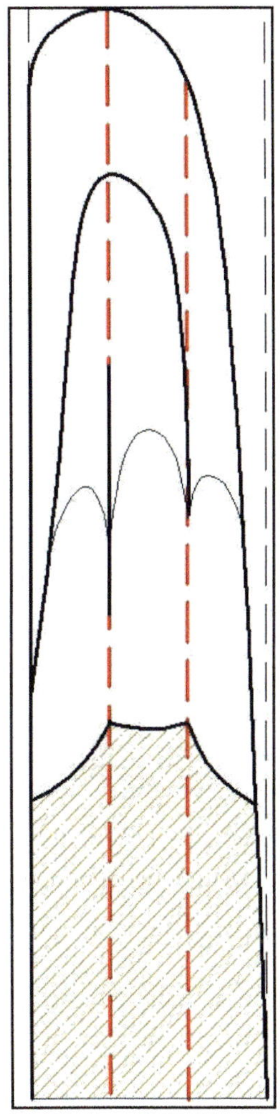

Cross-Section

A4 Template

A Norwegian Woodcarving Textbook: Fauske, Odd; ISBN: 978-1861518637 (2020); Amazon

Project Six – 17th Century Panel Carving

This project is designed to illustrate the simpler form of earlier oak carvings as it evolved towards the later complex forms of the Renaissance.

At the start of the 17th Century, the domestic oak was still the common timber used for the construction of furniture and fixtures, produced, with or without traditional domestic stylised carved decoration. By the latter part of the century, domestic oak was slowly giving way to the new imported timbers and decorative styles, developed on continental Europe. This evolved quickly and by the end of the century, has risen to its zenith with the furniture and realistic carvings of the Renaissance. Here the likes of Ginlin Gibons in demand and the use of lime (also known as or Linden or Basswood) for the new style of highly realistic carvings. In the early part of the century, during the Jacobean period, while the professionally produced oak furniture of the rich became even more ornate than the Elizabethan period, the vernacular decoration remained much simpler, moving slowly on from the simple incised chip-carved patterns of the earlier years to what is more recognisable as low relief carving. There are plenty of examples of this style from the later Victorian revival, but genuine examples are not that hard to find, as many of the really solid coffers built then have survived to this day, although many of the oak church pews in this style are later Victorian revival. The panel I have to decorate is part of the structure of a replacement balustrade that is at the top of an original vernacular oak stairs, so will need careful finishing to fit in with

10
20
30
40
50
60
70
80
90
100
110
120
130
140
150
5
4
3
2
1

the patina of the old panel boards above which it will be installed.

1 With the pattern transferred to the centre of the board use a knife and a straight-edge to mark the lines delineating the pattern. These can be deepened with a V-tool, but by using a knife first, you will have a greater chance of the tool flowing in a straight line with the V-tool.

2 Now the edges of the pattern are set-in, work can start on shaping the ovolo surround, starting with a bent fish-tail

N°1 to rough-out the shape, much in the same way as taking fine shavings using a plane to round over a larger board. Unfortunately, with the effective changes in grain direction between the inside and outside of the pattern, there will be much movement round the board to get the right angle of attack.

3 With much of the hard work done, the final shape can then be refined with he use of an otherwise little used tool - the back bent N°7, although the edges of the pattern will have to be continuously trimmed

back with a knife or straight chisel as the N°7 digs a progressively deeper channel into the timber.

4 As the Back-bent is not commonly held, much of the work can be achieved with an up-turned N°7, although there are some corners that are difficult to finish this way, so at the end of the chapter, I have given some advice on a work-round to get a relatively inexpensive but useable back-bent gouge for the project - see page 148.

5

5 With the surrounding ovolo diamond complete, the work on the main pattern starts by transferring the centre pattern to within the new ovolo surround then scooping out the four main cross leaves. It is well worth giving the N°5 a little "tickle" on the strop before starting the horizontals leaves, as the cross-grain cut required is very challenging to keep "clean" unless the edge is in first class condition.

6

6 The oval button at the centre of the pattern will need to be set-in before finishing these primary leaves as a careful cut down into the button with a N°7 is required to get the stems well down into the base of the button, as all the minor stems have to start from here as well.

7 Now that you can "see" the leaf patter, it's time to give them some shape. The technique is broadly the same for all of them, starting with a vertical stop-cut on the tip of the outside edge of the leaf, using the tool with the profile closest to the leaf shape. Often the curve of the leaf will change along its length, so start with the tightest profile at the tip and then change to the wider profile

7 A

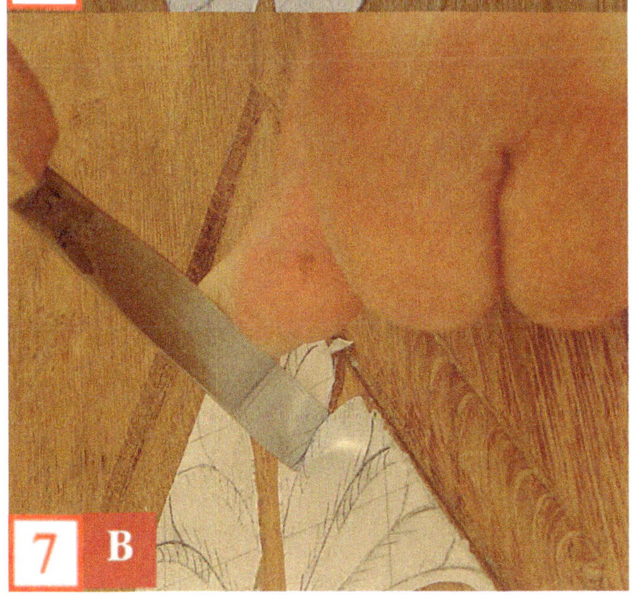
7 B

8

9

10

and run the stop-cut into the centre with a slicing cut.

8 With the edge firmly delineated, the chip can released with a smooth cut by rocking the blade firmly from the leaf tip towards the centre - this should leave behind a smooth surface as the chip pops out. Should this not work cleanly, a judicious paring of the exposed surface can clean it up.

9 Where the centre of the leaf cannot be simply profiled by the above slicing cut, it may be necessary to scoop it out with a cut along the leaf. However, this will require the tool to be rotated with a slicing movement toward the end of the stroke, so that its wings do not touch the leaf below.

10 The main horizontal leaf was scooped out earlier and as a result will take some care to establish its edges. As oak is friable, a good stop-cut will be needed to ensure the grain is severed beyond the depth of the scoop. Again the chip is eased out with a careful slicing cut. If you are competent with a knife, this is the sort of curve that can be knife cut, as it puts less strain on the fragile cross- grain.

11 The top edge of the leaf is rounded over by using an inverted N°5 - but remember to watch the grain direction as it will be critical with the different leaf orientations. For example, most of the top edge of

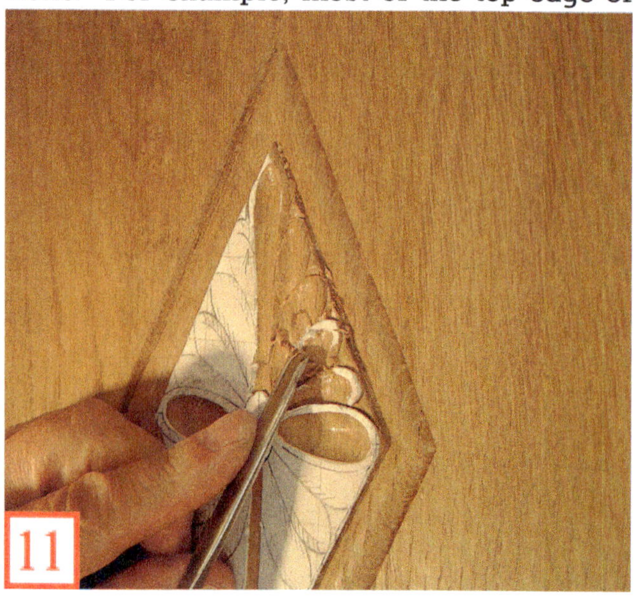
11

the leaf will probably get away with a single cut running outwards from the centre, with just a careful rotation towards the tip.

12 However, the change of grain over the tip of the leaf will need a change of approach. Change direction and come at it from outside with the leaf tip being cut inwards to meet up the earlier cut at the change of grain direction.

13 With the outside edges complete, attention can turn to scooping out the inside shapes. First make sure that you have a good stop-cut (as yo don't want to take the whole leaf out by mistake). By starting at the apex this will leave the maximum support in the subsequent un-excavated leaves to resist any untoward splinters. Find the right gouge for the shape - the top leaves will need a Nº7. A clean cut should bring out the clean chip to define the inner shape.

14 Progressively widen the radius of the gouge as you proceed away from the apex towards the centre leaves. The increasing width across the grain will necessitate more of a rotation to be added to the slicing action to bring the shape towards the centre in a single cut.

15 Counter-intuitively, a tighter gouge may be required for the last leaf, as it may need to be run as a cross-cut from

12

13

14

15

16

17

18

the tip, as this is getting into the cross-grain at the centre of the board.

16 This process is repeated for each of the four quadrants, which will leave the button in the centre as the only remaining un-carved piece of paper. Having been carefully delineated by a series of vertical cuts with both a N°7 and N°5, This has to be carefully rounded off, first with the N°7 now reversed on the ends.

17 With the ends rounded, the N°5 is then taken to round the top. This will a careful cut out from the centre, which is then repeated fin the other direction, to reflect the change in grain at this point. Some gentle pairing will be required to round all the edges until a smoothly rounded button is left prominently in the centre.

18 When all of the patter is complete, it just remains to tidy up the edges. A clean chip is required at the border with the ovolo band. To achieve this, tun a vertical knife cut along the inside edge of the band, then along take the gouge that best fit at the end of the leaf and make a stab-cut into the knife line to clear the chip.

19 This project limited the choice of where to locate the carving in the available timber, as a wide panel was required. As a result, part of the carving was located over a fault in the timber, which resulted in

19

the carving failing. Whether it is a gain fault like this or a human error, it is a simple task to use a piece of suitably matched scrap, cut to shape, to be glued into the area. Leave it as long as you can (best left over-night if possible) before trimming with a flush-cutting saw.

20 When firm, the repair needs to be pared flat to the original surface, which is where a bent fishtail N°1 really comes into its own.

21 If care is taken to match the patch to the colour and grain of the original, when finally carved, the insert should merge into the background pretty much seamlessly. Should there be any remaining miss-match, some adjustment to the finishing of the area can be made, as required.

As this is apart of a restoration project, when the carving is complete, all that remains is to colour it to fit in to its new environment. As the title suggests, this is a period panel designed to fit into a stair balustrade. As the old farm house had attached animal accommodation, all the original oak has been naturally "fumed" by the aroma from the barn, so the choice for this project is the same - ammonia fuming. Post fuming and installation a protective coat of coloured French Polish was applied, enabling a final adjustment to be made to match the colour of the surrounding original, with a final coat of wax polish to round it all off.

A There was a time when a the "one off" requirement for a special tool could be met by the inexpensive purchase of a tool without a handle. Unfortunately, few tools are currently available in this format as I suspect the combination of users wanting a "finished product" and the decline of skills once taught in schools (such as fitting a handle), have resulted in such tools being only economically viable as "show specials". There is one remaining easy source of tools without handles and that is from the basic concept of the Flexcut® range, where all blades are sold without handles, as they are designed for machine use, or in their comprehensive range of handles.

B However, as a temporary measure, to mount a single blade in a handle is trivial - requiring just a handle, a saw & a ferrule (brass pipe olive).

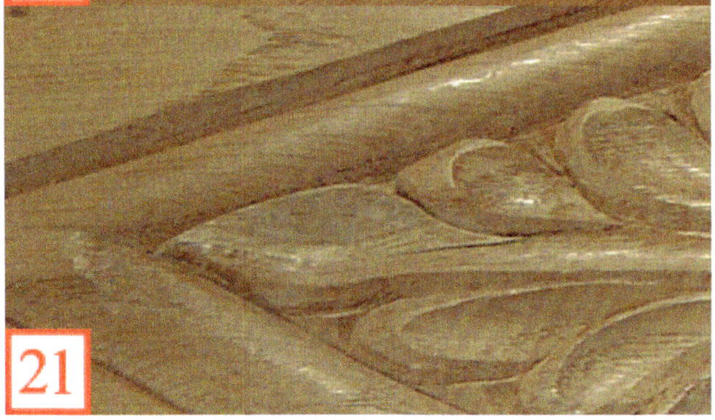

Quick-Handle

1. Select saw with kerf nearest to blade thickness
2. Make kerf cut in handle end
3. File end down to diameter of pipe olive
4. Boast pipe olive onto end.
5. Insert Blade
6. Optionally - fill remaining saw kerf.

Project Seven - Woodspirit

The Woodspirit - a cousin of the Greenman is a caricature of a face often glimpsed in the wild forest or more often now as the domesticated spirit of the garden.

The Greenman or Woodspirit has been around for as long as there has been woodcarving. They can still be occasionally glimpsed in the wild, sharing the forests with the Trolls and Pixies, but now, like the Fox, it is more often seen in the more domesticated environment of the garden. With thoughts of summer and, of course the sunshine, plans turn to the garden - in my case the construction of a Fruit Cage, As the structure was to be reasonably substantial, it would need to become a "feature" in the garden - so what better than to add some character(s). In this case, a couple of "Wood Spirits" to assist in keeping the birds off the soft fruit. The timber was purchased for the primary use, hence I found myself with a 200mm x 200mm (4" x 4") post of pressure treated, fast grown softwood as the carving material - somewhat less than ideal. As a result, the underlying requirement was to keep the design simple and the tools very sharp, and, weather permitting, I could and enjoy carving for and in the great outdoors.

1 This generic design for a Woodspirit will work on the edge of any square cut timber, and uses the right-angled edge as the profile of the face and nose. So for the purposes of the description, I will be assuming that the timber to be used is of square section. The initial rough shape is derived on the square edge of the timber from a large 60° "V" cut into the edge of the timber, about as deep as half the size of the square section - this forms the nose profile and the start of the eyebrows. To this is added a smaller "V" cut below, about half as wide as before and spaced about the same distance down as it is wide - this is the upper lip.

2 The large nose "V" cut is then extended up the log a similar amount to form the eyebrows, Pencil in where the nose will be, making sure to make it generous in size as pressure- treated timber will not take fine detail.

3 The initial rough shape is derived, using either a saw or a wide straight chisel to form rough 60° "V" cuts into the edge of the timber, to form the nose profile and the start of the eyebrows. To this is added a smaller "V" cut below, about half as wide as before and spaced about the same distance down as it is wide - this is the upper lip. The large nose "V" cut is then extended up the log a similar amount to form the eyebrows. The sides of the nose and cheeks can be cut in also with the large N°1 so that, with this rough shape of the nose defining the face, you can sketch in the overall shape of the face that will be bounded by the hair line and the upper lip's shape,

4 Still with the large N°1, finish the sides and the base of the nose, then insert the nostrils with a small N°7 or the tip of a knife blade.

5 Make a stop-cut along the top edge of the moustache with a suitable large curved gouge such as a N°5. Before moving on to setting in the lower edge of the cheek with a rotating cut with the N°1. You

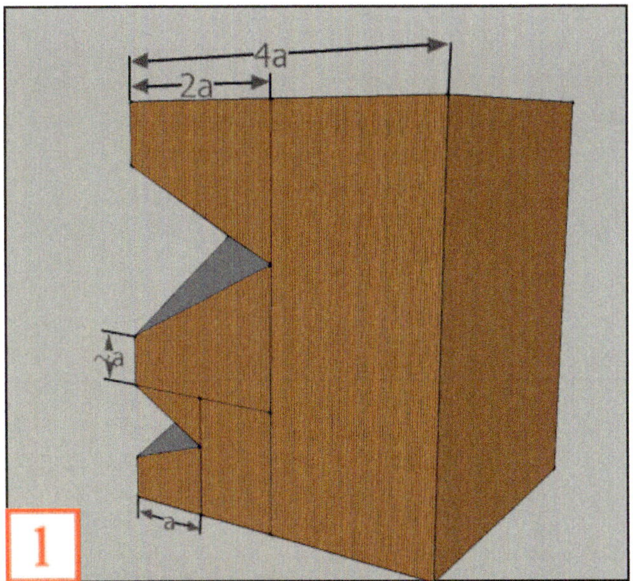

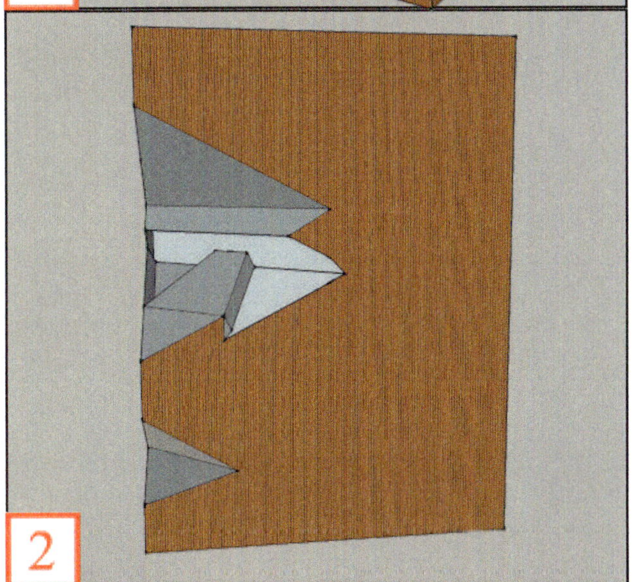

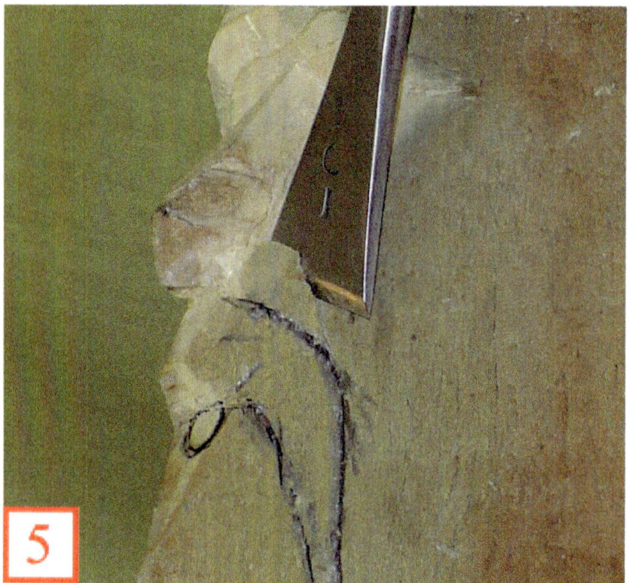

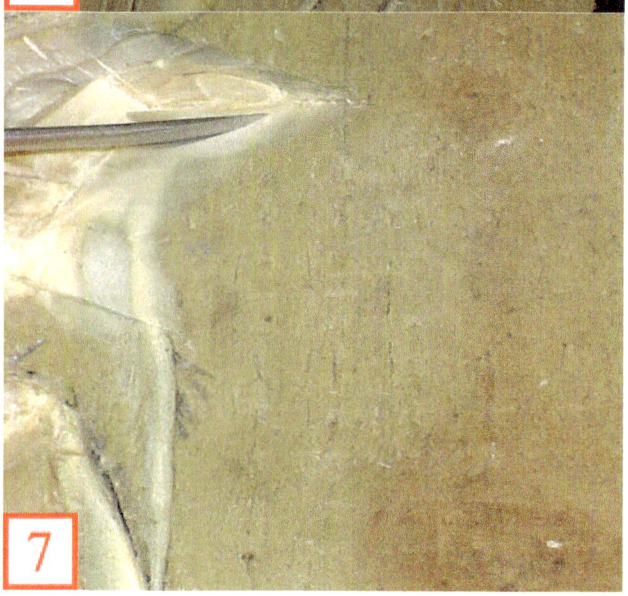

can then run a groove with a V-tool along the pencil line that shows the outside of the eyebrows and moustache, which will bound the carved area of the face.

6 The mouth is a simple triangle, above an accentuated lower lip. This is made by two deep cuts with a small chisel or N°1 for the apex of the triangle, underlined with a small N°7 for the base of the triangle. The lower lip is then outlined with a slicing cut using a N°5.

7 With the mouth defined, next comes the eyes - for which a large N°5 is used with a pair of cuts, the first slightly slanting away from the eye and the second slanting towards the eye (to pop-out the chip). This defines the upper and lower eyelids, for both left and right sides.

8 With the oval shape of the eye formed, use a sharp, pointed Slöyd Knife (a Scandinavian craft knife) to cut a slit across the eyelid to form the impression of the eye itself.

> Tip:
> Use a pencil often to sketch in the next bit of detail. This way you will be able to "see" what you want to achieve before you start to carve, so avoid errors. Also look at the carving from side-to-side and top-to-bottom to try to maintain symmetry and balance.

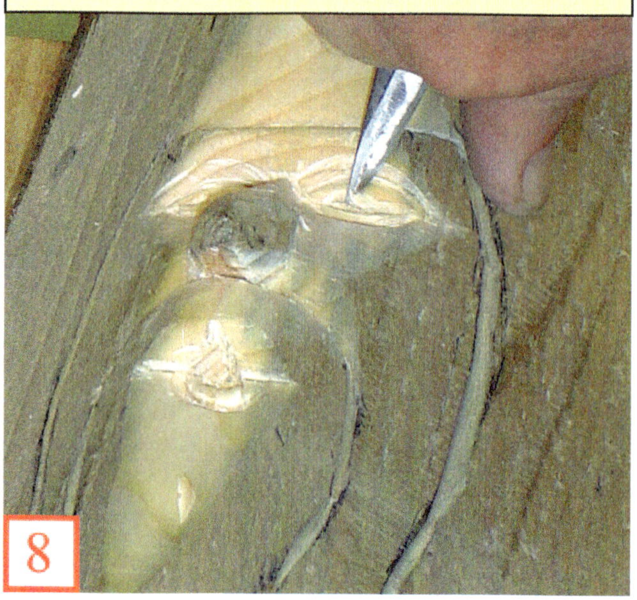

9 Next the area for the eyebrows are firmly established using a large No5 to make again a couple of complimentary angled cuts to define the shape, first a stop-cut above the eye-brow line, then the slicing cut down through the brow area,

10 With the bottom of the brow defined, move on to wasting away the rest of the brow area with any large curved gouge - quickly taking away a large quantity of waste, working across the grain, up towards the hairline. You will return to smooth this area after you have establish the hairline.

11 With the brow area lowered, the actual hairline can be established with a few bold cuts with the large N°1. In effect, these are the stop-cuts to establish the arch of the receding hairline, to enable you to turn back towards the face to shape the brow itself up to the hairline - still using the large No1 or the long blade of a carving knife or even a small draw-knife.

12 Finally finish the brow with a few cross-cuts into the eyebrows, leaving a smoothly convex shape joining the eyebrows to the hairline.

13 With the final shape of the upper face complete turn you attention to the lower face. Pencil in the shape and style of moustache and beard that you want and, if necessary "improve" the bottom lip to make

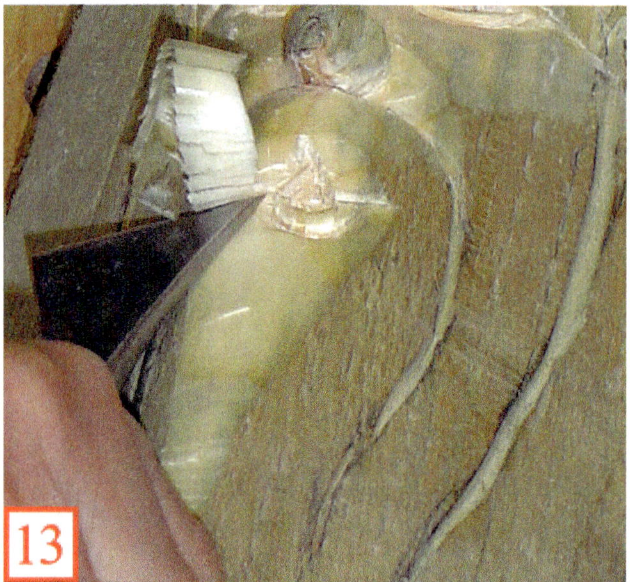

sure that it is well cut-in so that the subsequent work on the beard will not damage its shape. Then you can form the area of the moustache and beard with wide sweeps of the large N°1 into the base of the moustache.

14 Now take the largest and sharpest V-tool you have and carve away artistically at all the hair and beard that you have sketched in (or even go for it free-hand if feeling really creative). If you have a smaller V-tool as well, the brow can be gently "furrowed" with worry lines and the eyes accentuated by "crows-feet" in the corners. Make sure the hair has a random or "wind swept" effect to it, as the old fellow will live outside.

15 Before moving on to any staining and finishing, view the carving outside "in the wild" make any adjustments to perspective that this reveals.

16 Finally add a coat of preservative (or other appropriate finish). In my case, the finish applied was a creosote substitute, which not only restores some of the benefits of the tanalized coating that has been carved away, but also accentuates the dark and light of the hair and face. Then the pair of them were ready to take their place in the pile of timber that the Pixies were going to turn into a fruit cage that night.

Tip:

One way to provide "depth" to the pupil in a rough carving such as this, is to just drill the actual pupil (causing a dark shadow just below the upper lid and in the centre of the eye) or to drill and then fill the pupil with a dark wood dowel. If it is to be mounted, drill and screw through - the screw heads will reflect as pupils that follow you - see below.

16

Project Eight - Green Man

This project is inspired by the designs in the Lora Irish Book "A Source Book for Woodcarvers".

1

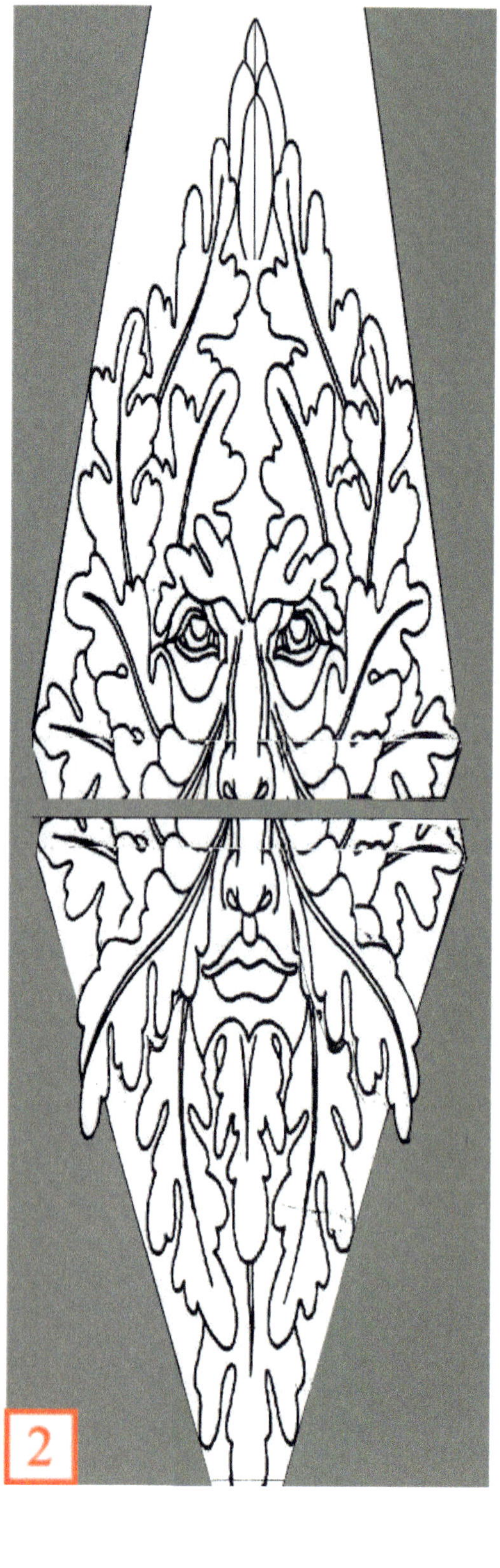

2

1 The design for this Green Man was developed in Chapter 10 from the "***Sacred Oak"*** drawing by Lora Irish to suit a lozenge (trapezoid) shaped project on an external Barge Board. As such, the best material to use is English Oak as it has natural preservative qualities (see below) and is "***in keeping***" with the age of the building. I had an off-cut originally sourced from a local saw-mill for barge boards.

2 Guidance was given in Chapter 10 on the printing of the pattern onto two pages, having made sure that the margins have been adjusted to ensure there is a suitable over-lap to enable the pattern to be accurately re-assembled.

3 With the two page paper image re-assembled onto the carving blank, cut round the outside with a band-saw (or coping saw) and file the saw marks off the edges. With the blank now secured to a suitable bench, rough out the major dividing features with a V-tool.

4 Set-in the first part of the patter, then take the set-back area down by 5-10 mm (¼") using a wide gouge with a suitable sweep rather than a chisel, as you are trying to leave a contrasting textured finish straight from the tool, and a chisel will leave a smooth, featureless background, more suited to a piece of furniture rather than an eternal architectural carving.

Both English (European) oak - *Quercus Robur* - and American Oak - *Quercus Alba* - are species known as *"white oaks"* Much of oak's longevity can be traced to the relatively high tannin levels within the wood, which acts as a natural pesticide. Tannins are what give the grain it's distinct and contrasting colour. In general, European Oak has roughly double the tannin content of American Oak. The higher tannin content makes European Oak more durable (rot-resistant), which is why it was the preferred wood for timber framing and ship-building throughout history.

5

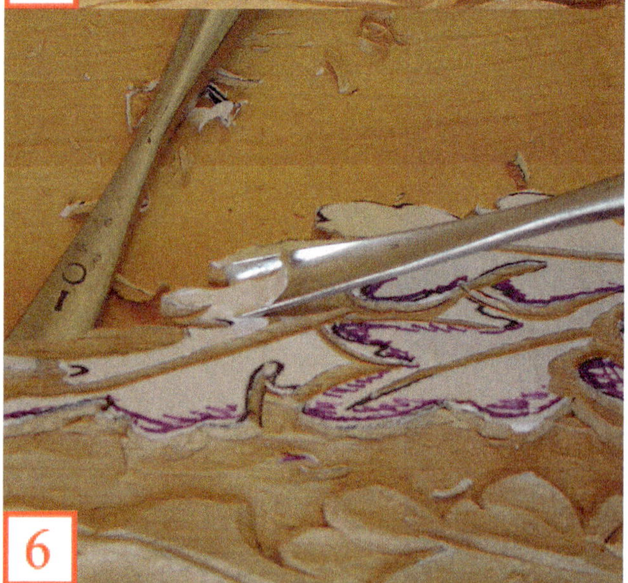

6

7

5 You can then set about carving the leaves through a series of stab cuts to define the individual outlets, followed by a single scooping cut with a deep gouge along the full length of the blade. The technique required for carving a Green Man is amply explained in the Lora Irish's book by Chris Pye, who is a much better teacher than I am. However, I would recommend that a beginner complete the carving of a "feature" be at a time, to learn the "feel" of the pattern and maintain consistency. This is less efficient than for a competent carver but in this case, I would suggest that you complete the carving of one side before staring on the other, as this then gives you the style to follow for the remainder, leaving you with a balanced carving at the end.

6 This shape of the run-out of the edge leaves can be scooped out with a deep gouge. While carving the first side, I lost my way from time-to-time, so here you can see the highlighting I've added to remind me of the run the under-cut leaves run.

7 With the outside of the leaf now clearly defined, you can move onto the inside, where a leaf underlay should be established through a stop cut at the tip of the next leaf before slicing into the cut to ease out the chip.

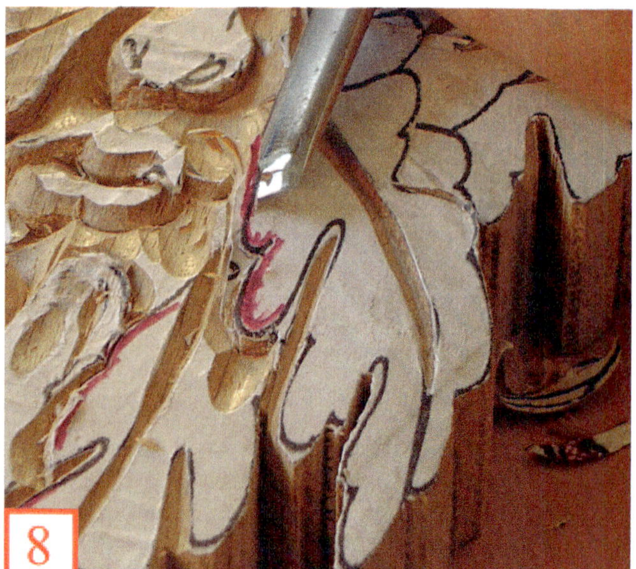

8

8

9

8 The edges of the leaves will need finished by gently rounding them with the inside edge of a tool. Where possible, this should undercut the leaf to provide the hard shadow that will be needed to emphasise the feature when seen from afar. With oak, some care is needed as sharp undercut edges can be brittle due to the wide grain.

9 The facial features are carved in a similar manner to the leaves, but without the undercutting. In contrast, features like eyes and eyebrows will require sensitive rounding while retaining the "feel" of the surrounding leaves, while the outline of the nose will need worked well down into the carving to generate deep shadows if it is to appear to stand out from the face.

10 As this is an architectural carving to be secured well above eye height, I have "cheated" with the pupils in the eyes and drilled them for the securing screws. This gives a slightly staring look from the deep shadow from the holes, which can be plugged later with a suitable dark wood dowel after mounting, should it offend. However, as this will need to be dismounted periodically for painting, I have just screwed it thorough the pupils, using stainless-steel screws (or brass), to avoid iron staining when weathered.

10

11

12 A

12 B

11 A When finished, I usually coat external oak with a clear wood preservative, to aid in its weather resistance, prior to mounting it in its final location.

12 When deciding on the wood to use for a "naked" external carving, it is as well to consider not only its durability, but also how it will weather.

A In my case, with a historic building to maintain, there are plenty of unfinished external features.

B These can give a guide to how the timber will age.

The pattern for this "Sacred Oak" finial is opposite, together with a similar derivation of the "Gothic Diamond" pattern from the book by Laura Irish - see Page 81, also adapted for use as a finial.

Sacred Oak

Gothic Diamond

Project Nine - Barometer

This is a design to replicate the small travelling weather station of the 18th century, that were subsequently to find favour with the Victorian middle classes, as the science of meteorology was to enter the home of the better educate.

The mercury column barometer was invented in the mid-17th century in Italy, using a 33"(840 mm) glass tube with an open mercury reservoir at its base. This remained the basis of the scientific measurement of atmospheric pressure in Europe until an EU Directive in 2007, on the sale of mercury, effectively ended the production of the venerable instruments. The length of the glass tube governed the size and shape of the wooden case used for the mounting – effectively to slightly more than 33" and "long and thin" . Prior to the invention of the aneroid barometer, in the mid 19th centenary, only the rich and the scientific community had the interest and resources to own a mercury "long tube" barometer. However, the aneroid barometer, with its round case and clock type dial, lent itself to adoption by a wider community and met an increasing interest in an expanding awareness of a scientific approach to weather prediction. It gave rise to the "banjo" barometer – which was still generally based on the 33" length of the wooden case from the "old" mercury column. As the manufacture of the aneroid barometer became wider spread and the instruments themselves became more robust, with the size of the dials becoming smaller, so the "travelling weather station" became possible. In its simplest form, this was a small aneroid barometer mounted with a thermometer, in a smaller "suitcase" format than the long "banjo" barometer. However, the inclusion of a hygrometer with the other instruments further increased the ability to forecast

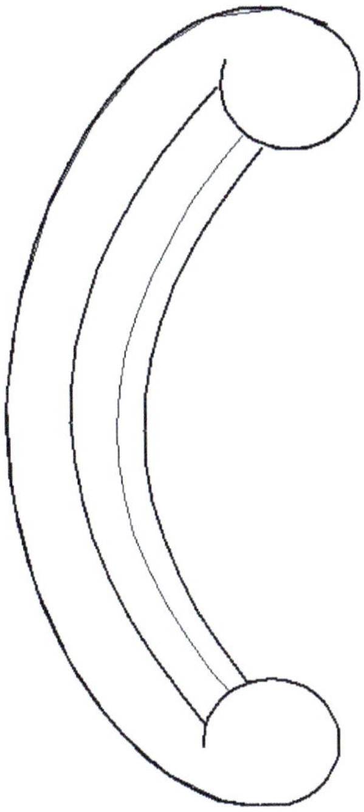

Standard 'C' Shape

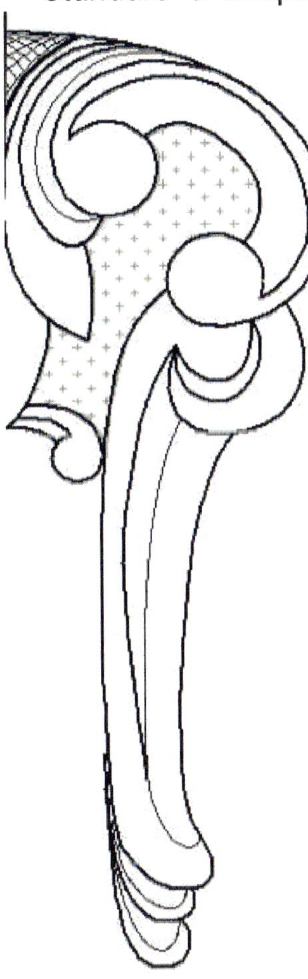

Crown with drape

rain accurately — a vital capability for the "travelling gentleman". What had started as the invention of the "gentleman adventurer" soon migrated into the wider population, adopted by those interested in robust weather prediction, whether farmers, fishermen or simply the increasingly better educated masses. As the original "portable weather station" developing into a more static piece of wall furniture, it also became more ornate, going full circle to imitate the larger (and more expensive) banjo format — complete with carved ornamentation.

The design of a small barometer is ideally suited to acanthus embellishments. The dimensions of the instruments available guides the proportions, with the size of the crown being chosen, so as to finish elegantly off the whole in a finely balanced group. In my case, the carving was sized to house a 100 mm (4") brass cased barometer and a 60 mm (2⅜") brass cased hygrometer resulting in a design that was overall some 500mm x 170mm (19½" x 6½"). To achieve this, the outline was drawn with a 175 mm (6⅞") circle at the centre with 115 mm (4½") top and bottom circles, linked with a 150 x 35 (6" x 1⅜") neck box. The main circles are mainly decorated with linked acanthus 'C' shapes, with the two bottom circles being linked together with an 'C' shape (be careful to consider your grain directions when you place the 'C' shapes, to avoid a grain change half way along the pattern). These are linked by the thermometer "neck" which is decorated with a series of inverted "fishing rods" topped out with a small semi-horizontal 'C'. The top is formed by a pair of reclining 'C' shapes, in turn supporting a central plume or alternatively a drape. You can "play" with the components and sizes to suite your own design, even using them to create a simple "banjo" design by dropping the bottom hygrometer circle out altogether and closing the centre circle by moving the compound 'C' up into the gap. My pattern size was also influenced by the practicality of being able to print it out from the computer onto two sheets of A4 paper. Armed with a suitable

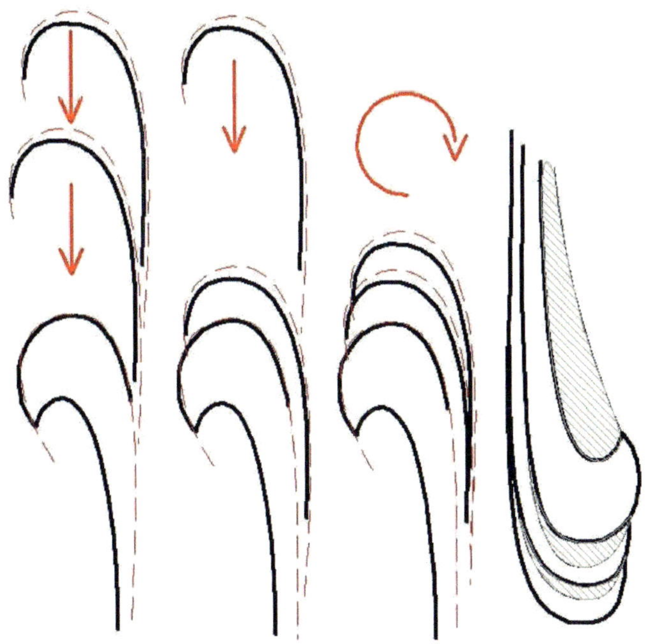

piece of wood 500 mm x 170 mm x 70 mm thick (19½" x 6½" x 2¾"), the final pattern and a can of spray adhesive, work can begin.

1 With the pattern stuck down, I used a Bandsaw to cut off the waste - note the relief cuts to stop the blade from jamming (a jig-saw, coping saw, or even any available apprentice can be used to equal effect if no suitable power tool is available).

2 As I am not going to carve the sides, I have used a drum sander to finish as much of the profile as it will reach, before finishing the sides with a file.

3 The seating for the instruments should be drilled out next, either in a couple of goes with a hole saw (the outer circle for seating the rim and the inner circle clean through to the back), or failing that, with a conventional drill marked with a drill stop and some work with a coping saw then some "wasting" work with a chisel and mallet. As the main part of the "instrument deck" is some 10 mm (⅜") below the rim, I then use a router to take out the centre to this depth (this can be either a power router, or a hand router - either way it pays to "set-in" the pattern first, so as to reduce the chances of mistakes). As the crown area is not as deeply rebated (and also to be patterned), I left reducing the level here until later — so that I

could get the "feel" of the pattern round the thermometer neck. While on the rough stuff, mark the final depth of the instrument seating on the inside of the circle and then also mark the mid-way between this and the "instrument deck" so you can clearly see how much still needs to be taken out.

4 You can then take any large gouge (I used a N°5) to roughly waste the base down to this mid-line, leaving enough thickness to later carve a smooth circular rim, which will enhance the view of the recessed instrument. Remember that cutting round in a circle like this need the cuts to be taken in four different directions on each of the arcs if the round, to allow for grain changes round the circle.

5 With all the preparations now completed, at last you now have reached the stage where you can start the "real" carving. I started with the 'C' patterns on the central ring, where the ball-ends are set in with a vertical slicing cut using a small N°7. This is followed by an angled cut to "pop" the chip out. For ease of illustration, I have taken each 'C' in turn, but greater efficiency will be achieved if you go round all of the 'C' shapes in the centre while you have the N°7 in your hand, before you change to the N°5 next

6 A small N°5 is then used to take out the full length of the inner curve (making sure you are cutting the appropriate arc for the grain at this point).

7 With the N° 5 still in your hand, the tool is reversed to shape the outside of the design on the return trip. (Before putting the N°5 down, have a look at how you are going to approach the next step of reducing the centre ring, as you may have put some shape into the large ball-end on the adjoining 'C' on the neck so as to be able to get a good swing at reducing the centre). Do not forget to go back to the N°7 to complete the 'C' shapes by rounding off each the ball-end in turn.

8 Moving on to reducing the base of the centre of the banjo, use the small N°5 to cut in towards the centre, again taking the grain change into account, so that a smooth finish is achieved. I am leaving the tool marks as the final finish, to lead the eye to the barometer that will be insert in the centre.

9 As it had already been getting in the way of reducing the centre, I had started on the top edges of the 'C' shapes with a reversed N°5 (above), so I went back finish these next. The two circles of the base are linked together with these 'C' shapes that are compound leaf shapes that reverse on themselves round the 'C' to eventually just "kiss" in the middle. The approach uses a very similar technique to the 'C' shapes in that the ball end needs defined by an initial stab which will isolate it from any subsequent accidental damage, then cut into it to release the 'C'.

10 This is followed by running the outside leaf grooves into the ball ends with a No7. This groove will have to extend from the cross-over in the middle of the 'C', in both directions and on both sides, to eventually establish a saddle in the centre of the 'C'. It is this "saddle" that will later provide the location of the transitional "kiss"

at the change of direction and orientation of the two arms of the compound leaf system.

11 The top shape of the 'C' is defined by taking a crescent chip out at both ends - N°7 to ease the chip on the small ball ends followed by a N°5 for the larger ball ends. The external shoulders of these crescents are rounded over with a reversed N°5 with a groove run round the inner edge with a 'V'-tool to establish the edge of inner leaf shape. This inner leaf is then carved with (or at least "finished with") a single careful run of a deep gouge, such as a N°7. This has to be repeated at both ends, with the two grooves just overlapping in the central "kiss" in the saddle at the middle. The additional secondary leaf on the lower inside of the curve should have its free end rounded to give it a clean finish.

12 As this is difficult to describe it is illustrated by the juxtaposition of the drawing with the finished item, to better relate the drawing to the above description.

13 The compound 'C' round the bottom edge only differs from the side patterns in that it has a grain reversal at the base, that requires considered use of the gouge, especially on the inside bottom curve. As the whole shape is more relaxed, a N°5 is suitable for both inside and out, as the difference in radii can be accommodated within the curves. Here again, the inside ball ends need defined with a stop-cut before the N°5 is run round the inside to give a smooth curve.

14 The same tool can be retained for rounding the ball-ends and for the two indents that are, of course, there to add subtle shape to the detail. As is often the case with traditional designs, they also nicely reduce, to a manageable length, the section of inner curve that you have to shape with a single run of the gouge.

15 With the inner curve finished, the same tool can be simply reversed to round-over the outer edge, where, apart from

12

13

14

15

16

17

the grain change half way round, there is no flimsily detail to get in the way of bold strokes of the tool. Before you put the tool down, the sides of the instrument-well will need to be reduced in much the same way as at above para 8 incorporating a small ridge-line between the two instruments.

16 With the bottom half completed, attention can be moved to the thermometer neck before finally moving on to the crown. Working from the outside top edge towards the centre ensures that the thickness of the remaining wood gives structural strength while you take bold sweeps with the gouge along the line of the leaves. With a stop cut made at the base of the top curl with the N°5, the sweep of the inside can be removed with a couple of bold cuts with the N°7, finished into the stop cut.

17 The underlying fronds that are formed by the inverted "fishing rods" (see page 162), can then be cut in with the N°6, using the combination of a rotating stab cut and then a 45° slicing cut to "pop" the chip out. This is repeated for each of the layers, before reversing a N°5 to round the ends over.

18 Having worked your way down the neck establishing the outside shapes, on your way back up these leaves, you can now apply the inside edge shape with the

18

reversed N°5, first to round the ball ends and the sides, then through a series of slicing and paring cuts, to define the edges of the individual leaves along the neck. A similar technique is then used to repeat this work on the lower portion of the neck, together with its final concluding 'C'.

19 To give some emphasis to the crown, the area to be patterned is taken down by about 6 mm (¼") using a ***"old hags tooth"*** hand router (or a bent chisel), as it is separated from the rest of the carving by the small horizontal 'C' that tops off the neck area.

20 Define the ball end and sweep of the dividing 'C' with the small N°7 before turning a small N°5 over to shape the outside – a similar process is then followed with the reclining 'C' s that supports the top plume.

21 Before starting on the feathers of the plume, carefully set in the small band in the middle with the small N°7, to make sure that it is not damaged by subsequent work. Starting on the bottom feathers of the plume, these are then set in with a sequence of cuts with the N°5, initially a rotating vertical stop cut at the lower edge, followed by a slicing cut to release the chip. The tool is then reversed to shape the lower edge – the whole sequence being repeated as you work up the plume. Finally, the top feather is given some depth by carefully cutting down with the large N°7 from both directions, to meet in the middle – which, unless you are very skilful, will probably need some work with the small N°7 to clean up the join, before finishing the external shape with a revered N°5. With all the detail of the plume now safely finished, finally round the top and bottom of the central ring carefully with the small N°7.

22 Go round the carving to make sure that you have not left anything out before texturing the background of the top with a suitable punch.

19

20

21

22

23

24

23 The final part of the carving is the insertion of the leaf veins to give "life" to the pattern. Care should be taken to get into a position that will allow a single sweep to be taken, from start to finish of a vein, as any join in a vein will be highlighted by any subsequent application of a finish, such as oil or wax.

24 When carving is complete, turn the carving over, find the centre line, then cut a 25 mm (1″) groove just below the crown to take an 8 mm (¼") fencing staple to provide a safe and secure hanging point. Having completed the carving, any inadvertent marks that have been made (such as clamp impressions on the sides) can be carefully removed before the application of a transparent finish. The insertion of the instruments then leaves you with a fully functional weather station that you can pack in your suitcase for your next expedition to the Matterhorn or just hang in your hall way.

25 **A** This carving used a plume as the top motif:.

B However, the same carving can be complete with a top "drape":.

With the carving complete, use a suitable "finishing oil" to seal it and add a coat of wax polish, before inserting the brass-case aneroid barometer in the centre, a hygrometer in the bottom of the "hour-glass" body and the thermometer in the neck.

The Aneroid Barometer can be used to predict the weather through relative pressure changes. If you set the movable arm at the same time daily, you can note which way the pressure has moved in 24 hrs. Rising pressure indicates improving weather, falling pressure, worsening weather. Tapping the glass will get the main arm to move to indicate if pressure is currently rising or falling.

"Standard" pressure is measured as "Mean Sea Level Pressure" (MSLP) and pressure changes with altitude - the higher you go the lower the pressure - (giving rise the the "altimeter"). A barometer usually has an adjustment screw on the back, that will allow you to set it to accurately measure pressure, locally adjusted for your height above MSL.

A

25

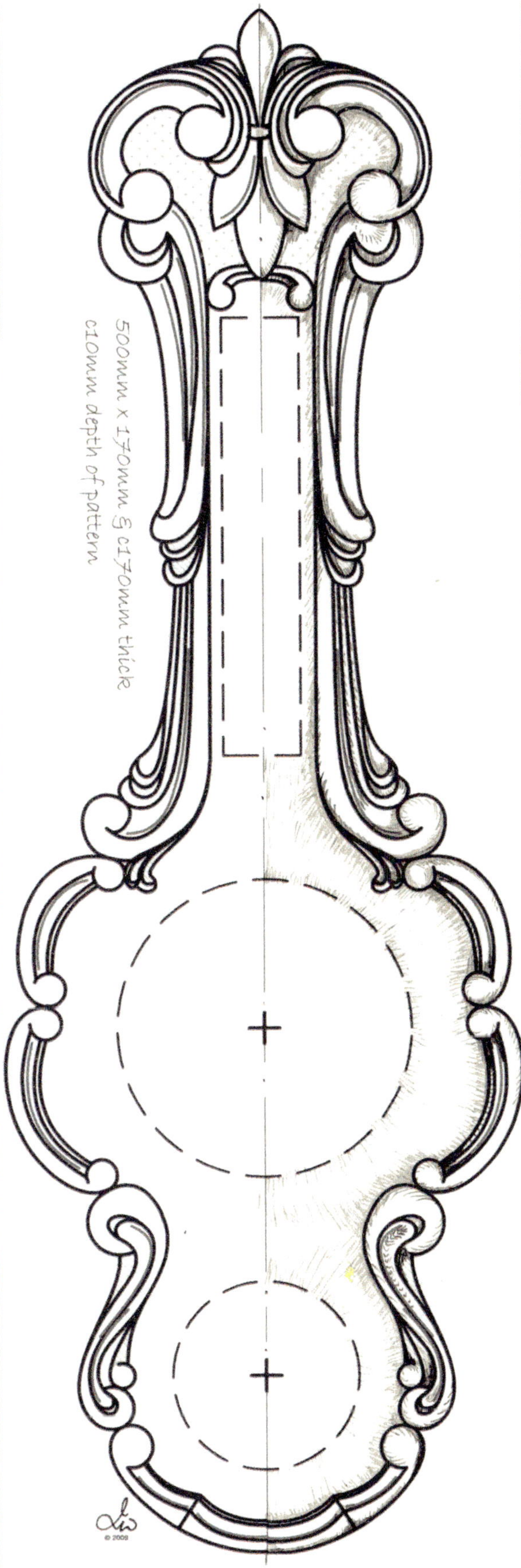

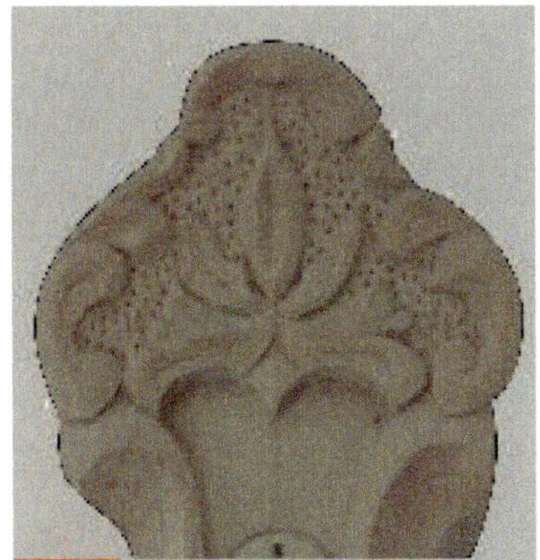

B

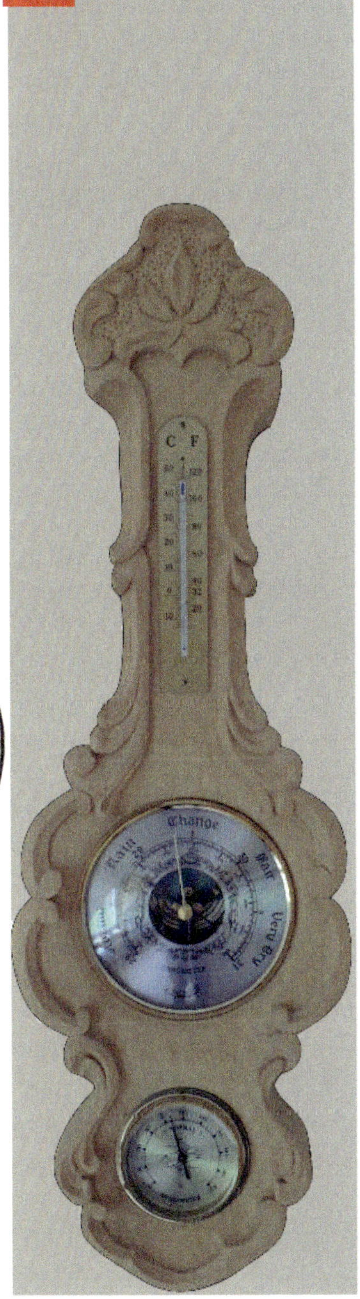

Project Ten - Norwegian Style Wall Clock

This is a traditional design
taken from those of the Norwegian master carver
Johan Amrud 1913-1997.

You my have to adjusted the pattern[1] to suit your clock mechanism (in my case a 160mm (6½") clock face), so that it will fit within the carved bevelled ring. As my timber was not thick enough, I have used the off-cuts from the birch slab glued to the back to increase the thickness of the piece and to bulk up the side profile. The enlarged pattern was stuck to the blank, using spray-mount and then the hole for the clock mechanism was cut with a hole saw, prior to roughing out the pattern with a thin blade on a Band-saw (although a coping saw can also be used). Just remember to make "relief" cuts at suitable points round the pattern, to allow the waste to drop away without jamming the saw blade. In this case, I have undertaken what could be called an "initial finish" on the sawn edges, as the pattern will be carved over and round the edges, so a near final edge is needed.

1 The edge preparation should be undertaken with a straight chisel to remove the worst of the saw marks, then use a set of files or tungsten carbide coated tools. (As the work is yet to be carved, do not use conventional sheet abrasives for this, as they will leave an abrasive residue that will dull the edges of your tools). Select the curved gouge that best suits the arc of the pattern,

and set-in all the lines round the pattern and both sides of the circular bezel.

2 The easiest way to then "ground" the carving is with a powered router, to take out the bulk of the waste round the clock face. If such a tool is not available, then mark a drill bit with the necessary depth stop and drill multiple holes and carefully cut out the waste with a chisel.

3 In either case, the subsequent lowered base level can be tidied up with a chisel or an "*old hag's tooth*" router such as the Stanley #271 (or easily made from a suitable block of hardwood and a Stanley blade[2]).

At long last the carving can commence. Start at the middle top or bottom and carve out towards the edge. To minimise the chance of an unfortunate slip, take a "V" tool and quickly outline the main dividing lines between the leaves. I would recommend that you carve symmetrically – that is, carve a bit on one side, then immediately carve the same bit on the other. That way you will be using the same tools more efficiently and reduce the challenges of remembering which way to carve with the grain.

4 With the acanthus, the technique is to match the sweep of your gouge to the curl that you want to carve, in this case a N°7, starting at the tightest "ball" end, then

5

6

7

change gouge to your next wider sweep progressively, until you reach your N°3 at the leaf tip. The first cut is a vertical stab cut, rotating the gouge to get a clean cut in towards the start of the ball. Then, in the reverse direction, run round the whole circle of the gouge profile to set-in the rest of the base of the ball end.

5 This is followed with angled slicing cuts, to clear around the ball end, taking care to rotate the cut with the grain. The same process is repeated with the next lower numbered gouge then the next, to follow the unfurling line of the pattern out to its end.

6 With the convex outline of the leaves now established, the upper concave shapes can be started. Makes sure that your N°5 is really sharp, check the grain direction and make a bold (smooth) curve along the top outside edge of each of the leaves in turn. Should you not be able to take the first cut all the way, it is important to try to make a "finishing" pass in a single cut.

7 You can then turn the gouge over and come back along the outer convex sides, ideally, with the two cuts meeting along the ridge line. Clear the waste and clearly re-delineate the base of the valley with a slicing cut along the join with the adjacent leaf, before repeating the process

8

again — N°5 or N°7 for the concave top and then the N°5 reversed for convex side.

8 Towards the base of the leaf curl, where the whole stem cross-section is convex, the inside will shape will need to be developed through a whole series of fine cuts with a straight blade — if you have a bent back chisel (see Chapter 11) this is ideal. Slowly shape the final curve that needs to be developed by moving from one side of the stem to the other, to build up the convex cross-section, while leaving an impression of a smooth surface from the many small flat plane cuts.

9 The valley between leaves needs to be to develop to give depth of the carving, This is best achieved through a series of slicing cuts along the length of the feature, to clear the waste and leave an impression of movement and depth. The tool selected will have to progress from N°1 through N°3 to N°5 to suit the progressing curve in the alignment. This whole sequence is repeated, leaf by leaf, for the rest of the pattern on both sides.

10 When you get out towards the bottom corners, you will have to set-in the final curls with an angled cut using a N°7 and then clear the pattern with a rotating cut to pop out the waste, followed by a N°5 to take out the "eye" towards the end.

11 The outer edge will need chased to a smooth convex surface with an inverted N°5, all the way round to the end - but remember the grain change at the outside of the large curve. where it just touches the edge of the groove, The top of the leaf is given a bit of depth with a groove along its length, put in with a single cut of a N°7.

12 To start the crown at the top of the pattern, first outline the small "***bobbles***" on the crown's ring by rotating a small N°8 or similar in an exact circle. Having established these circles, then set-in the curve far enough away from them to ensure that your timber can take the necessary fine

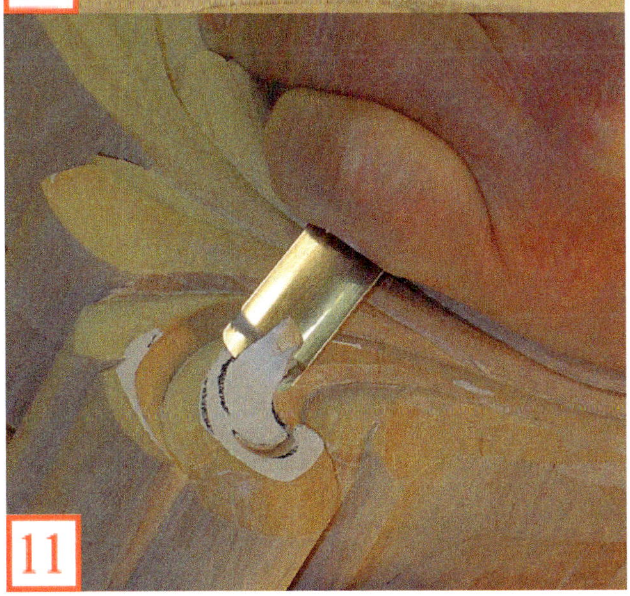

detail. (The carving of the "***bobbles***" and the rest of the ring on the crown is by far the most demanding part of this pattern for the timber grain. If you have doubts about it, or you are carving the pattern for a smaller clock face, leave the crown as a simple ring).

13 After the ring, you can then move onto establishing the outline of the plume, with the curl of the top feather being achieved by fairly coarse removal of waste with a N°5 successively cross-grain then along-grain from both directions,

14 This is finished by carefully clearing down to the stop-cut at the crown-ring with a small N°7.

15 The bottom edge of the crown plume is developed in the same way as a leaf end, with its outside edge over the top of the first large leaf. The shape is started with a bold sweep of a N°7 to make a convex outer edge, followed by a N°5 for the top of the next leaf,

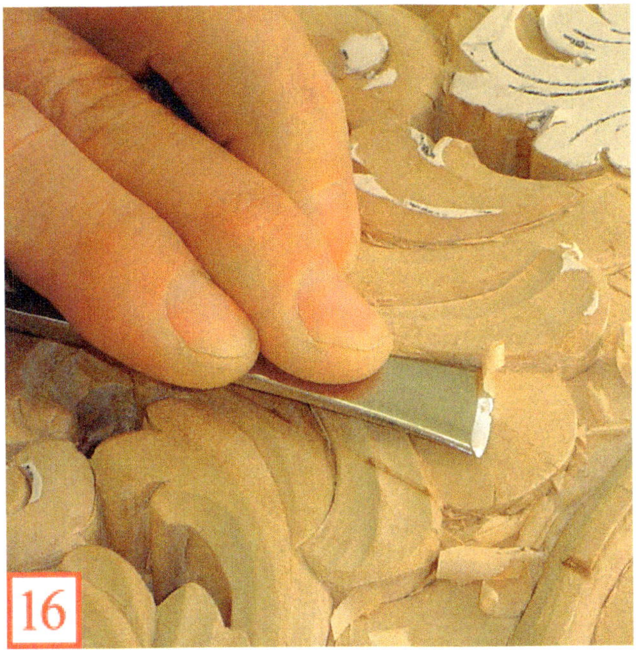
16

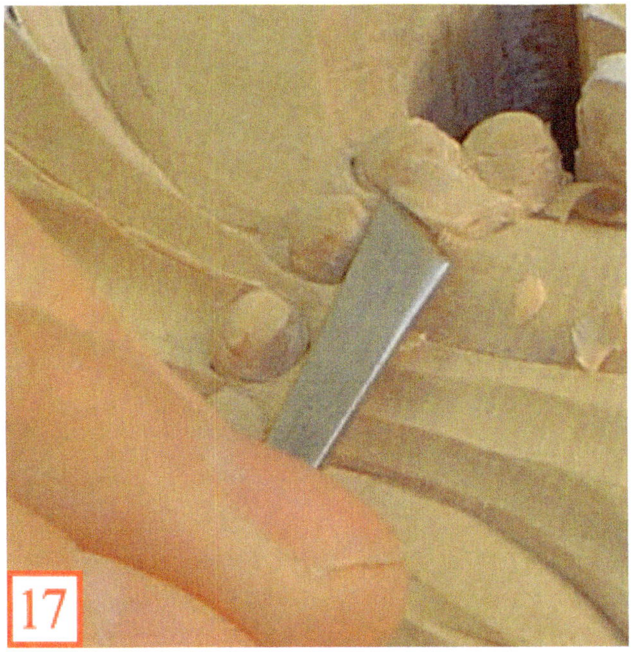
17

16 The base of the plume is then finally finished by running the central "tail" of the plume downwards with a reversed N°3. to give it the smooth undercut shape of a lobster tail.

17 With the plume finished the first of the large leaf curls either side of the central plume can be carved. They have to start well below the plume itself, to appear to be going underneath the crown-ring, to re-appear ending at the highest level on the top edge of the carving. To achieve this illusion, they have to be heavily cut back so that they reach up from the lower level of the clock face, This necessitates the bold removal of waste and as the crown-ring is in the way, you will be initially working across the grain needing a sharp straight or skew chisel,

18 This root end of the stem is a curved ovolo shape, so unless you have a back-bent tool available, you may again have to nibble away at it with a chisel or skew, until the correct levels have been established,

18

19

20

21

19 When you have the rough shape you can return with the N°3 & N°5 to establish the convex curves of the outer sides Again, in the absence of a back-bent gouge, the inside concave ovolo shape will have to be worked up in a series of small shavings with a straight chisel or skew.

20 The top supporting plumes, while developed in the same way as any other leaf, need to be finished with a single run of a N°5 on their inside edges, leaving a smooth concave curve along their length. This edge needs to be steeply raked so that it will cast a strong shadow, to help to make the plume really dominate the top of the design. Ideally, a single run should also leave an uninterrupted sharp ridge line to give a hard edge to the dark of the shadow.

21 The outside edges of the large leaf curls have to be a rounded ovolo shape. As the grain direction changes along the leaf edge, remove the outside edge from

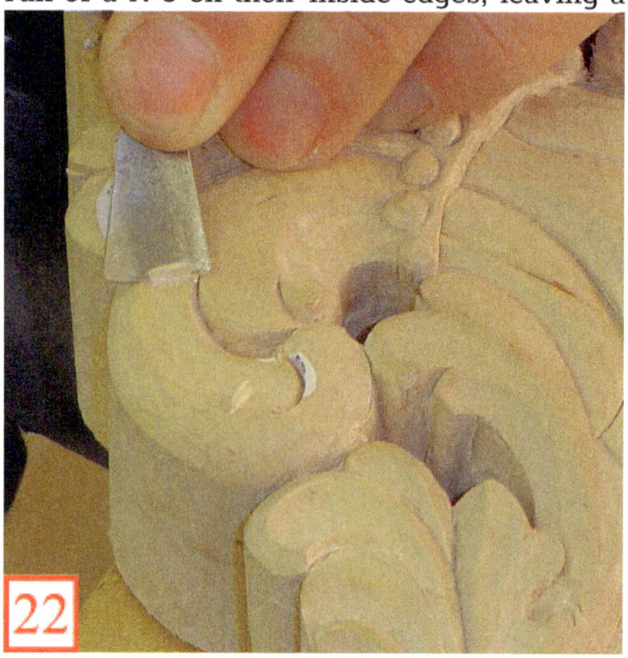
22

23

24

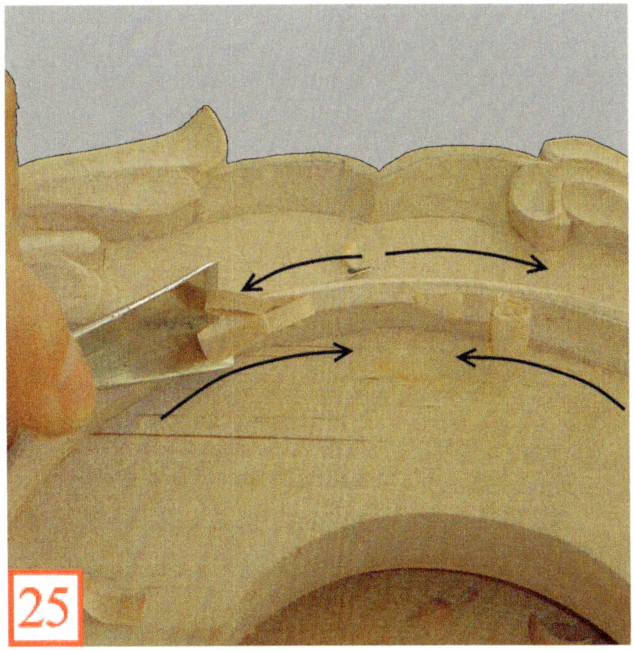
25

either end using an inverted N°5, to meeting cleanly in the middle.

22 The shape of the leaf is finalised with a shallow groove along its top edge. This is put in with the N°5 - the right way up this time. From here, move systematically outwards to carve the supporting leaves before finally, when there is no further danger of accidental damage, return to the crown-ring;

23 Clean up the crown-ring by removing any remaining waste between the bobbles, carefully with a small skew, so the smoothly rounded bobbles stand proud of the supporting ring, which itself is now clear of the plume leaves running beneath it.

24 The central bezel is shaped with a N°5 to make a convex moulding on the outside and a concave moulding on the inside.

25 Remember that the outside is worked systematically, taking into account the changing grain, as illustrated in the diagram.

26 Now put the carving end-on in a vice and shape the back of it with a straight-edged tool, to give it a subtle curve that lightens the profile and accentuates the crowning plume. Although clocks are designed to be viewed from the front, I also go round the edge with appropriate gouges to round the pattern from the back to front - that way it will retain more character when viewed at an angle.

27 A Finally, carefully re-draw the leaf veins from the pattern and follow them round with a 'V' tool, before using some form of pattern punch to mark the clock background.

B After dusting the carving off, apply your

26

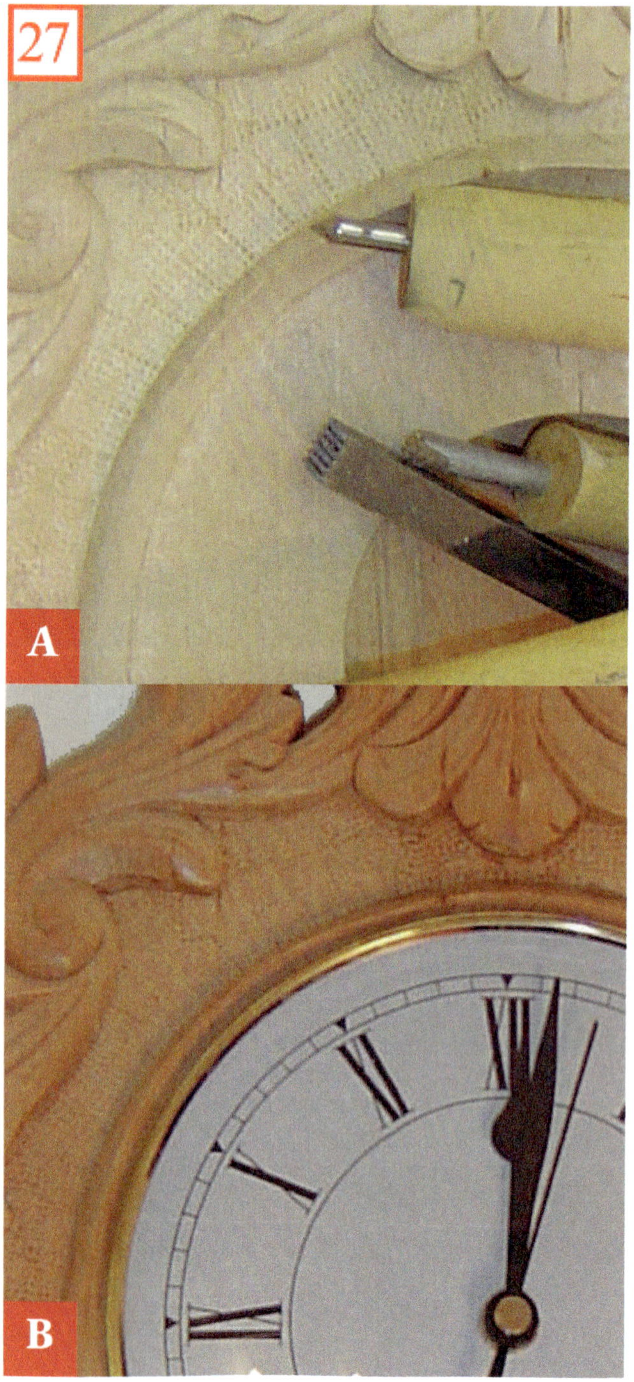

favourite finish, and fit the clock mechanism. Before you finish, some form of hanging mechanism needs to be provided, I have seen all sorts, from a simply carved slot, through a strategically placed fence staple, to conventional picture hangers - the choice is yours, then hang it on the wall and stand back to admire your work.

Norwegian Carving in a Modern Context

In common with many of the woodcarving cultures in Europe, there has been a tradition of decorating household items in Norway, such as clocks. This is shown from early long-case (or grandfather) clocks, through shelf (or mantel) clocks, to wall-clocks. Splendid examples of these can be seen, in the context of original old wooden buildings, at the open air museum of Maihaugen[3] near Lilehammar in Norway.

Here you will find not only the old wooden buildings, but also their associated furnishings, many of which are painted or carved – or both. The various ornate styles of these are well illustrated in the seminal work on ornamental carving by Johan Amrud (in Norwegian) and in the repertoire of the instructors at the "*Senter for Bygdekultur*[4]" - at Hjerleid Technical High School (see Chapter 9), where Amrud taught for many years and where you can go to learn the style.

Sadly, Johan Amrud is no longer with us, and his original book is out of in print in Norway, as is the English edition in USA, but his patterns are still available by mail order in Norway and the USA[5]. Other Norwegian clock patterns are available in Odd Fauske's compendium of plans[6] available from Amazon.

[1] *Pattern reproduced from TRESKJÆRING – Johan Amrud, (Universitetsforlaget 1983), with the permission of Gyldendal, Litteratur, PO Box 6860 St Olavsplass, NO-0130 Oslo.*

[2] *Hag's Tooth Cutter http://www.stanleytoolparts.com/12-305-1-02-a-04.html*

[3] *The open air museum of Maihaugen near Lilehammar: https://eng.maihaugen.no*

[4] *"Senter for Bygdekultur" - at Hjerleid: https://www.hjerleid.no/english*

[5] *Patterns available in Europe from: Amrud (Treskjæring), N-2634 Fåvang, Norway and available in North America from: Vesterheim NorwegianAmerican Museum Shops, 523 W. Water Street, P.O. Box 379, Decorah, IA 52101: http://vesterheim.org*

[6] *A Norwegian Textbook; Fauske, Odd,Mereo Books, ISBN-10 : 1861518633, ISBN-13 : 978-1861518637: https://www.amazon.co.uk/Woodcarving-Norwegian-Textbook-Lærebok-*

Project Eleven - Mangle Board (*Mangletre*)

This is a project for a typical low-relief carving using a traditional Norwegian acanthus pattern.

Low Relief carving is a common early form of woodcarving and is also known as bas-relief. This is where the impression is given of a three-dimensional object through the illusions of perspective created by the shadows and shapes created through a shallow carving that is predominantly two-dimensional. It has been widely used for ornamental carving in many materials, but in wood was common in the 16th and 17th Centuries, being a steppingstone to the complex high relief styles of the Baroque and Rococo styles of the 18th century. The background of a low-relief is typically reduced by 10-12mm (½") and can be etched or punched to create more emphasis, although a "tooled" finish is also common. Leaving the background completely level, for example as a smooth routed finish (not uncommon in stone carving), does little to enhance the depth effect, so is not recommended.

1 The pattern used for this project is derived from one of those in Odd Fauske's compendium of plans[1], where there are another six designs from which to choose:

A in this case, I have added some embellishments in keeping with the Acanthus style of the original. Odd Fauske's plans are reproduced in his book at full scale, so all that is required is to print the relevant pages then trim and assemble them on your blank. As this is an embellished design, I have included a two-part view of my design at the end of the chapter which can be re-scaled to suit your needs. In keeping with tradition, I have used Norwegian Birch for the project-

[1] Fauske, Odd - A Norwegian Woodcarving Textbook - ISBN 1861518633

Index Sheet from Odd Fauske's Book (pg 373)

2

3

4

5

660mm x 115mm, & 30mm thick (2'2" x 4¾" x 1¼"). This Norwegian birch is slow growing, so fine grained, giving a timber that carves relatively easily while still taking the fine detail of the acanthus style and, historically, the punishment of frequent use.

2 Assemble and glue the pattern to the timber with sufficient offset for adding the handle to the finished board,

3 The first task is to set-in the external lines, to give a hard stop-edge to avoid accidental errors while clearing the background. If you have a cutting gauge handy (see Chapter 1), this is ideal for setting-in the base line on the edge of the work, as the incision made by the gauge, not only gives you a hard starting groove for a straight chisel, but also helps to reduce untoward edge splits.

4 The background can be removed by hand - a task traditionally allocated to an apprentice. The modern "***tailed apprentice***" can be used to expedite this work, such as a router (as this will give a flat base to the background).

5 If you only have a drill, a suitable forstner bit will do the job (as long as you make an extra depth allowance for the mark left by the small brad-point). It's always a good idea to leave a little waste to be removed by hand, as this will not only give you a (small) margin for errors but will also leave the possibility for a "tooled" surface finish should this be desired.

6 There are a number of alternative ways of keeping the pattern "safe" while providing a guide for the subsequent roughing-out work that include:

A taking a 'V'-Tool to run round the pattern.

B using small skew will gives a good view of the line-ahead as you carefully push it round the pattern, or even a .straight blade chisel or chip-knife can be run round the lines of the pattern.

7 In this case, I ended up with a gentle nudge towards using a router for the bulk of the work, as working with a chisel quickly showed that the blank had a "shake"[2] along one side that started opening up when I applied any force, with the potential for later disaster:

A to avoid future problems I had to carefully glue the crack I had inadvertently opened.

B then, after leaving the glue overnight, I set-to with a router to rapidly cut-down the background by about a third. After setting-in the sides, the waste, left as a margin for error, was then removed with a bent N°1.

C The old Hag's tooth (Stanley #271 hand router) is also a handy way of removing this waste on internal relief. It has the benefit of leaving a level surface at a consistent depth, without the drawbacks of the electric router.

8 It is difficult to use the hand router on the edges without undermining the pattern but it is still worth setting-in the edge. With the repaired shake in mind, the setting-in was modified to the use of a slim knife-blade in lieu of the wedge shape of a carving chisel. With a bit of repetitive work

[2] *A shake is a natural crack in a log that can open when sawn timber is seasoned. As it lies along the grain, it is often imperceptible unless activated by an edge tool. As it is along the grain, the glue-line of the repair will blend well with the grain and will become imperceptible in the finished product.*

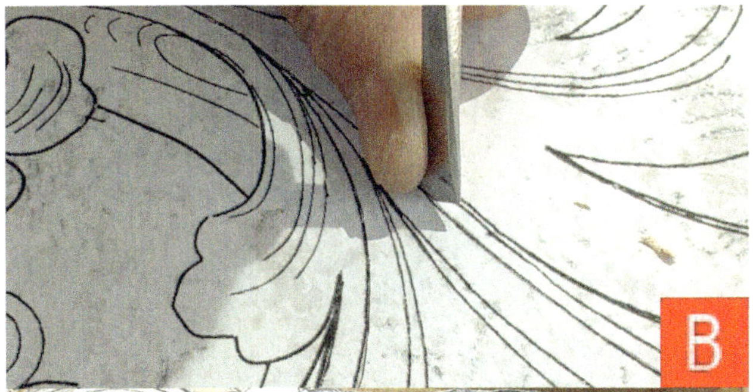

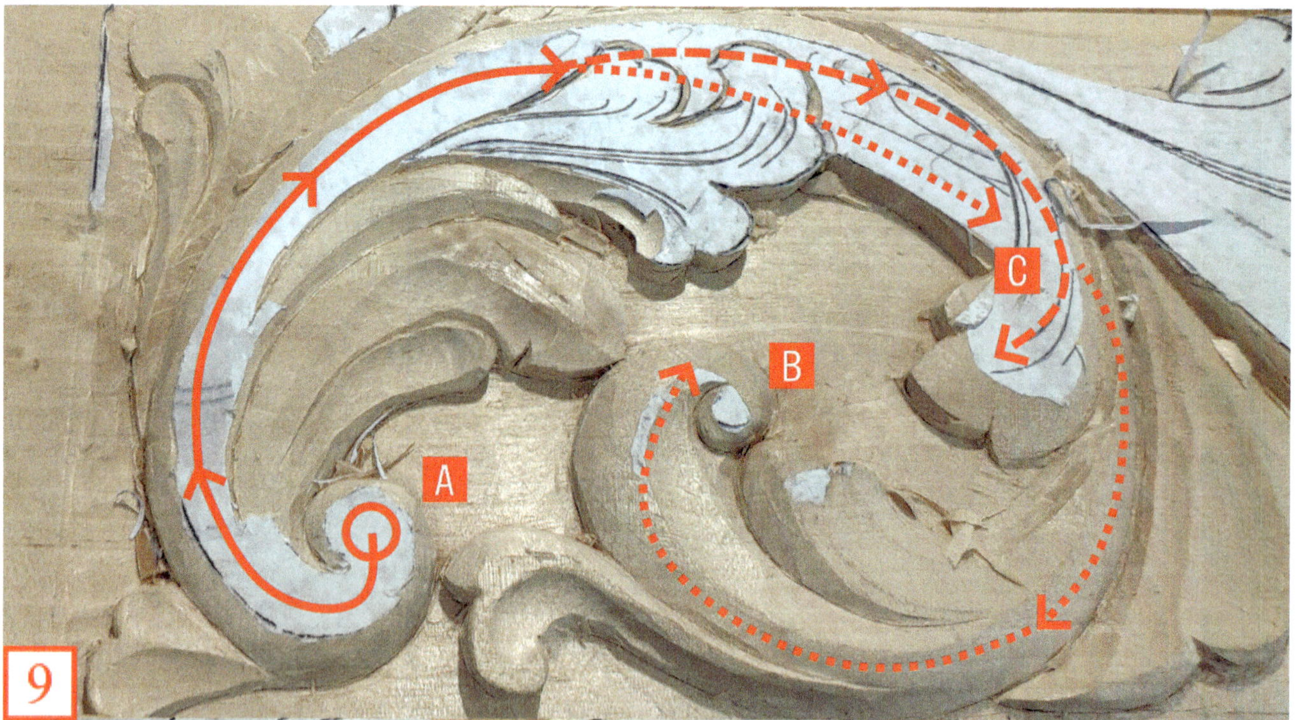

you can finish the set-back evenly at 8-10mm (¼" to ½") deep, alternating between setting-in and clearing out along the whole edge.

9 When it comes to the main pattern, there are some principal components:

A first the stem, which runs from a large snail-curl at the root in a smooth arc, all the way to the top;

B the top is a (smaller) snail-curl, that emerges from the foliage at the end

C en route the stem has side branches that use the same main stem as the base so they have a dominant vertical cross-section using the full depth of the carving.

10 These primary stems are the main three-dimensional component, standing proud of the background, with a solid cross-section, casting a strong shadow that sets the visual depth of the low-relief format. Bearing in mind that the whole is designed

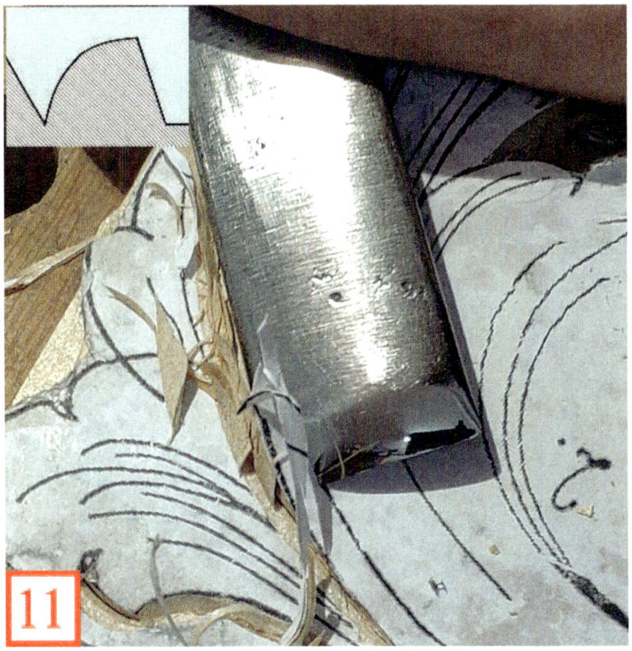

round a series of interlocking curves, it is a complex piece of geometry, so the stem itself needs to be cut down boldly to the base level. This is achieved by a deep, curving groove to outline the outside edge. The shape of this curve is initially set-in with a mallet using a N°3 followed by a N°4 if you have one; then delineated by a series of slicing cuts along the outside of the curve towards the centre-line.

11 The profile is then cut down, into the groove, and beyond, still width the N°3, but now reversed, with its wing guided by the earlier groove, giving a side profile

12 This is followed through, right round the bend, the stem shaped and cut down level with the outside edge that was prepared earlier.

13 The N°3 is used to chase this outside of the tightening curve, all the way to the top curl, where it is used to start the round-over of the end, a process that will be

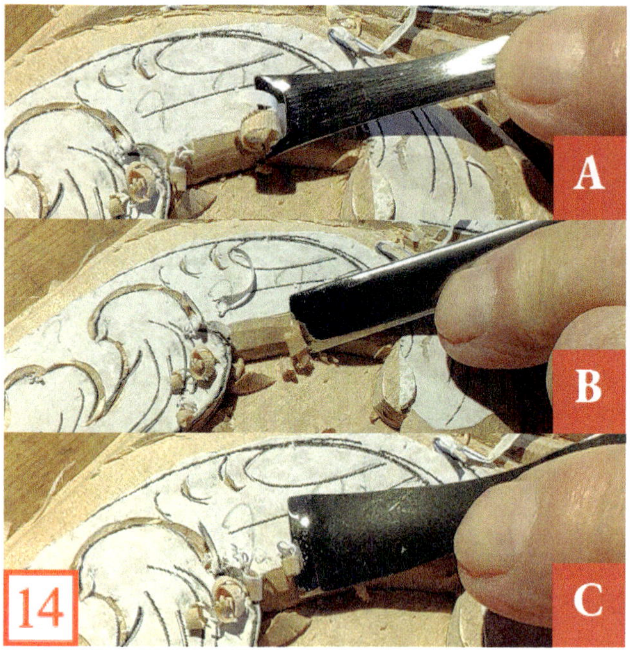

developed during the detail carving phase.

14 This process, for defining the shape of the main stems, is repeated three times along the length of the pattern. The three inter-linked stems form the backbone as they support the branching foliage. This pattern uses one of the "tricks" of the Acanthus style, where the second stem passes over the foliage at the end of the first. This gives depth to the carving and generates a short length of "hard" stem on the first branch that provides some challenges in carving a semi-circular profile onto the top of a curve, all in a confined space. There is a short length of "pure" stem where the pattern goes over-and-under. This can pose quite a challenge to refine the convex profile, due to restricted space. The approach needed remains the same, but the tool selected can depend on availability:

A a bent N°1 can be used to gently whittle away, in the same way as a bench plane is used to form a "round".

B a reversed small gouge , a N°5 or N°7 as best suits the profile, although this may give problems with access.

C alternatively, this is the situation for which the Back-Bent gouge was developed see page 143, as its swan neck is ideal for such a tight location, as it will keep the handle well away from the work.

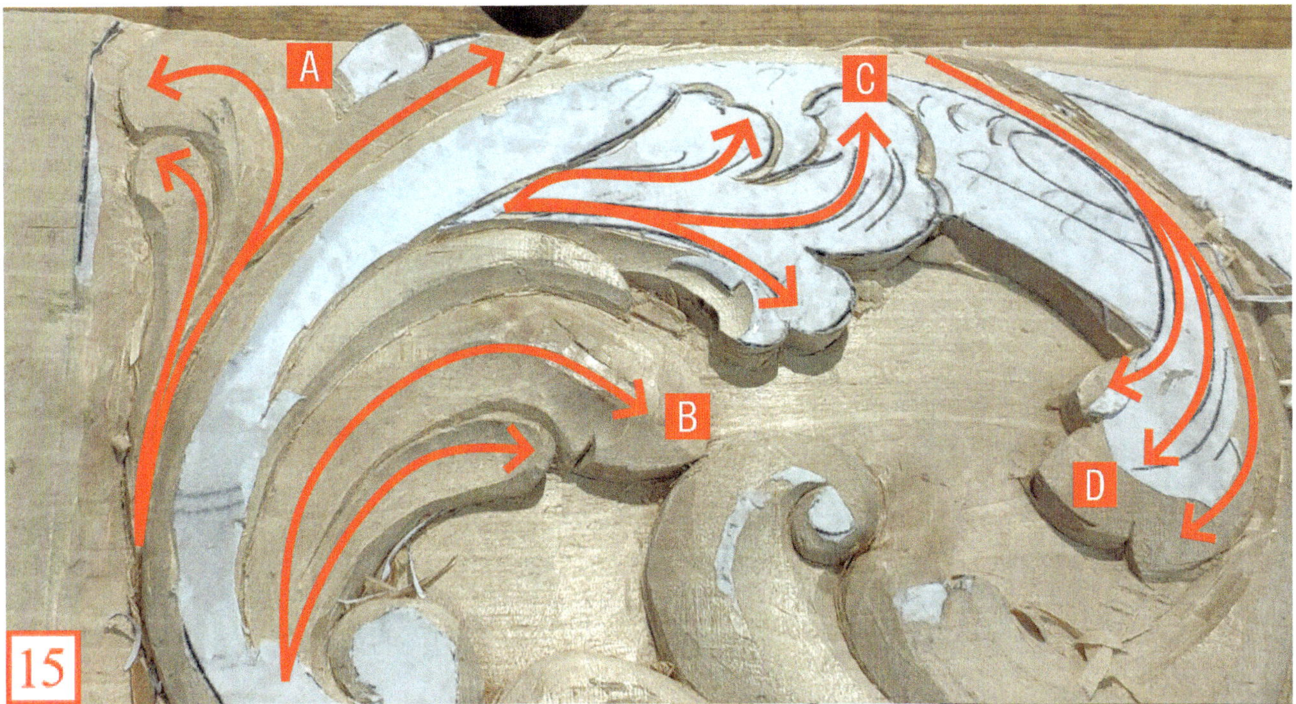

15 As you work through the main stems, you can make a start on the associated "leaves", which can go over and under the stems as the pattern demands. These are The second principal component of the style, where, in most cases, their construction is broadly similar, with variations on the number of leaves and relative orientations - See Chapter 7 page 162 . This pattern shows the variations in their orientation, often designed for balance and as infill for the open spaces, such as:

A at the start of the pattern, a leaf from the outside base of the stem bends back to fill the empty space by the handle, so balancing the first curl of the stem.

B a second leaf from the start balances the first on the inside.

C the next builds on the second, but goes up and over the stem

D the final one comes from behind, over the stem, to dive down again and fill the space in the centre of the main curl.

16 For example, use the outside of a N°5 or N°7 for the concave inside and the inside of a N°3 to form the convex outside edge and face of leaf **D**.

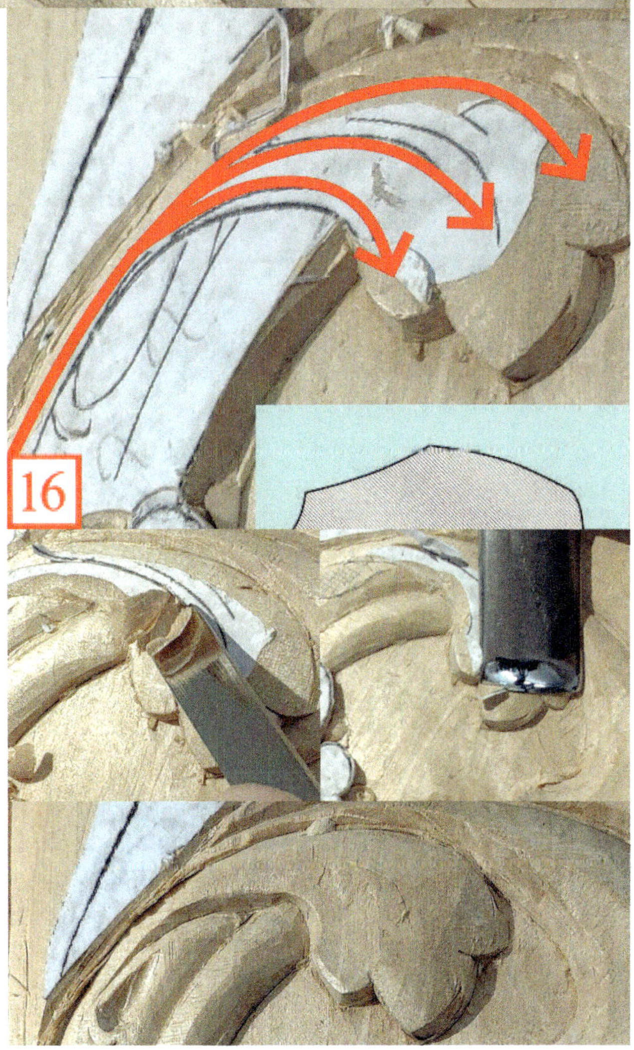

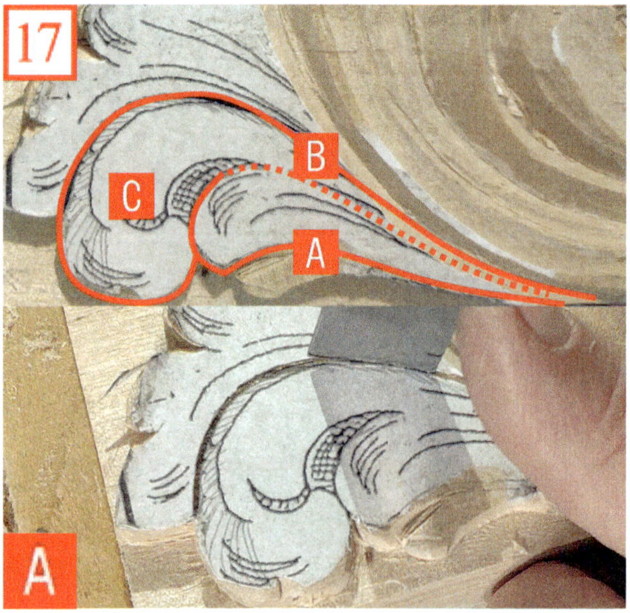

17 Leaves also round the end of the pattern off where a group of leaves come out from behind the last stem as a finishing touch, to square away the end. Here we have a twin-blade example, that illustrates:

A the setting in of the leaf edge, here with a thumb-assisted slicing cut with a N°3

B followed by a series of rotating cuts to enable the adjacent leaf to undercut the leaf below,

C then by following a similar routine to para 16 above, you can build up the depth and profile of the compound leaf structure.

18 Another recurring technique is the round-over for the terminals. The technique is the same, whether for the large initial "root", or the smaller end shoot:

A the shape is formed by the inside of a N°3 or N°5

B initially by rounding over the top surface,

C followed by chasing the edge all the way round the outside, which will need constant changes in orientation to accommodate grain direction.

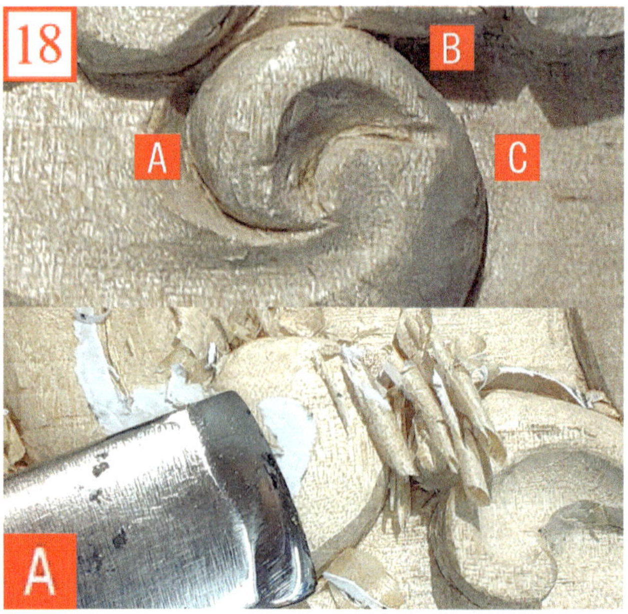

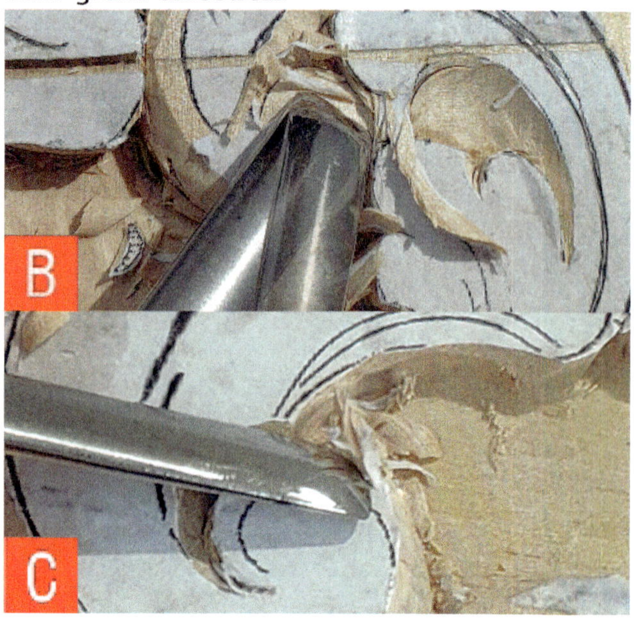

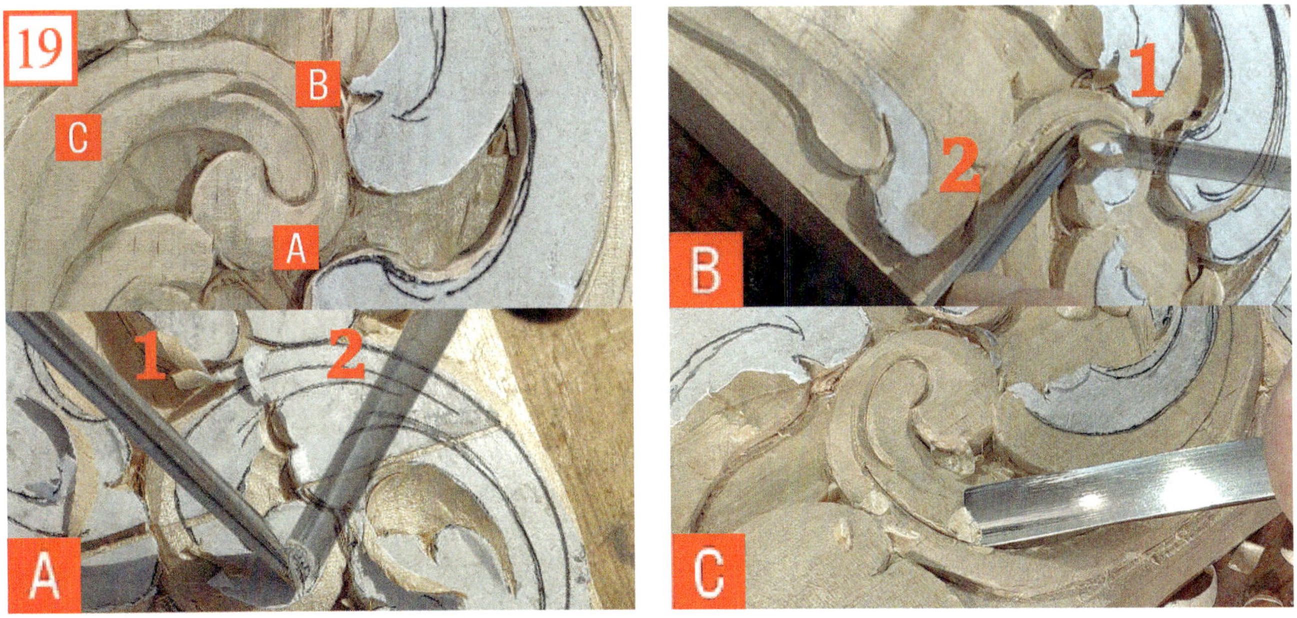

19 The end-curls can be made more "interesting" by embellishments such as:

A the inclusion of half-moon to accentuate the tip -

1. with an initial stab with a small N°7
2. then a slicing cut to pop the chip,

B from the half-moon, the top of the blade can be slanted towards the centre along the inner curve in a similar way with -

1. an initial stop cut with the small N°7
2. then with a slanting groove into it,

C to accentuate the twist, carve the outside with an opposing bent using a N°5.

20 The leaf tops can also be given a series of twists in a similar way, re-ordering them to appear interlaced:

A starting at the tip, using a N°7 or N°5 groove the inside with the grain,

B then go to the other end and groove in the opposite direction on the other side, so that the two grooves meet in the middle,

C finally, depending on the location you are embellishing, you may need to re-establish a "clean" leaf edge, using the tip of a N°3 to run round the inside or outside again.

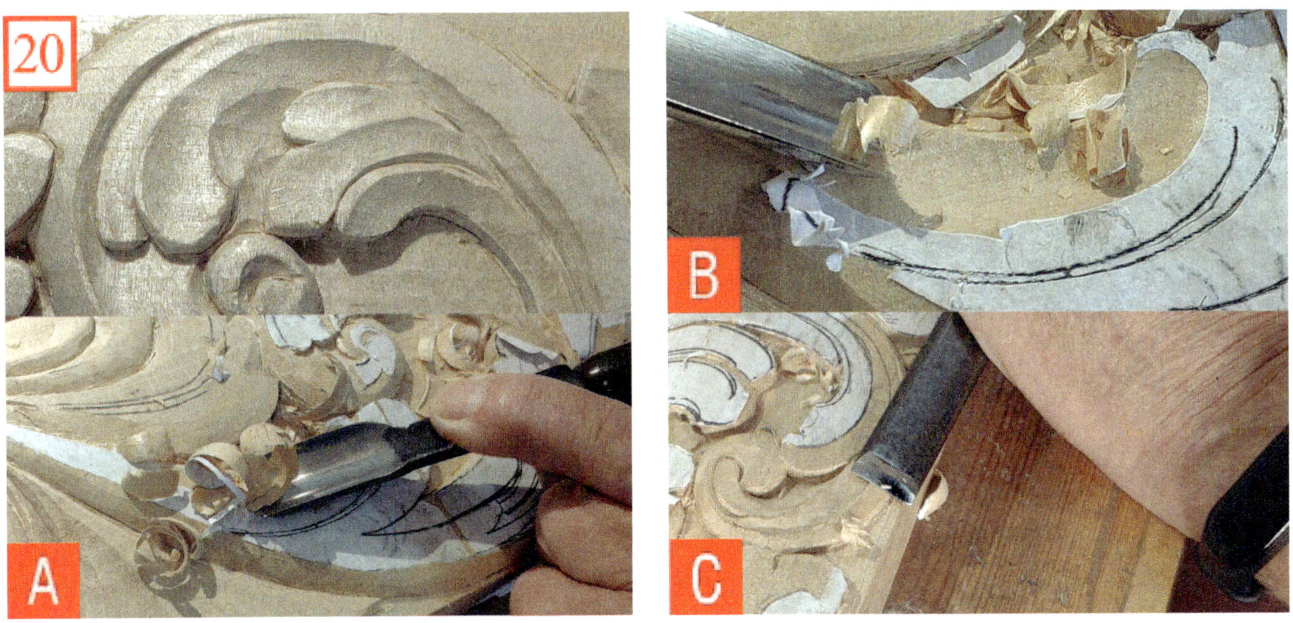

21 To a large extent, this carving is comprised of the above elements, repeated in three interlined and reversing 'C' curls along its length. After removing the background, a start can be made on these curls:

A starting at the root tip, using a N°3 or N°5 rough our the outline,

B then clean out the groove for the in-fill leaf at the base of the carving, so that the outside of the main curl can be shaped,

C at the other end of the curl, you should rough out the "flower", then you can move on to the detail of the leaves.

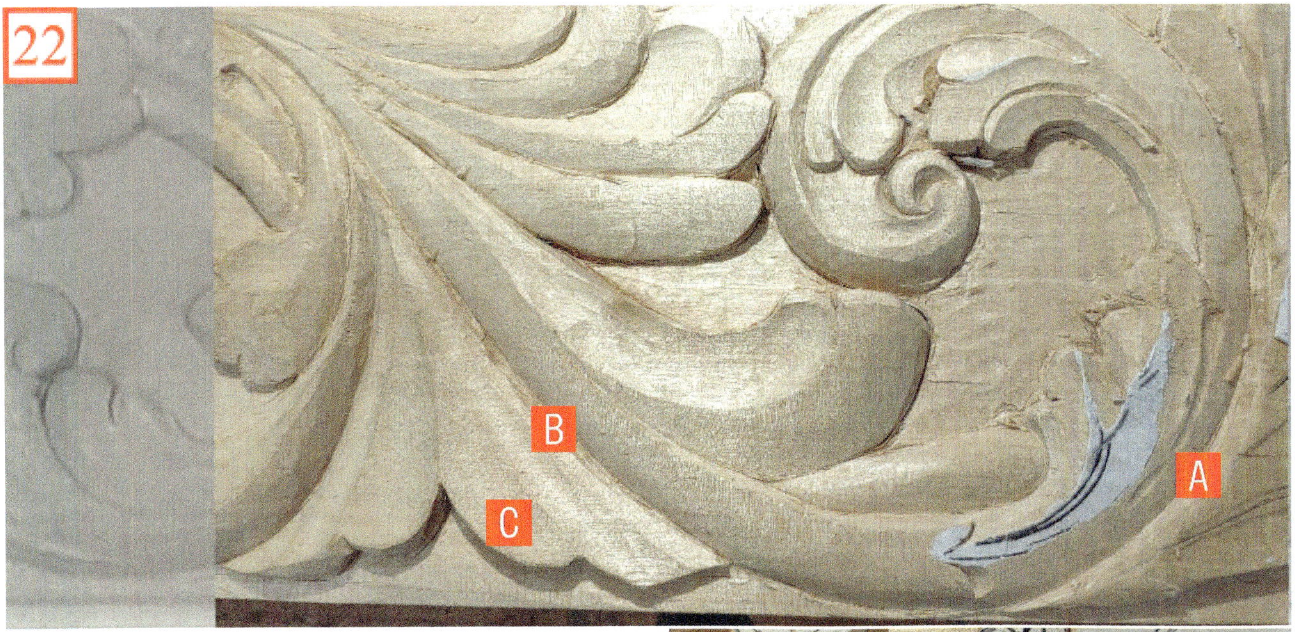

22 As you move onto the second curl there in another the whole process is repeated :

A again, using a N°3 or N°5 rough out the outline - this will need repeated change of direction as you chase it round the curve,

B then, as both sides of the “flower” are now clear of the curves, the final shape can be applied, running N°5 or N°7 from the intersection of the two curves out to the tip, with a suitable twist towards the outer edge,

C the top petal is carved last with a N°3 to leave a slight crest in its junction with the other side.

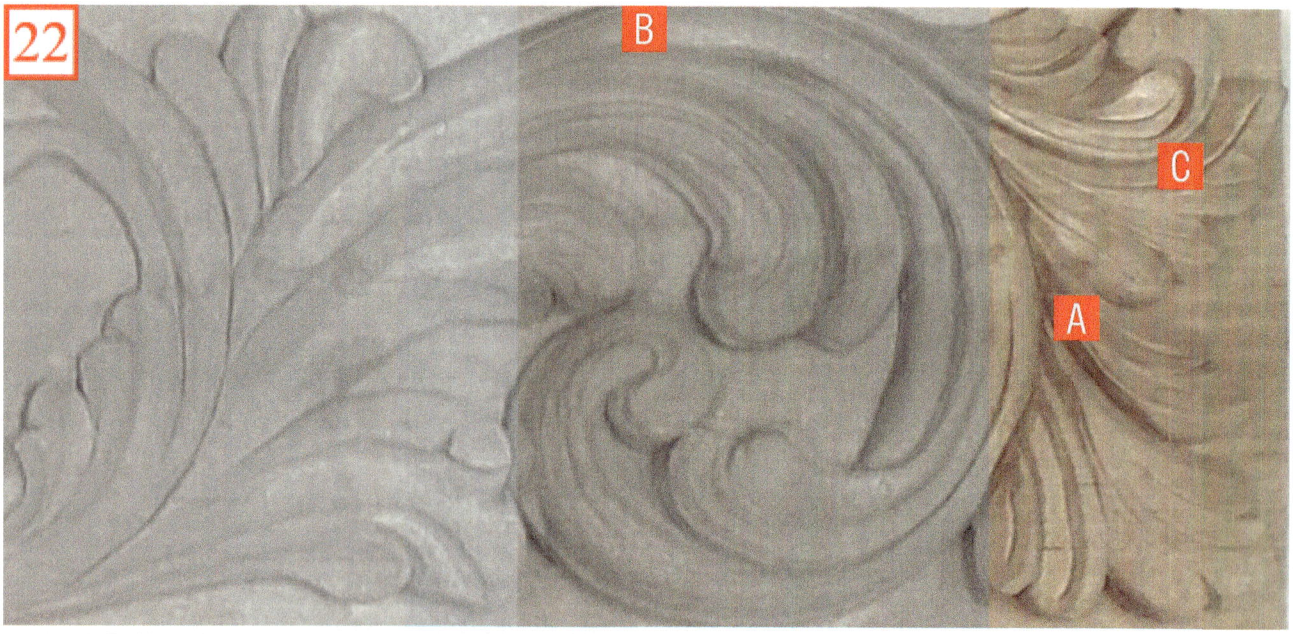

22 The final curl - which leads into the decoration that comes from behind its curl:

A again, using a N°3 or N°5 rough our the outline ensuring that sufficient depth is provided for the subsequent end carving;

B then, carve the two supporting leaves that flow from under the previous curve, filling the space to the edge;

C finally, move to the tip of the carving, there start with the short length of stem that links the other leaves, where you will also have a 'tip' to round over, before carving the spray of leaves that fill the end.

23 Here is a lot of under-cutting with these final leaves, as they fan out across the end. Fortunately, as it is the end of the carving, there is plenty of space to move around, to accommodate the ever-alternating approach angle required to care the multiple leaves.

24 When it came to the background, the end-grain behind these leaves proved challenging, but was eventually tamed by resorting to some low-angle slicing cuts that are the stock-in-trade of the carving knife, by slicing neatly into the leaf edges.

25 When the bulk of the pattern is complete, there is one feature of the style still to be addressed - the leaf eye. This is a representation of a natural fold as the leaf turns back over the stem. This is what the small U profile "Veiner" or N°11 is for (see page 3). The back of the eye is formed with a single stab cut with the N°11 or made up with a combination of skew stabs for the shoulders and a small N°9 for the back.

26 Again, the best tool for the groove into the eye is the Veiner, N°11, as this gives a single smooth cut from the mouth to the back of the eye, to pop out a clean chip.

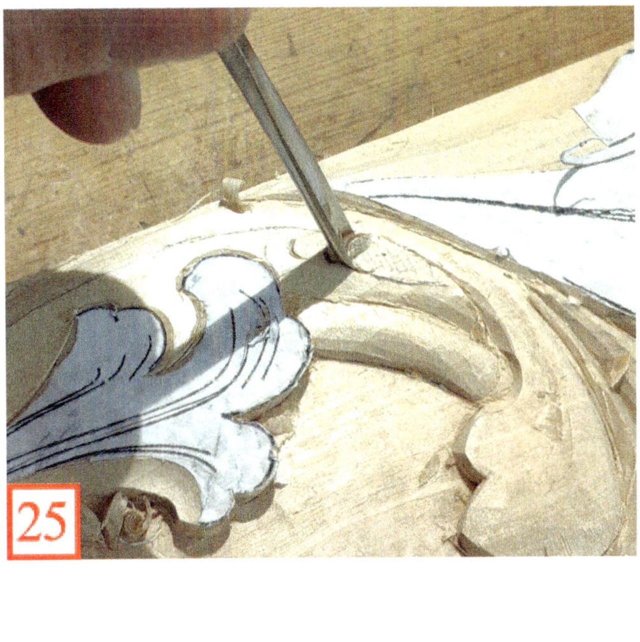

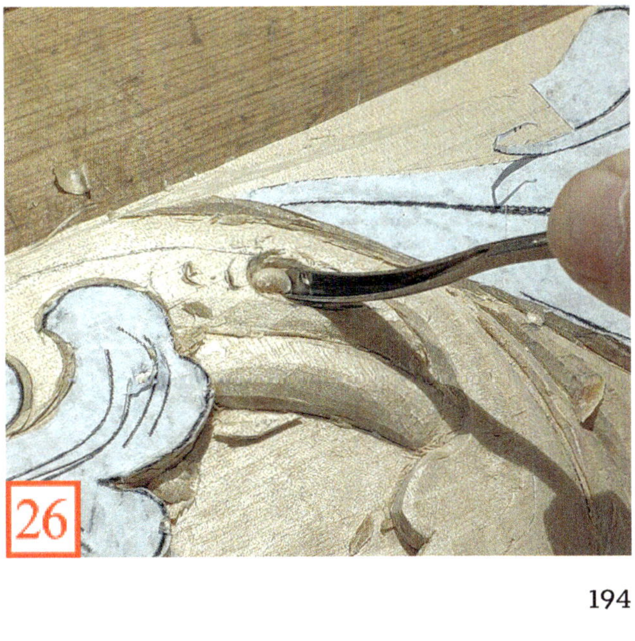

27 With the body of the carving complete, it's time to get out a pencil and copy the leaf veins from the plans onto the carving and to go round them all with an appropriate 'V' tool.

28 Then all that remains is to assemble the horse-handle and the board, add a coat of oil (in this case Walnut-oil), and finish it all with a coat of wax polish, together with a final buffing.

The Mangle-board (*Mangletre*[1]):

The Mangle Board - In the 17th and early 18th centuries, mangle boards were common household items and were often carved or decorated with painted figurines - to reflect the virtue of hard work, biblical motifs were especially popular.

To use the mangle, the damp garments were rolled tightly around the pin-log, the smallest garments on the inside and a larger one on the outside. With the right hand on the handle and the left hand on the board, the mangle is pressed against the roller while it is pushed back and forth to "iron" the clothes.

[1] *i Photo: Norsk Folkemuseum, CC BY 3.0, via Wikimedia Commons https://no.wikipedia.org/wiki/Mangletre*

2.

Project Twelve – Round Acanthus Box-Lid

This is a project for a round box-lid decorated with a traditional acanthus pattern.

1

1 In my case, the size was set the diameter of the box, but, as it a circular design, it can be scaled as necessary. Acanthus is a good pattern for decorating a circle, as the basic leaf is drawn on an arc - akin to the shape of a lucky fisherman's a rod with a large fish on the end of his line. Several of these primary leaf curls can be carefully arranged around the required circle and then embellished with secondary leaf structures as in-fill.

2 I have shown the starting circle with the preliminary arc running away from the centre point out to the circumference then subdivided into four equal quadrants,

3 This is followed by its secondary leaf added in blue, as an off-shoot near the half-way point.

4 The second leaf is them positioned in the next quadrant starting tangentially from the circumference.

5 The whole procedure is then "step & repeat" round the circle, with new leaves and sub-leaves being added progressively in each quadrant.

6 Finally take it full-circle around the whole circumference, again to include variations and sub-leaves in alternate quadrants.

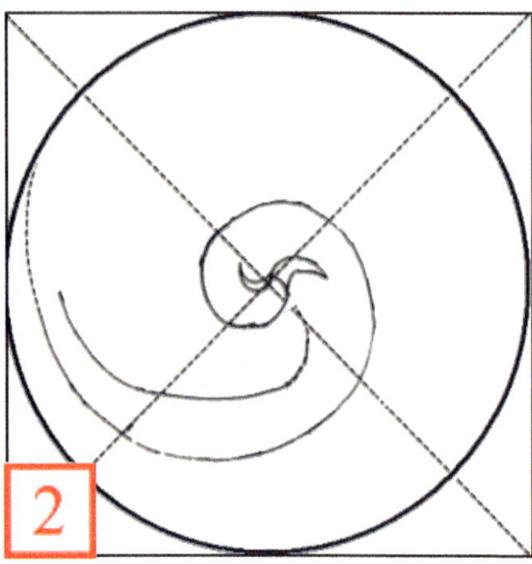

2

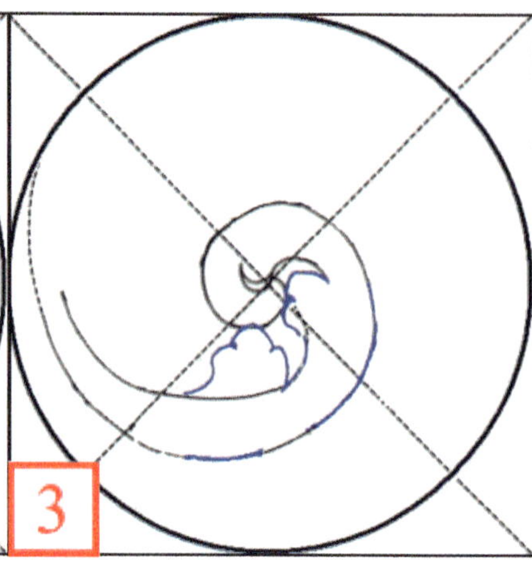

3

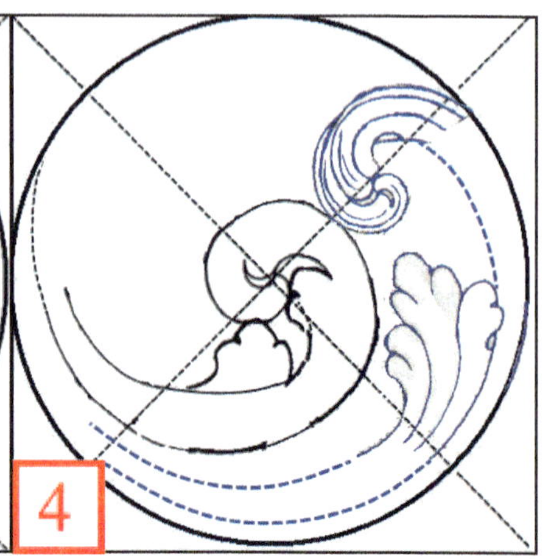

4

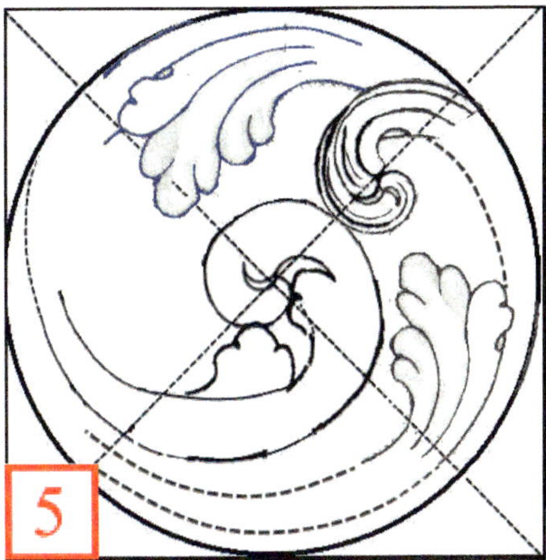

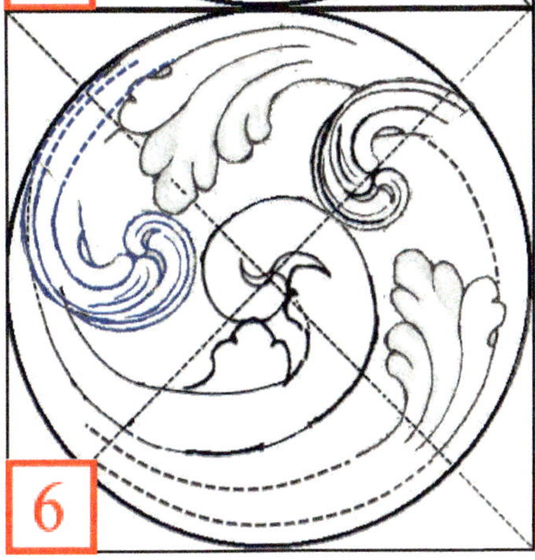

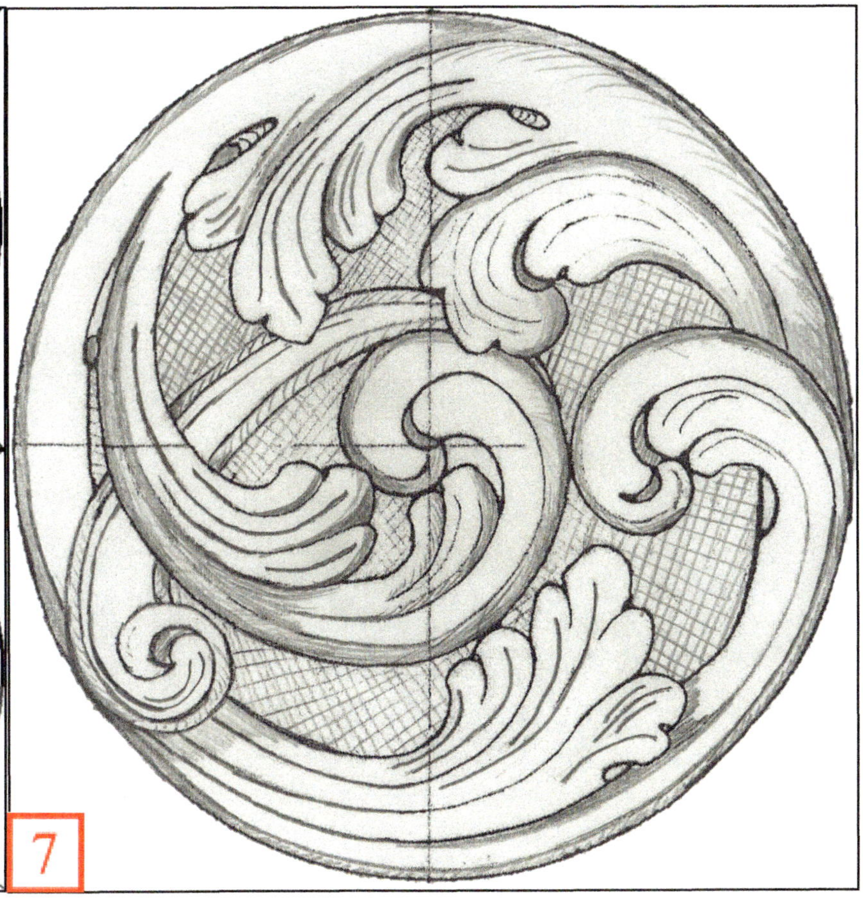

7 Hopefully that gives some ideas for your own design progression, with the full design being scaled as required - in my case, enlarge to a diameter of 117.5mm (4 $^5/_8$") - or whatever you need or want. When finished, it can then be printed onto paper and glued onto the chosen blank.

8 For materials, in my case, I chose an off-cut of European Birch about 10mm ($^3/_8$") thick, as luck would have it, nearly quarter-sawn - see side panel.. The circular shape for the blank can, either be produced using a tank-cutter mounted in a pillar drill, or, as I my case, on a lathe. Either way, unless quartersawn the grain has to be setup correctly, with the carving undertaken on the side towards the heart of the tree.

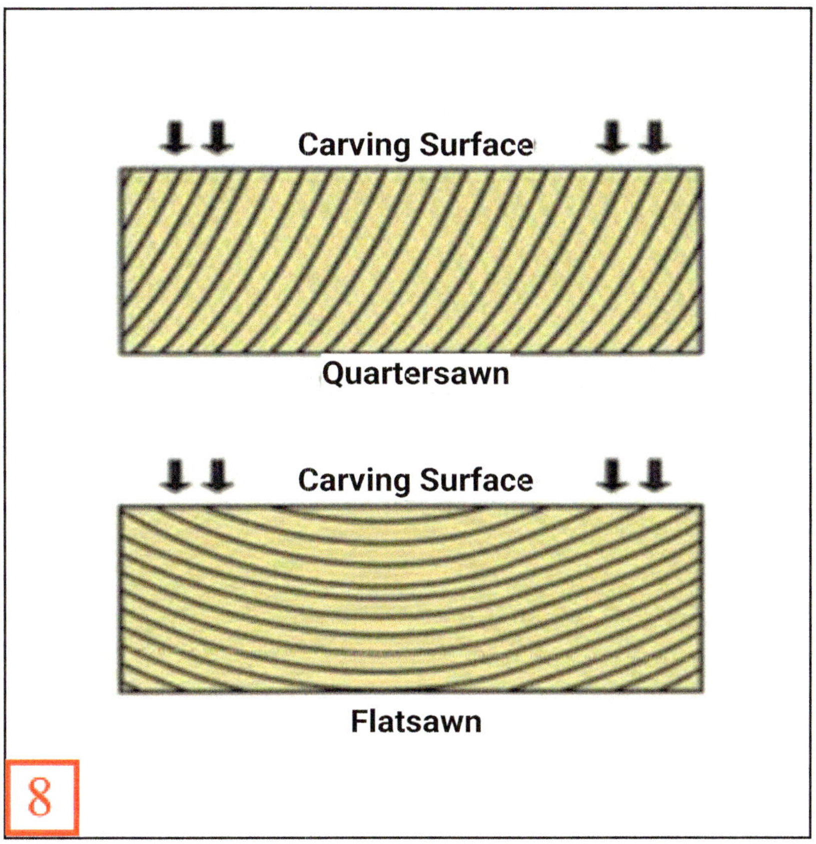

9 I started by roughly cutting the blank circular on a band-saw,

10 Then moving onto the lathe, to turn the blank round with a lip to fit inside the box and recessed the underside then turned it over, and slightly domed the carving surface, - all to try to limit the potential for the lid warping later. While the inside surface is best finished on the lathe, remember not to sand the carving surface, as grit will inevitably remain in the grain, with predictable bad results in shortening the life of the finely polished edge of any carving tool subsequently applied to it.

11 At this point, the carving can actually begin with the bosting-in[1] of the pattern, or in plain English, reducing the background by a couple of millimetres ($^1/_{16}$") to leave the pattern proud. The process starts with a vertical stop-cut with a suitable curved gouge (here a N°5) all along the appropriate pattern edge,

12 When the whole pattern has been set-in, the overall shape can then can be isolated by all the chips round the outside being gently eased to free before carefully cutting back towards this hard edge with a bent straight edge fishtail chisel.

13 "Best Practice" recommends that this bosting-in be undertaken for the whole

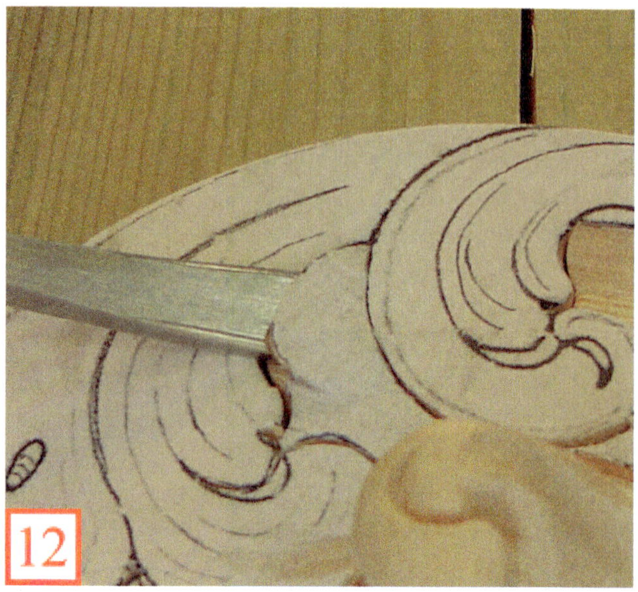

pattern area, so that you can clearly "see" the area to be carved standing proud, although some of the smaller areas may need to be left until better access is gained through the carving away of the surrounding detail.

14 With the background removed, carving the detail can now start, by setting-in the edge of the rest of the pattern in the areas to be carved, using a slicing cut, powered by the thumb. With the curve of the pattern in mind, this can start with a N°3 or N°4 at the outside edge, progressively followed up with a N°5 and then finally N°6, to link in to a terminal stab cut made with a N°7. Alternatively, with a limited number of tools, the transition from a N°3 to N°5 can suffice, with a bit of dexterity using the edge of the gouge carefully steered to make a leading cut along the line of the pattern - it's slower this way, but saves on the price of tools.

15 With the edged defined, the adjacent leaf stem, which runs underneath, can be cut back with a N°5, taking care not to cut too deep as the finished depth needs to remain proud of the lowest background level

16 While you have the N°5 in your hand, simply invert the tool and a smooth curve along the outside edge all the way to the end, When rounding the outside edge, you need to take into account the grain direction,

13

14

15

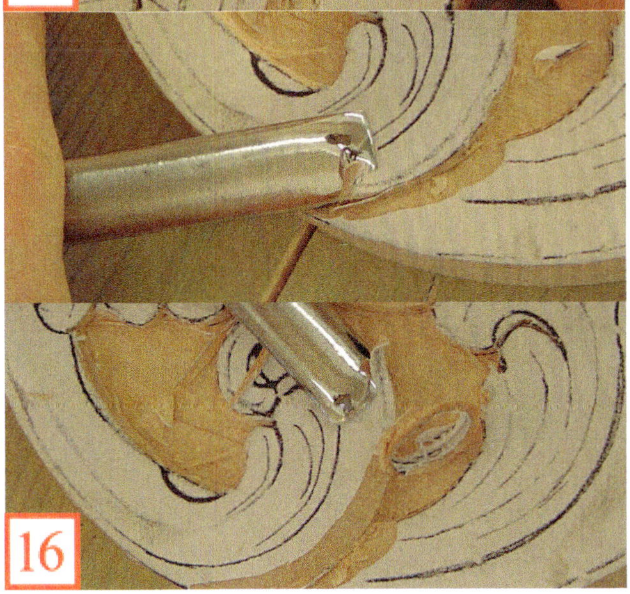
16

17 When you reach the end of a leaf it will be time to finally rounding the end off with a small N°7.

18 The curve has to be brought round the end of the leaf and the return defined through careful removal of a chip with a small N°7.

19 You can then start on the "return journey", with the same tool on the inside edge of the leaf, initially with the lower terrace then the same method on the higher terrace with a N°7.

20 The attention can then move to the outside edge, running a reversed N°5 round the outside, to provide a smooth convex curve tangential to the box's circumference, the inside edge of which providing, if you like, the "***watershed***", as the highest level on the pattern, with finished surfaces sloping in two directions - in towards the centre of the lid and outwards to the rim.

21 The top of the leaf then remains to be defined, starting with a slicing stop-cut along this "watershed" line, here with a N°3.

22 The length of the feature is defined with a reversed N°5. When you get to the end of the sweep, it can be cleanly rounded over with the N°5, before you turn it up the right way again to run back along the top, lightly recessing it so that it slopes

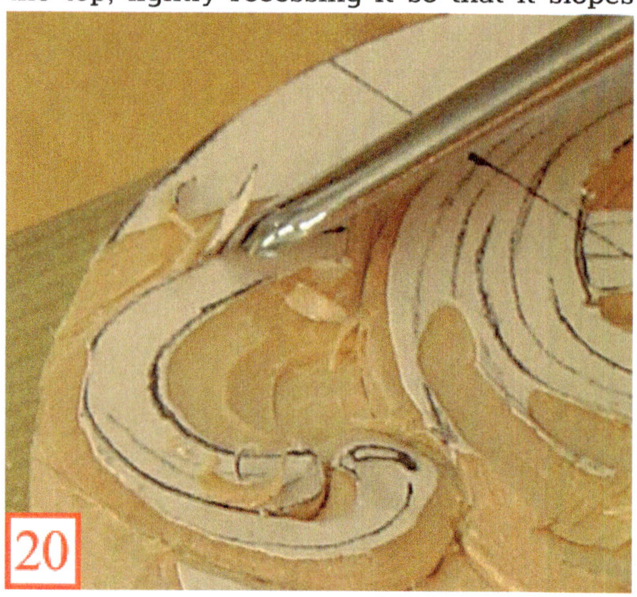

21

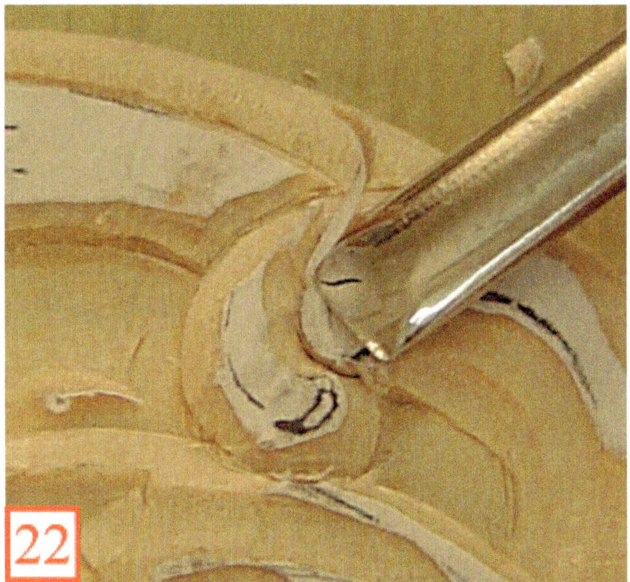
22

in towards the centre and down along the stem.

23 The resulting highs and lows can be seen on the finished leaf.

24 A similar technique is deployed in a "step & repeat" round the lid to define and carve the whole pattern. With the whole pattern complete, the outside edge needs rounded I into a smooth ovolo shape, by using a reversed N°5, taking care to adapt your direction of attack as the grain changes round the circumference.

25 Then you can stand back and check your finished carving for symmetry.

23

24

25

26

27

28

26 You may have to go back and clean up any "dings" that have magically appeared in the otherwise uniform background level, before giving the background depth by accentuating it through a random pattern of punch marks,

27 The punch marks may, initially, seem to add very little to the presentation, but after a coat of finishing oil has been applied, these will greatly add to the "depth" of the finished product - compare this **[27]** and "***with oil***" in **[28]** below.

28 Finally, before finishing with oil, add the fine detail, such as leaf notches (a couple of careful stab cuts with a small N°8) and leaf veins (added by a "V" tool tracing the curve from leaf base out to its end).

29 I do not use any abrasive to "finish" a carving, as I follow the theory that it take away fine detail, but that's your own choice. To bring out the background and the fine detail, a liberal application of finishing oil is recommended - but as this is a lid, where the inside surface finish could taint the box contents, I used walnut oil, as this does not leave an unpleasant smell inside a container. A light application of wax followed by generous buffing with a soft brush mounted in a drill finally completes the job.

29

30 A lid may need a knob to make manipulation easier, so I included one. The easiest solution is to turn a matching knob and fit it through the hole left by the screw-chuck. An alternative is to include it in the carving, by gluing an off-cut from the blank to a dowel placed in the hole in the centre. This can then be carved to key in with the patter. The key to a smooth transition between the knob and the lid surface is the careful alignment of the two grains when you glue the knob blank on. The "ski slope" side of the knob is finished with a smooth downward cut, so the gouge needs to be able to move from the vertical to the horizontal without a dig-in - only possible with common grain direction.

30

Project Thirteen – Acanthus Barge Board

This project is taken from the book "A Norwegian Carver's Textbook" by Odd Fauske. Although a traditional Norwegian acanthus drawing, it is a pattern that you could find anywhere in Europe.

This carving pattern, derived from a book of traditional Norwegian acanthus drawings, is one that you could find anywhere in Europe, especially in the repertoire of the Victorian revivalists in English churches. However, the original pattern is for a fully carved Barge Board in the Norwegian style[1], so has been reduced to the terminal leaf only as more suited to the English oak frame barge boards it is to decorate. The pattern is reproduced in two mirror-images to fit either sides of the gable end and then scaled to the correct width for the target oak planks - in this case locally source 1" English Oak planks from a Devon saw-mill. Although supplied so green it was wet to touch, it had been left stacked in stickers during a particularly dry English summer for a few weeks to air partially-dry before preparation.

1 Once the pattern is fixed to the blank, the first task is to make tactical relief cuts before trimming the outline, then

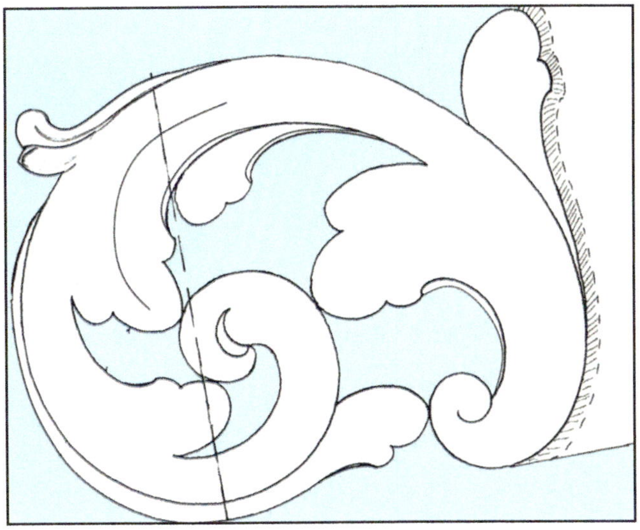

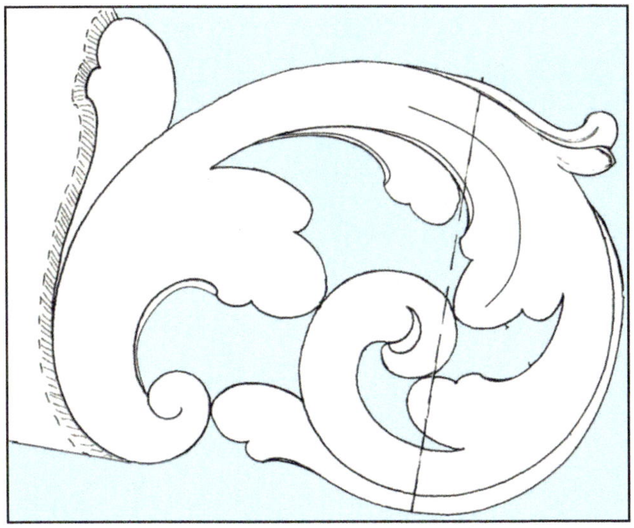

NOTE: Full size pattern Fauske Book see pg 217

rough out the piercings by drilling through the blank to enable a saw blade to be inserted.

2 You can use a fret-saw, coping-saw or electric jig-saw, depending on the finished size of the carving and the tools available in your workshop.

3 With the outline established, and before starting the carving, it is well worth chasing round the outside with a V-tool as insurance against the pattern becoming degraded, but it also gives a good visual reminder while carving. Carving can then start on the outside edge, to establish the overall depth of the patterning. However, it's worth take the precaution of inserting a few stop-cuts round the outside, especially where external leaves depart, to make sure they are

1

2

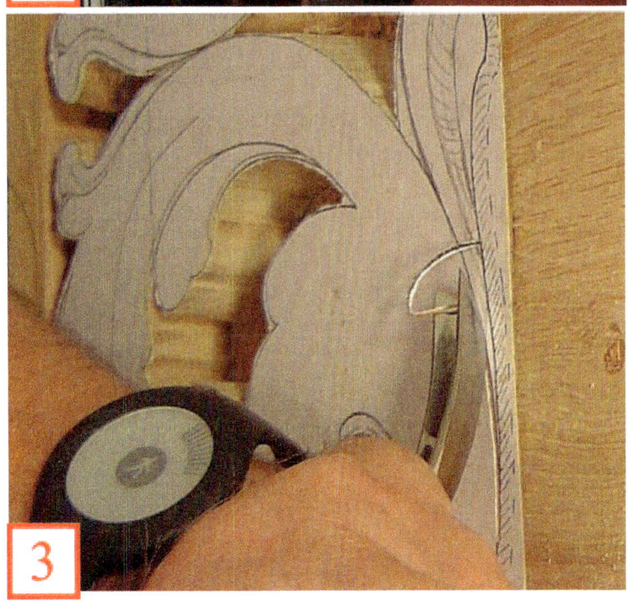
3

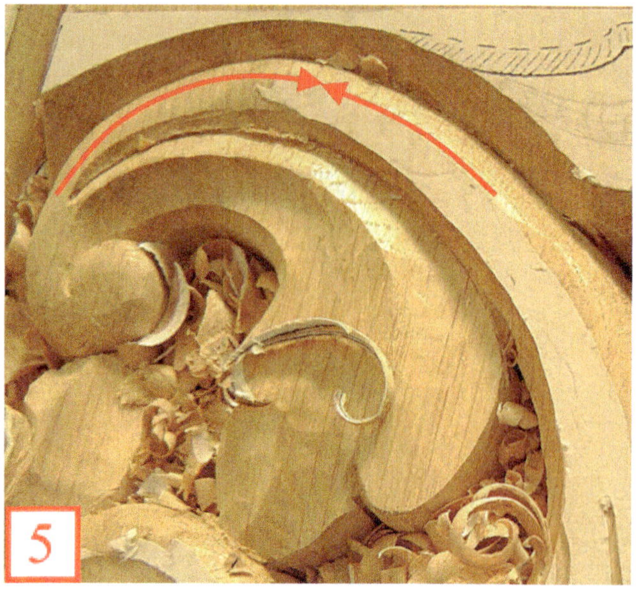

not broken off by over-enthusiastic roughing out.

4 The root is the lowest part of the pattern and the leaf tip is the highest, with the outside edge curling downward to the root. To achieve this, carving will start by reducing the pattern at the root to establish the low point. Initially use broad chisel, either a reversed N°3 or N°5 and boldly remove at least half the thickness of the root (in the background of the picture you can see the other side with a finished profile for comparison).

5 On a large carving like this, where the leaf curl goes across the board and back again, you have to remember that the grain is going to change direction four times and adjust your line of attack correspondingly. So, while you have the large, broad tool, start to rough out the outside curve. You won't get far before you are caught by the first side- leaf that needs to be roughed, out as it originates below the level of the outside curve.

6 This means that you have to turn your attention to the first inner leaf. The curve that this follows to diverge from

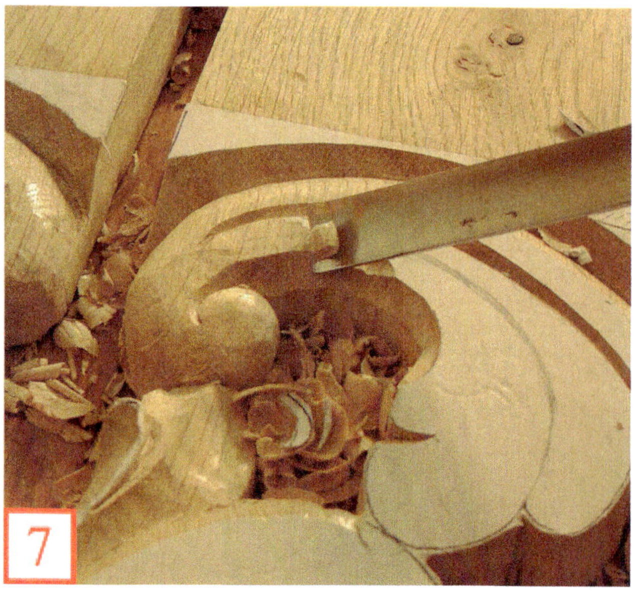

the stem can either be established with a series of cuts with a V-tool, or by running a N°3 from the root out to the tip followed by the reverse side of a N°5 to take out the waste and to establish a smooth ovolo shape on the outside edge.

7 This will also run into trouble catching the inside edge of the reversed N°5, so you will need to take first a N°7 to rough out the bottom inside curve from the tip to the root, then a N°5 to put in the upper inside curve in the same way, with the line of attack then reversed to start cutting down towards the tip.

8 About half way down, as the leaf approaches the tip, the N°5 is replaced by a N°3 to chase the profile down, so that by the time it "kisses"2 the top end, it is about half way down the depth of the timber. This then requires the tool to be reversed to avoid undercutting the end, with attention paid to trimming back the end cur as a stop-end.

9 With the first inner leaf now well below the outside edge, a return can be made to its shaping, without any more danger of snagging the inner tip of the reversed N°3. A series of fine shaving cuts can be made with the N°3 before revering to a N°5 to carefully join this new work to the earlier work where the grain direction changes.

10 A little roughing out on the second internal leaf is needed before turning attention to the tip. This intermediate leaf starts behind the first leaf so needs to be taken down below both the rim and the pattern's tip to enable caving to continue from both ends. The basic shape is roughed by running a groove along the back of the first leaf to start the bottom edge of the second. As the grain changes, this has to be done in stages from both ends.

11 The back edge is then defined with a slicing cut from the start to end, followed a reversed N°5 to define the back-side that is run all the way to also take the tip to ensure it's down below the level of .

8

9

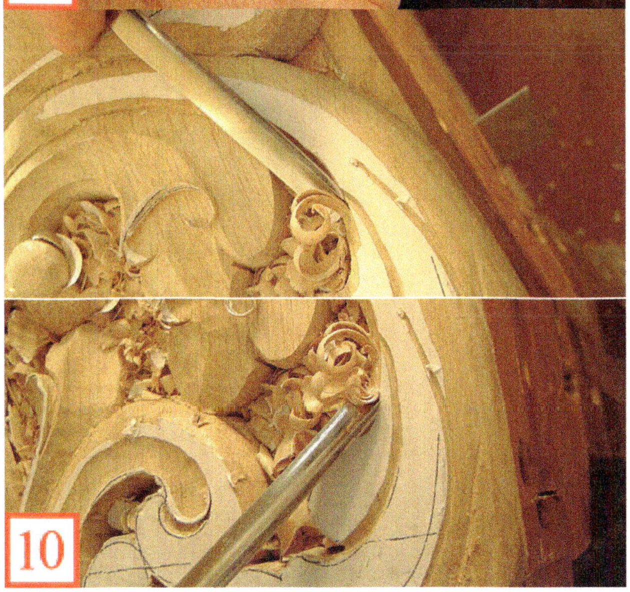
10

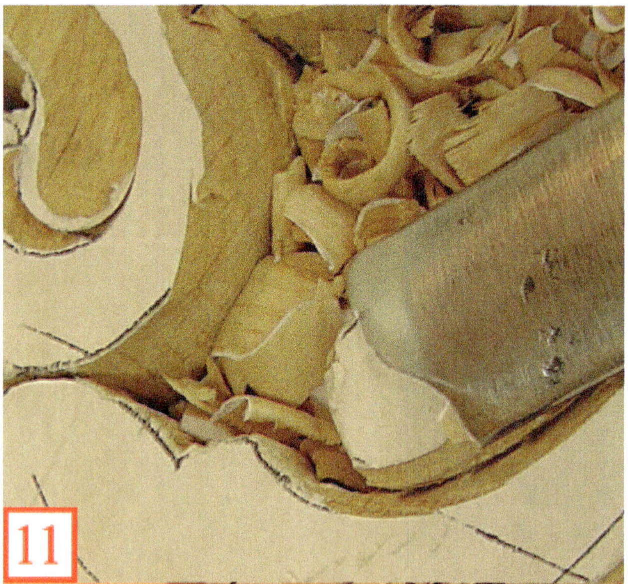
11

12

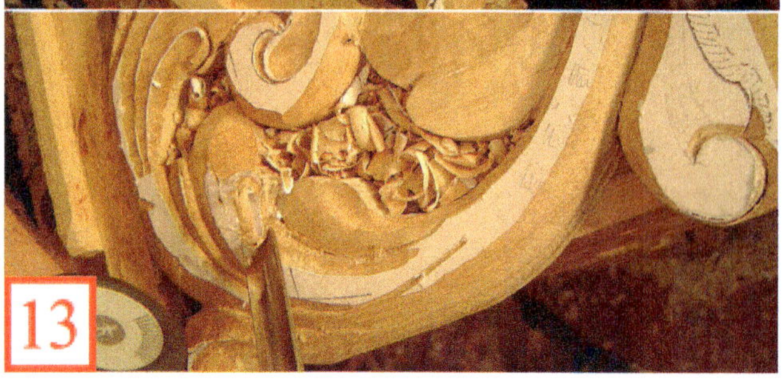
13

the main tip, in much the same way as was achieved on the tip of the first leaf.

12 The centre and back edges are separated from the external scroll by a series of alternating slicing cuts the first vertical cut defining the alignment and the subsequent angled cuts removing the waste along the alignment, until a smooth groove has been established along the back edge, together with a delicate mini-leaf behind it.

13 With the shape now defined, all that remains is to finish the detail with a channel along the top of the leaf, that tilts slightly in towards the centre. Take a N°7 and start the groove from the tip and when the grain starts to change, move your approach to the other end and run the groove, as smoothly as possible, over the tricky cross-grain where the two meet.

14 This has taken the leaf well below the danger zone for returning to the outside edge with a broad reversed N°3, enabling with final rough cutting of the curl from the root to the tip. Not only are there challenges with grain changes, but inevitably also with the end-vice I was using to secure the Barge Board to my bench. In the picture you can see that I have has to use a composite "block" to secure the piece, with a lower front edge to enable the tool to reach round both sides at the apex.

14

15 With the outside of the top well established, work can start on the detail. A key element of this is the terminal "eye" that separates the top from the sides. This is formed by a vertical stab-cut with medium N°7 followed by a slicing cut into it, generating a semi-circular chip that should cleanly "pop" the eye out.

16 Using the eye as the origin, the groove along the spine of the feature can be run out along its length. However, this groove will have multiple grain changes along its length, so will have to be done in sections. Using 12 o'clock as the top of the pattern, first run the medium N°7 from 9 o'clock back to 6 o'clock then move to the eye and carefully join it back to the end of your first cut at 6 o'clock.

17 Before you can continue with carving the outside edge, more depth has to be gained on the inside by lowering the end of the final interior leaf below the level of the top curl. To provide for some variation in shapes, a concave curve is given to this one by running a N°5 along its spine and down into a stop-cut on the inner edge of the main curl, By running the end on a downward slope it will stop the end-grain from coming off as an untidy chip.

18 Round the end that "kisses" the centre curl in the same way as before, then

15

16

17

18

19

20

21

move back along the inside of the spine with the medium N°7 to groove it, before adding an “ear” to the leaf. This is done by inserting a vertical stab-cut with a small N°7 at the relevant point on the pattern, followed by a rotating cut at the base of the leaf bellow to ease out the waste.

19 With the top and the bottom levels now established, the middle leaf can be completed to bridge the gap. This leaf has to different part to it, with the lower level tied to the bottom leaf by a long stem carved with a small N°7 running from its tip right round the back of the lower leaf.

20 The upper level initially defined by its top groove being run into the rim with a corkscrew shape that transitions from the horizontal top through 90° to run along the spine above the bottom leaf. Both these grooves have the added problem that the meet the rim at the grain transition, so will need work from both ends to join in the middle. The leaf profiles are carved using a blend of the earlier techniques, You will know when these levels have been established, as you will be able to finish the shape of the rim with a revered N°5 without damaging the inside carving.

21 With that leaf now ell below the outside rim, attention can return to shaping the external surface to stop the external

22

leaves from looking as if they've been stuck on by cutting the stems into the side of the large ring. If necessary mark with a pencil line where you want the stem to run from (which should be say half way down the depth). If in doubt over your ability to chase this line with the edge of a N°3, the it can be set-in with a V-tool. Take the N°3 to run the stem down across the grain and into the outside ring, using a series of slicing cuts to progressively advance and develop the groove.

22 Now that the external leaves are well rooted and their shapes defined, the smoothing of the profile of the external ring can be finished, working round the outside starting with a N°3 round the base of the profile and smoothly transitioning to a N°5 as you turn the profile over the top.

23 The external leaves are all carved with a mixture of the techniques used for the internal leaves, with care being taken with the "sight lines" for the joins to the main ring, as the whole will be viewed from below, so all the small "Twiddly Bits" are still visible.

24 As the end of the barge board over-sails the gutter line, this carving will be seen from the reverse side, so it has to be finished in three dimensions. The end grain will make the ring delicate, so rough carving

23

24

25

26

the reverse could be destructive. Just use a micro-plane file for roughing out and a gouge only to finish to the required profile.

25 The two "ears" also need to be rendered in three dimensions. When carving the ear on the top, you will be working with the grain, so the work should be simple.

26 The reverse is true on the bottom, so careful cutting from both ends will be required.

27 The obverse also needs shaped, so the pattern will need to be sketched.

28 The obverse of the leaves is a relatively simple rounded shape made with a N°3.

29 Then back ring profile can be finished by careful shaving with the N°3 or N°5 as required to match the front profile.

30 Unfortunately, the coarse end grain of the oak, combined with increased drying caused by reducing the thickness through carving, lead to a shake splitting the end of the carving. The board is external joinery, some strengthening of the fault is required. For decorative carving, toothpicks are ideal, so here we need to up-size to a kebab stick. To align the joint carefully for drilling and pegging, some "wet work" is required. So quickly open the crack, fill it with glue, then roughly re-align it with masking tape. A glue-line is still visible in the end

product, but this can be safely carved away as the tannin in the oak will self-colour any residual hairline glue, making

31 Then clamp the join using a suitable caulk to align the break until the glue has set.

32 A The glue-line is still visible in the end product,

32 B This can be safely carved away as the tannin in the oak will self-colour any residual hairline glue, making, it indistinguishable from any other end grain.

31

[1] A Norwegian Woodcarving Textbook: Fauske,Odd; ISBN: 978-1861518637 (2020); Amazon

32 A

32 B

Full Size Pattern

A Woodcarver's Textbook
Bargeboard/Vergerboard
Vindskie
305
©Odd_Fauske1973

Bibliography

1750 Diderot, Denis: *Encyclopédie, ou dictionnaire raisonné des sciences, des arts et des métiers*, Paris: https://quod.lib.umich.edu/d/did/
1769 Roubo,M. (André Jacob): *L'art du menuisier*, Paris: Académie Royale des Sciences, https://archive.org/details/gri_33125009321916
1875 Sawyer, George: *Fretsawing & Woodcarving*, Boston: Lee & Shepard https://archive.org/details/fretsawingwoodca00sawyiala
1886 Page, James: *Guide for drawing Acanthus* London: Quaritch, https://archive.org/details/guidefordrawinga00pagerich
1891 Leland, Charles G: *A Manual of Wood Carving*, Project Gutenberg http://www.gutenberg.org/files/42949/42949-h/42949-h.htm
1892 Salomon, Otto: *The Teachers Hand-book of Slöjd*. Boston: Silver, Burdett & co. https://archive.org/details/teachershandbook00salo
1895 Bruhns, Alois: *Die Schulwerkstätte ..... mit dem theoretischen Unterrichte*. Vienna: Hölder https://archive.org/details/dieschulwerkst00bruhuoft
1896 Phillips, Joseph: *Wood Carving*. London: Chapman & Hall https://archive.org/details/cu31924031276151
1903 George, Jack: *Wood-carving*. New York: Appleton NY https://www.gutenberg.org/files/22107/22107-h/22107-h.ht
1976 Fuske, Odd:*Lærebok i treskjæring*. Etnedal, Norway: Fauske Forlag, ISBN 82-990953-0-147
1981 Mader, Joseph: *Vom Kerbschnitzen ......Reliefschnitt*. Vienna: Oberösterreichischer Landesverlag ISBN: 978-3852142913
1987 Mader, Joseph et al: *Chip Carving & Relief Carving*.:London:Collier Macmillan London, ISBN: 978-0020007203
1993 Amrun, Johan: *Ornamental Woodcarving in the Norwegian Tradition*.Whitewater, (WI):Heart Prairie, ISBN: 978-0962266393
1996 Bigton & Odden, Else J. & Phillip: *Treskjærerkunsten*. Oslo: Universitetsforl. ISBN 82-00-41754-9
1997 Stana, Lars: *Norsk Treskjæring*. Oslo: Libri Arte, ISBN 82-445-1068-5.
1998 Engeland, Knut: *Treskjæring*. Oslo: Teknologisk Forlag, ISBN 82-512-0408-9
2007 Skånsar, Tom *Enkel treskjæring*. Oslo: Borgersen,Boksenteret, ISBN 82-7683-301-2
2009 Engeland, Knut: *Treskjæringsmønstre*. Oslo: Cappelen Damm, ISBN 97-88-24-9607624.
2011 Schwarz,Christopher:*Workbench Design:The Art & Philosophy* Des Moines, (IA):Popular Woodworking, ISBN: 978-1440310409
2014 Irish, Lora S, *Wood Spirits and Green Men: A Design Sourcebook*. Mount Joy, (PA): Fox Chapel, ISBN: 1565238567
2015 Tweedale, Geoffrey: *Addis: A Famous Name in Carving Tools*. Sheffield UK: Tweedale, https://docplayer.net/65140897-Addis-a-famous-name-in-carving-tools-by-geoffrey-tweedale.html
2016 Refsal, Harley: *Scandinavian Figure Carving*. Mount Joy, (PA): Fox Chapel, ISBN: 978-1565238756
2017 Williams, Donald C *Roubo on Furniture Making (Translation)*. Covington, (KY): Lost Art Press, ISBN: 978-0-9978702-2-0
2020 Fauske,Odd, et al: *A Norwegian Woodcarving Textbook*. Cirencester UK:Mereo Books ISBN: 978-1861518637

INDEX

If you enjoyed this book and are looking for further inspiration for carving patterns, have a look at "*A Norwegian WoodCarving Textbook*" by the same author.

The book includes Fauske's full sized patterns for a variety of common carvings; 14 different spoons-carvings (many in 3 sizes), 8 different mangle-boards and a variety of previously widely used household items from, a porridge pail to log a chair, plus a variety of panel designs, from small boxes to doors, together with patterns for carving a full sized linen chest; they will provide plenty of inspiration for carving projects, from a simple key-rack to detailed plans for a traditional acanthus style mirror frame, together with many traditional Norwegian items of folk art, such as mangle-boards, spoons, ladles and furniture, fittings plus architectural items. All plans are reproduced full-size to enable them to be copied easily for personal use, either in the traditional tracing paper method (described in the book), by photocopying, or through scanning & printing by computer. Iain Whittington has brought his experience of map production and the writing of woodcarving articles to the editing of the old material and has added a new introduction - a guide to the history and special place in Norwegian life for woodcarvings. Fauske's original words have been professionally translated by Evaline Whittington.

Proceeds also go to SSAFA, The Armed Forces Charity.

Printed in Great Britain
by Amazon

74403761R00129